MW01255134

ROBERT HUGH BENSON

Life and Works

Janet Grayson

University Press of America,® Inc.
Lanham • New York • Oxford

Copyright © 1998
University Press of America,® Inc.
4720 Boston Way
Lanham, Maryland 20706

12 Hid's Copse Rd.
Cummor Hill, Oxford OX2 9JJ

Library of Congress Cataloging-in-Publication Data

Grayson, Janet
Robert Hugh Benson : life and works / Janet Grayson.
p.   cm.
Includes bibliographical references and Index.
1. Benson, Robert Hugh, 1871-1914. 2. Catholic Church—
Clergy—England—Biography. 3. Catholic converts—England—
Biography. 4. Authors, English—Biography. I. Title.
BX4705.B46G73 1998   282'.092—dc21   98-19992 CIP
(B)

ISBN 0-7618-1152-4 (cloth: alk. ppr.)

To

Bernard Bonowitz, OCSO

Sacerdos Catholicae et Romanae Ecclesiae

CONTENTS

List of Illustrations

Preface

Introduction

Appendices:

Illustrations

Preface

With profound gratitude I acknowledge the assistance of these libraries and collections that provided many letters and documents in whole or in part: the Bodleian Library, University of Oxford, and the estate of the Rev. K.S.P. McDowall for Robert Hugh Benson's letters to Mary Benson and diary entries, and for the Hare Street Chronicle; the Harry Ransome Humanities Research Center at the University of Texas at Austin for the Rome diary 1903-4; the British Library for permission to reproduce the last known photograph of Benson published originally in the Benson Memorial Magazine, Buntingford; and the Rev. Dr. Simon Tugwell, OP, custodian of Elizabeth Antice Baker's papers at the Domincan Historical Institute, Rome. I am especially indebted to the Master and Fellows, Magdalene College, Cambridge, for permission to use material drawn from the incomparable Arthur Christopher Benson diaries (for which Mr. David Newsome has provided an invaluable index), and wish to thank particularly Dr. Richard Luckett, Pepys Librarian, and library assistants Mrs. Coleman (now retired) and Mrs. FitzSimons for their cooperation during my many visits. Magdalene College also provided the photograph of the Benson family taken at Tremans, 1903. To the custodians of these library and university archives I am also indebted for miscellaneous letters and newspaper articles: the Berg Collection in the New York Public Library; The University of Notre Dame; Boston College; The College of the Holy Cross; The University of Pennsylvania; Princeton University; the Archdioceses of Boston, Chicago, New York, and Philadelphia; the Isabella Stewart Gardner Museum. Thanks also to Mr. Donald Weeks for valuable insights into Frederick Rolfe's connection to Benson. Also to Father Fenlon and Sister Isa of Our Lady of Lourdes Church, New York, my thanks for opening to me parish records of Robert Hugh Benson's visits in 1912 and 1914, and for providing a photograph of Mgr. Benson taken during his 1912 visit.

I have made use of C. C. Martindale's two volume biography *The Life of Monsignor Robert Hugh Benson* (London, 1917), and also Arthur C. Benson's *Hugh: A Memoir* (London, 1915). Father Martindale called upon Mgr. Benson's friends for letters and personal recollections, and I have dipped into the sea of correspondence that he amassed. Benson's many friends and admirers eager to send their letters to his biographer if only to link themselves to his presence in a book that they expected to be a lasting tribute. In the interest of abbreviated notation, I have for the most part cited references to these letters within the text rather than in endnotes. I have done the same for Arthur Benson's diary entries and the letters of Hugh Benson and Mary Benson.

Introduction

"He maketh His minister a flame of fire."

Does anyone read Robert Hugh Benson any more? He has been dead since 1914. His star like a comet hurtling across the sky, drawing all eyes to it, passed out of mind almost as rapidly as out of sight, though in his moment of glory, his fame burned so hot that it seemed all but inextinguishable. It may be that more than 80 years after his death Benson admirers are still to be found among Catholic readers exposed as youngsters to his historical novels or to his stirring apologetics that did much to advance the Catholic revival that had begun with Newman and the Oxford Movement. While he lived, from first novel to last, Benson enjoyed an immense audience, an international audience drawn from all classes including royalty and stretching across two continents. His admirers were not satisfied with a novel a year, or even two. It was rumored by those who did not like him that so smoothly oiled was his creative machinery that he had contracted with publishers to crank out three novels a year.

Sic transit gloria mundi.

He was indefatigable. Within the space of a single year, 1913, there appeared *Come Rack! Come Rope!*, *Confessions of a Convert*, another novel *An Average Man*, and a book of printed sermons, *Paradoxes of Catholicism*. It was true that he wrote with incredible speed and intensity, for that was how the creative urge moved him--to set him furiously to the task, to write and write until the thing was done and then to collapse into a week of sleep. It was true also that he was often careless, and thus left himself open to criticism, some of it deserved. But his public remained faithful, rapt in Bensonmania, and seemed not to mind the faults big and little, satisfied that yet another opus was waiting to be savored. The appetite for Hugh Benson was unabating.[1]

In 1915, his uncollected poems were edited; and there was one more novel yet to appear, for a grand total of 20 novels alone published in eleven years, the span of his life as a Roman Catholic. Besides his novels, children's books, plays, and poetry, books put together from articles, lectures, and sermons also saw the light of day. At the same time, he was writing prefaces and introductions to the works of other writers and keeping up a voluminous correspondence. As a speaker, he drew enormous crowds and was much sought after in England and in America as well; at the time of his death his engagement book was filled up with sermons and lectures on two continents for two years to come. He was besides this and above all, a Catholic priest.

His official biographer, C.C. Martindale, also an Anglican convert and priest, commissioned to write the massive two-volume biography (probably unprecedented for a man not yet 43), had met him, did not like him, and liked him even less as the work developed, yet managed the task honorably, to the satisfaction of Father Benson's family, his friends, and the untold numbers of admirers clamoring for yet one more memorial to the beloved priest.

It was the suddenness of his death, cut off midway in life--and what a life it had been!--that was improbable and unacceptable. They would not let him go. Robert Hugh Benson was simply there, a part of English life, ever writing, ever preaching. Open a newspaper, and the announcement of a sermon in Kensington or at Westminster Cathedral or away in Salford or Liverpool or Edinburgh jumped out of the page; pick up a monthly or a quarterly and there was a Benson book or Benson lecture being reviewed, or an article by him of some length on any number of subjects from Spiritualism to German War Atrocities in Belgium to Miracles to Christian Science. He was ubiquitous, a part of the landscape, a celebrity in high vogue, with more ink spilled over him than over any other English priest or bishop, Church of Rome or Church of England. That such a familiar presence was cut away so suddenly was an effrontery to the proper order of things, like losing a favorite brother. So the panegyrics poured forth in a stream of articles and books and poems and letters and from church pulpits. The public could not get their fill of Robert Hugh Benson dead or alive to the extent that finally the *British Weekly* clamored for the worship to cease in a headline *No More Hugh Benson!*

The greater the wound the longer the convalescence, but the public recovered, and before long, deprived of his personal magnetism, cut off from his stunning sermons and without the benefits of a sympathetic press to keep Bensonmania alive, the public let go and he was allowed to rest at last.

Hugh Benson was many things, but above all a preacher, the best in the land, many held. In the decade of Catholic life allotted to him hundreds of thousands heard that low rough humorous voice transformed in the pulpit as by miracle, so that the words poured out in a torrent so powerful and passionate that he pulled everyone in the church into the torrent with him. In Rome in 1912 when he preached the Lent, every English-speaking priest and student came to hear him. On one occasion fifteen Cardinals sat transfixed. It was estimated that 50,000 men and women saw him and heard him speak later that year when he visited the United States, and many more thousands in 1914--this without the advantage of radio and television. Many who did not care for Benson the novelist (but read every word he wrote) admired Benson the preacher, for in that art he had no equal. Not even the brilliant Basil Maturin, an eloquent contemporary and himself an Anglican convert, could pack the churches to overflowing time after time.

In 1903 while an Anglican he had taken the public by storm with *The Light Invisible*, a collection of curious stories told by an aged Anglican priest. To many readers a mystical side of religion was revealed for the first time, full of insight and transcendence, of angels intervening in human affairs, of priestly intuition of Divine purposes. The effect on the public was electrifying. Rational piety, sensible doctrine, flailing controversy over what is and what is not reasonable to believe--the condition of Anglicanism at the time--all fell away before Benson's stunning "*O Altitudo!*" He was by then in Anglican orders, the only son of three surviving sons to follow the father into the English priesthood. The book was greeted warmly. Here was potentially the successor, the 'right hand' of the father, a visionary with a vocation. Not surprisingly this book written while he was a priest of the Church of England was judged by Anglicans to be his work of works upon which his fame was destined to rest. In 1914 the official Anglican reaction to his life and death was genteelly cool. With a sigh of relief they bade him farewell confidant that his real literary success had been *The Light Invisible,* the book he had written as an Anglican. Try as they might, Benson's achievement as a Catholic novelist could not be dismissed, for he had been a powerful influence in prodding legions of English readers to rethink deep anti-Catholic prejudices, and if after having the case put before them in Benson's inimitable fashion, they were not convinced in all points, at least their hostility was the less; some even called for a rethinking of the Catholic position. Writing for the *Church Times* (the publishing arm of the Church of England), an old friend and colleague of Benson's from those early days described his riveting mission sermons as thrilling to the crowds who responded easily to the simple "man next door" reductions of lessons of Scripture. But Anglicans never forgave him his defection because in the course of his short life through his books and preaching he drew thousands into the Catholic Church, and they knew it.

Physically, Benson was not impressive: small, with a lot of brown hair flattened down, quite boyish looking to the end of his life, with a low raucous voice and a definite stammer that went away only when he stood in the pulpit. "A pink-cheeked boy with china blue eyes," he was once described: irrepressible, with "the look of the mad hatter." In photographs of the Benson family group the cassocked priest in biretta stands out distinctly, in size, in features, in dress. He stares at us from the rear, standing between his brothers--at his right, Arthur Christopher Benson, the anchor of the family, bushy-browed and solid; at his left E. F. (Fred), slender, elegant, handsome--Cambridge men all. In front sits his sister Maggie the Egyptologist, dark and a little grim, and darker still for the mental turmoil going on under the surface, and next to her Mary Benson, adored *materfamilias*, brilliant and witty, bulkily regal, spread over the lounge chair like a recumbent silvery Victoria Regina. There is finally the beloved aged nurse Beth looking on vacantly, bewildered by the suspended motion of her highly animated darlings. In looks the Bensons are remarkably familiar--we have seen such a picture and such lives a thousand times before--the well-educated fairly prosperous English family enjoying a Sunday afternoon, durable yeomen stock making their mark in the world, whether in business or the business of empire or belles-lettres, staring at us with a kind of horror at being swallowed by the lens. They appear a typical unsmiling group, without being (outside of this flat representation) anything of the sort, even remotely of that sort. Still, the priest leaps out at us, by his conspicuous dress and his littleness, and the sense conveyed in the concentrating eyes that here is more nervous energy and determination compacted into a single heart and soul than in all the rest.

Nothing in his childhood except a vivid and sometimes wild imagination prefigures the priest and inspired preacher he was to become; nothing in the slight body suggests the capability, emotional and physical, of bearing up under the enormous weight of multiple and simultaneous careers, any one of them draining of the energy of many men, how much more so of a man subject to the cravings of an artistic temperament. A late bloomer, one might say in looking over those early years. Friends recalled that he had done little work at Cambridge, but remembered a certain charm which he always had about him. By all accounts he gave no indication at the time that he would develop into a brilliant preacher and lecturer upon contemporary issues as well as one of the most compelling of novelists.

Hugh Benson loved to tweak the noses of modern writers--H.G. Wells (whom he admired) and G.B. Shaw (whom he did not admire), for instance. His eccentric habits added to his "mystique." He believed in ghosts and actively sought them out--to no avail however because they never appeared for him; he loved play-acting and the theater always and wrote a number of plays though as a priest he was forbidden to go to the theater. In personal appearance he was notoriously dowdy--put no store in his appearance, ate sparsely, denied his body small comforts-- yet he took full advantage of favors handed to him by others: he loved the simple life of the solitary, yet he was frequently the guest of the great and powerful who sought him out and who in a few cases created a private chapel expressly for his use in their homes. In his affections, he walked the line between detachment from others and dedication to their spiritual needs--and demands made upon his time and talents were unremitting.

Chivalrous and charming, he claimed no strong mortal attachments, never appeared to regret or mourn a loss, never looked back, ever single-minded and intent upon going his own way. He loved solitude. "When I am alone," he wrote, "I am at my best; and at my worst in company. I am happy and capable in loneliness; unhappy, distracted, and ineffective in company." The truth was in company he was charming, brilliant, and funny, easily winning over men and women who disliked his religion and disbelieved what he believed. On the other hand, he was a controversialist, ironic, cutting--yet possessed of an eager and winning sort of courtesy even in the midst of brisk debate. He was magnetic, indestructible, forever youthful, and never, never dull.

His conversion was the single most important act of his life, reducing all other realities to dust.

His brother Arthur frequently accused him of ignoring the scientific method, of relying upon authority, of arguing cleverly but with a surface logic; of charging him with narrow-mindedness when it was not he, but Hugh, whose mind was closed. The truth was that Hugh Benson saw the logic of his position because he felt a deep need to anchor his faith in imperishable stuff and recognized the dangers in speculation that challenged orthodoxy. In the battle of authority and free inquiry, he took the side of authority always, not because he had abandoned all claims to formulating and defending his position by reason or that in this issue as in matters of dogma, he as a Catholic must hold with orthodoxy. To give himself up to dogma and obedience was to Benson no mere escape from the difficulties of real life, as his brother Arthur claimed. It *was* life. It was not only yielding one's heart and will to an inflexible institution, unmoved and unchanged by subjectivism, it was joining himself powerfully to the body of Christ on earth, the Church, as a living limb of that perfect body. For him, as for Catholics of his day, the point was that "the Will should adhere, and the Reason assent." The English Church, its music, its dignified liturgy, its beauty--these were externals, lovely and sentimental graces of a temporal institution which in real life was divided by uncertainty and pain. He was acutely aware of the obligation laid upon him as the son of the Archbishop of Canterbury, particularly as the other sons were not cut out to follow his father's footsteps to the altar; but once having decided Rome was the answer, there remained no question where his future lay. All the doubt and anguish lay in breaking the news to others, particularly his mother Mary whom he adored.

The controversy he sparked during his life and especially in the wave of emotion following his death is the stuff of legend. He was a saint, he was no saint. He was pious, he was subtle. He was not a true priest but a child playing at religion, an artist who thrived on external sensations. He had betrayed his father's church; his love of the truth brought him back to the true faith of his fathers. He rushed headlong into Catholicism as a boy rushes into a playing field; he loved the Catholic faith heart and soul, and gave his heart and strength and finally his life for it. Love him or hate him, it was impossible not to have an opinion.

His influence upon the spiritual development of young French Catholic intellectuals like Jacques and Raissa Maritain and theologian Teilhard de Chardin, for instance, suggests a bolder strike than has been credited him by modern critics.[2] And then there is the touchy matter of his obsession with physical presences, death, pain, imprisonment, the body. Whatever morbid construction modern critics put on it, Benson and his vast audiences--Catholic and Protestant alike--accepted this way of grappling with the mystery of spirit and body, of soul contained in perishable matter, the eternal in the carnal, of life in a handful of dust. Of all miracles this, stretching from heaven to earth in the Incarnation, was the most astounding, for every possible good in human nature forever after was vitalized by it.

In recent years there has been a lot of interest in the Benson family, the result of the reprinting of E. F. Benson's humorous Lucia and Mapp confections. A number of biographies or sketches have appeared on E.F. (Fred), the last of the Bensons, and on the Bensons collectively. Another valuable biography of Arthur Christopher Benson is based on unsealed diaries, revealing his struggle with depression while shedding incomparable light on his contemporaries.[3] Robert Hugh Benson has not fared so well. Unfortunately, the habit of some modern writers approaching the life of any Benson is to dismiss the priest as an egoist who perfected a theatrical style to pack the churches and lecture halls in the self-serving aim of building a reading public for his novels. Any glance at his life, they say, will show that he was simply too self-absorbed. There are also lately the amateur psychologists who adduce from his priesthood an acceptable route of escape from married life, though he had as a very young man already decided that marriage was not for him. His motives for entering the Church he discussed again and again, in books and letters and conversation, and it does no good, and probably much harm, to challenge the claims he made repeatedly in public and private, claims never contradicted by any existing evidence, and, in point of fact, confirmed by the tireless work on behalf of her, that his interest first and last was the Church, not to hide behind, but to exalt as the living Body of Christ.

Hugh Benson reacted against a society mired in endless speculation that threw all into doubt, smugly confident in its ability to divine truth by denying absolutes or reducing them to arguable propositions: paths leading, as many suspected and as events sadly proved, to nihilism and despair. In fact, his world was not much different from our own. Intellectually the struggle was more acute in his day because the parade of "isms" that have over the years pounded our generation insensible--materialism, positivism, determinism, and the rest--were new and disturbing controversies, disturbing because they challenged received notions of the world and mankind and uprooted the divine hand in the act of creation.

The world of the late 19th century into which he was born was optimistic. It looked around at its great strides and was well pleased. Evolution had brought Europe to a veritable high-point of civilization if the use of rational powers was any measure. The scientific method was strengthening the materialist view that all is matter and that the universe once formed evolved under an inevitable process from which special creation or intelligent creation was excluded. In this utilitarian age, knowledge meant progress; but knowledge undermining dearly held creeds also brought a share of pain. Traditional religion and faith itself were suddenly at risk. Assailed by Geology which held that the earth had been fashioned by action upon nebulous matter for millions of years; assailed also by Biology which held life to be created and regulated by a mechanical process in nature; even by Psychology which adapted the mechanical model to intellectual and emotional processes of the brain as interacting electrical impulses without spiritual identity--

assailed thus on all sides, religion was suddenly confronted by challenges it had not faced before. In a mechanistic, self-regulating universe God and the immortality of the soul were irrelevant. Newman's caveat that with matter science began, with matter it will end was hardly detectable amid these bursts of intellectual progressivism.

The conflict of science and religion seemed irreconcilable.

At the same time, there were disquieting developments in Scripture study. Higher Criticism had done irreparable damage to the claims of the Bible as a reliable record of God's intervention in human affairs. Protestantism, relying heavily on Scripture as an unerring document of revelation and history, was unable to reply satisfactorily to the assault except by resorting to the very texts that Higher Critics had discredited and so was forced into creeping accommodation with the new science, particularly Archaeology. The Church of England, divided by doctrinal controversy, trying to keep step with Higher Criticism while holding to the Bible as inspired testimony, seemed helpless to resolve its difficulties. The immediate result was further erosion of faith.

Inevitably, religions as historical phenomena fell into the scholar's hopper. Archaeology and History were joined by Comparative Religion (an amalgam of several disciplines rooted in social history and philology) and marching under the banner of the Scientific Method they stormed the practice of religion, finding in religious traditions and liturgy glaring resemblances to the rituals of ancient fertility cults flourishing in Asia Minor about the time of Christ. Probably of all challenges this assault from Comparative Religion was most troubling. While the higher critics posed challenges to biblical texts as records of historical events, hitherto untouched were matters of revelation and the nature of the Divine Persons. Now came the army of comparatists led by the so-called Cambridge school (Sir James Frazer, Gilbert Murray, Jane Harrison, et al), who challenged the divinity of Jesus Christ by connecting Him to ancient vegetation gods--Attis, Osiris, Adonis, Tammuz. Great religions could be pared down to the bone to reveal their beginnings in primitive cults, thus demonstrating the tendency of human nature towards ritual magic and sacrifice--that tendency altered over the course of centuries by time and local traditions. Christianity, Protestant Christianity at least, was as yet unable to respond with one clear voice that Christ's sacrifice had been adumbrated in the gods of pagan religions; and that although every cult in man's history contained some bit of truth, Christianity embodied in itself *all* the vital elements of *all* the religious impulses of mankind. It fulfilled and completed the religious yearnings of the human race.

To the "progressivist," all movement had purpose. Knowledge meant progress. Rutted into the evolutionary determinate pattern, Christianity would go--it must go--the way of its predecessors, absorbed into the next stage of human development in the relentless forward surge.

In those post-Darwinian days, conventional interpretations of Christian revelation became increasingly inadequate for the highly educated layman with the result that religious faith was severely wounded, and for some killed altogether. That is not to say that for the English faith sank suddenly like lead in water. It did not. In fact, the strong evangelical tradition and millions of nonconformist Protestants and Catholics were unaffected by the Spencers and Huxleys of the day. Their faith remained intact. Catholic writers, particularly in *The Month*, picked up the challenge, separated truth from theory parading as fact, and made learned rebuttals.

In falling back on the test of individual conscience, in accommodating rationalist objections to Scripture, in temporizing essential pronouncements on doctrine where the stakes were the very faith of Christians, Protestantism had sacrificed its authority. Battered by dissension within its ranks, the Church of England was not able to defend religion, while Catholicism in holding fast to revelation and tradition was not nearly so vulnerable.

Early on Hugh Benson was lured by Absolutes, by a spiritual life undisturbed by changing times and opinions. The modern relativist dilemma, everything subject to change and personality, to the test of science, to experience, to personal taste, to proportion, and nothing to objective reality; everything adrift in that perilous subjective sea left him unsatisfied, but not despairing. Solid footing is what Benson sought, solid ground he found. To those Protestants who were arguing that truth is relative, or unknowable, or that truths had to be tested in the crucible of individual conscience; to those Anglicans ever insisting that authority must yield under pressure of changing attitudes and declining morals, he answered this: in the Catholic Church, and there only, man finds that which is unchanging because it is apostolic, absolute, and absolutely true. He left behind an English garden of gorgeous but fading roses in order to enter the desert, as the world esteemed it. Instead of vast wastes he found consolation and creative power; his thirst was quenched. Loneliness drove him deeper into the soul where God revealed all he needed to know. And when he had rested, back he went into the faded garden, ever alluring with a false fragile beauty of the kind that shows its temporality at the first cold blast.

Notes

1 Even characters in fiction read Benson. He is one of Amory's favourite writers in *This Side of Paradise*, F. Scott Fitzgerald's autobiographical novel of 1921.

2 "Trois Histoires comme Benson," in Teilhard de Chardin's *Hymne de l'Univers* (Paris, 1961). Father Teilhard had been deeply impressed by Hugh's tale of the contemplative nun of Malling Abbey in *The Light Invisible*. These three *histoires* or *contes*, written in 1916, "The Picture," "The Monstrance," and "The Pyx," have the sound and feel of Hugh's mystical tales where physical matter comes alive.

3 David Newsome, *On the Edge of Paradise* (London and Chicago, 1980). From the same author has come a biographical sketch of Martin, the first Benson son, who died at 18. It has opened yet another window into this extraordinary family. See *Godliness and Good Learning* (London, 1961).

AT TREMANS 1904
Arthur, Hugh, Fred, Maggie (with Roddy), Mary, Beth

THE BENSON BROTHERS 1882
Fred, 15   Arthur, 21   Hugh, 11

HUGH AT 5, WITH BETH

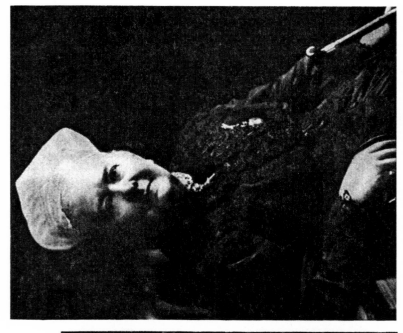

MARY BENSON AT 70

MARY BENSON AT 30

EDWARD WHITE BENSON, ARCHBISHOP OF CANTERBURY

1
The Bensons

"We suck out of all things a kind of essence that abides with us always"

It was an exceptional family and an exceptional birth. On November 18, 1871, the fourth boy child, Robert Hugh (Hughie, then simply *Hugh*) was born to Edward White and Mary Benson in the Master's Lodge of Wellington College, Lincoln. Five others had come before: first-born Martin, his father's pride and right hand, dead of brain fever at 18 when Hugh was just 6; Arthur Christopher, and high-spirited Nellie (Mary Eleanor), who has left behind so few traces.[1] There was brilliant, unhappy Maggie (Margaret), and Fred (Edward Frederic), whom Hugh had unseated as youngest child. Here was a lively thriving brood in a comfortable home full of games and creative merriment--a late Victorian family, yet not wholly typical, for the children were all energetic and clever, gifted with rapid minds and verbal felicity under constant encouragement.[2] The results are proved in the hundreds of essays, stories, novels, drawings, poems, and miscellaneous pieces streaming from the pens of the sons. Of the four surviving children, only Fred and Arthur were to reach old age. In 1916 Maggie died at the age of 51. She was the scholar, and had written two books on Egypt and several commentaries on the New Testament. Sadly her last years were spent in a sanitarium for the insane. Hugh died at 43 in 1914, just months after the outbreak of World War I. He did not live to see the world he skillfully depicted in his modern novels wiped out with the last of the brave young men who never made it out of the trenches. In 1925 after a long active life first as housemaster at Eton and then fellow of Magdalene College, Cambridge, a post he had held with distinction for many years, Arthur Benson died. Like his father, his life had been blackened by chronic depression. Depression ran deep in Benson blood;

not even Hugh was spared, but his bouts were rather infrequent and almost always brought on by overwork and chased away by rest.
Finally, there is Fred, the last Benson, dying quietly at Rye in 1940. And so the line was extinguished with this last of the boys. There had been no marriages, nothing of this brilliant family was passed on, everything has snapped shut and gone to dust. Such an absolute close was not foreseen when in 1871 Hugh came into the world. Of all literary families in Edwardian England, surely this was the most gifted. Unique to each member were his talents, and all made complete use of those talents to the limits their physical and mental powers allowed; so that in its heyday the Benson name attracted a huge following and gathered many honors to itself.

A Family Affair   Edward White Benson ruled the house in the manner of the kindly *paterfamilias*. He was a commanding figure, loving, intense, high-minded, introspective, demanding, painfully sensitive to the slightest offense, and incapable of hiding disappointment, which often dragged him into a deep gloom. Life was serious business to him. He loved his children and they loved back but were intimidated by his moodiness, by his mighty anger, with which he struggled all his life, by his vast knowledge of all sorts of things, by demands and high expectations so difficult for children to understand let alone satisfy. Even their recreation Papa expected to be wholesome and edifying, as for example, their frequent walking jaunts during which (Hugh complained) he was made to talk about poetry and civilization. Papa's appearance at the door threw a shadow over the children's play, and though they sought always to please him, and sensed what pleasure he took merely to relax into his chair and watch them sketch, or sit with them as they dined, and even join in their games, they were uncomfortable in his presence as they might be of a benign but watchful giant. And they too were vigilant, for a roistering prank, a word, a noise might throw him into such a disappointed gloom that dampened all pleasures. Something more was always expected of them, some intelligent profit to be made from every amusement. He was a man absorbed by details, wringing a dozen meanings out of an idea or phrase that the writer could not have intended; a simple Latin lesson from him Hugh compared to a waterfall spilling into a china mug.
Hugh was born at Wellington College where Edward was headmaster. All the Benson children were summoned to breakfast and when Hugh's birth was announced, their father received as on cue their awkward words of congratulations. Natural shyness in expressing his love divided him from his children; and awkwardness was often misunderstood as diffidence or irritation, though he was in Arthur's eyes ". . . so desirous

to be surrounded with love and joy, and yet so unable to see that people cannot enjoy by rule; so unaware how formidable he could be . . . And then too his dark mood, his sense that everyone was doing wrong, was acting selfishly and inconsiderately. His bringing much too serious motives to bear on simple situations. . . ." (*Diary*, Jan. 3, 1906). Martin was Edward's darling, a precocious boy with strong religious leanings, apt successor of the father. His death left the father a stricken man who never completely recovered from the loss of the one nearest his heart. In time Edward's hopes lighted on Hugh as the son destined for Holy Orders.[3] Though Hugh was to aspire to these heights later, it was not so at the time, for Edward alone of the family had religious enthusiasm. But he saw what he wanted to see in his Hughie, to whom ritual and ceremony were no more than splendid dress-up pantomimes to be played out for one's amusement. Even with Edward's high hopes for him, this son was spared the full yoke of intellectual demands imposed upon the precocious Martin; in fact, Arthur tells us Hugh was brought up on the opposite principle to that which had governed Martin's early training. The basic material was different: Hugh was high-strung and playful, and not nearly so intent on pleasing his father.

Yet for all their apparent differences, Hugh inherited many traits from his father, boundless energy, a spiritual nature tending to the mystical, the artist's fondness for ritual, a love of liturgy and church ornament down to the last detail, and finally immovable will. That hard streak, mitigated by touches of courtliness in the father, was passed on to Hugh the child though with a difference, as we shall see. Edward threw himself into the serious business of life; Hugh went about a project at hand with ferocious single-mindedness, but when it was over he relaxed and laughed; he was easy-going, full of good humor, with a genuine talent for conversation. In smaller matters of taste and habits there was remarkable likeness as well--a love of bathing, of horses, of travel; explosive temper when provoked although Hugh recovered quickly, while Edward, perfectionist that he was, slid into dark depression over trifles. Both had read classics at Trinity College, Cambridge, before becoming priests of the Church of England; and both believed in ghosts. This boy (Edward said) for whom he developed a strong affection would be his great friend as he grew old, and it deeply disappointed him when at 19 Hugh decided upon a career in the Indian Civil Service. Once Hugh's mind was set nothing short of Divine Intervention could budge him, for a strong will and determination were already rooted in his character just as they were firmly rooted in Edward's. As things turned out it was not to be the Civil Service after all--God's signature moved here as everywhere--so he was off to Trinity and after Trinity into the Church of England he went, to the satisfaction of his father and all the family.

Mary Benson, Edward's remarkable complement, was by all accounts loving, tactful, pious, intelligent. She warmed her children to the delights of fantasy and game playing, perhaps because she had been scarcely more than a child herself when she married. To her young children she was adoring and gentle, smoothing over the angles of Edward's daunting personality. In 1858 Mary Sidgwick had married Edward, who was by then a Fellow of Trinity and a priest of the English Church. He was 29 and she 18. A year later their first son was born. As a girl, she had prepared for marriage to Edward by educating herself in those specialized matters that would bring her intellectual equality with her husband (her older brother was Cambridge philosopher Henry Sidgwick). She was young, merry, loved by all, possessed of a sharp eye and an easy nature, very kind and loving to her children. Her sons loved her back to the end of their lives. She was Hugh's confidante, his vital support in the difficult year before he went over to Rome, but once he had her blessing, no power on earth could stop him. In everything she was the perfect wife, in everything the perfect mother.

With Wellington now established as a first-rate public school the Bensons removed to Lincoln Cathedral where as newly-appointed Chancellor Edward once again proved an indefatigable worker, stretching himself from project to project, and solidifying his reputation as a forceful and efficient administrator. From Lincoln they moved on to Cornwall, to the Kenwyn vicarage (thereafter dubbed by him Lis Escop), their newly remodeled residence just above Truro, in those days a small town sheltered by wooded hills. This was an untroubled happy time for the family, full of joys and evening walks and excursions to mystical places--Tintagel and Land's End and Rough Tor--and at home, games and shadowboxes and playacting, every diverting amusement to while away the hours. By this time Edward was Bishop Benson of the newly created See of Truro, a post offered to him by Disraeli with the warm approval of Queen Victoria. Before long he would become Archbishop of Canterbury.

The extraordinary circumstances of the Canterbury See--residence and receptions at Lambeth Palace, affairs of church and state in an atmosphere thick with dignitaries, from the Prince of Wales to such exotics as the Russian ambassador, might have created a different family character. It did not, and the children were untouched by self-importance or self-consciousness.

A word must be said about Elizabeth Cooper--beloved Beth--who completed the ménage. She was a family member not by blood, but by devotion and longevity. She had come as a young girl to the Sidgwicks to be nursemaid to their children, and when Mary Sidgwick married she went with her to the Benson household to care for the brood with great tenderness. There she remained until her death at the age of 92. By then she had been with Mary for seventy years. Hugh was her favorite, being the youngest, and she lavished him with love and favors, buying him little presents, seeing to his comfort, tidying up after him, and caring for him during Mary's absences. She was especially remembered in his letters home, and made an appearance in Benson's novel *The Coward*, as Benty, the old nurse Val Medd turns to in time of trouble.[4]

II

Hugh was a highly imaginative child with as keen an eye for details as for panoramas. And all about him were placed delights for eye and ear so that from the beginning his precocious imaginative faculty was nourished by romantic settings. Country houses and country gardens, cathedral closes, Tudor halls and turrets, granite tors under a night of stars--these impressions and more, fed by dreams and ghosts of long ago dragged over the landscape--supplied the fuel of a robust imagination. He feared the dark. Nothing could induce him to enter a dark room. "I see b--b--blood," he cried, terrified of falling over a mangled corpse--"squish! into a pool of gore."

Academic distinction, alas, was not in the cards. Mama tutored him, aided and abetted often by good-natured, motherly Nellie. At these sessions everyone's mettle was tested. Arthur writes that Nellie "would explain a rule of arithmetic to Hugh. He would assume an expression of despair: 'I don't understand a word of it--you go so quick.' Then it would be explained again: 'Now do you understand?' 'Of course I understand *that*.' 'Very well, do a sum.' The sum would begin: 'Oh don't push me--don't come so near--I don't like having my face blown on.' Presently my sister with angelic patience would show him a mistake. 'Oh, don't interfere--you make it all mixed up in my head.' Then he would be let alone for a little. Then he would put the slate down with an expression of despair and resignation; if my sister took no notice he would say: 'I thought Mama told you to help me with my sums? How can I understand without having it explained to me?' It was impossible to get the last word."[5] Daily Latin lessons were quite a struggle. Hugh was bored, inattentive, fidgety, his eyes lured away by the smallest distraction. Threats and mockery were wasted on him; he could not be intimidated. Of course, the Bishop's turn at him in Greek Testament brought better results, but when a similar duty fell to short-fused Maggie (supplied by Hugh with "temper tickets" beforehand), she was soon out of patience and showing it. "Intractable!" she would howl, throwing up her hands. Still, Hugh was "so dreadfully funny that nobody could possibly be angry with him for long, and when he had reduced his sister to distraction by his disobedience and inattention, he would anticipate the final threat the moment before it came, and, with shut eyes and a face inexpressibly solemn, would chant, 'Mamma shall be told!'"

What life was like for these children of the Archbishop was related by Fred later on in several books. They played together in the summer-house where the mystical "Chapter" was held. Arthur was warden, "Nellie, Maggie, and myself, sub-warden, secretary and treasurer, and Hugh was Henchman. . . . We all subscribed to the funds of the Chapter (my mother, who was an honorary member subscribed most) and the money was spent in official salaries, and in providing decorations, chains and crosses and ribands for the officials. The largest salary, which I think was half a crown, was drawn by Arthur as warden; he also wore the most magnificent jewel, while Hugh, the menial, drew but the salary of one penny, and had every poor gaud to console himself with. As Henchman, his duty was chiefly to run errands for the rest of the Chapter, to summon my mother when she was allowed to appear, to kill wasps, and to fetch the warden's straw hat. He was the only member of the Chapter who dared to dispute the will of the warden, and was known to exclaim, 'Why shouldn't Fred?' (the treasurer) when he was tired of running about. Even more subversive of canonical discipline was his assertion one day that he would not be a member of any more societies, in which he was only deputy sub-sub-bootboy. But I secretly (though treasurer) rather sympathized with him, for I considered then, and consider still, that the Chapter was rather a soft job for Arthur."[6] A fair in the village, his dog Watch leaping outside the window, an ailing goat, all these distractions were lures to tempt Hugh. Edward too could be charmed by his youngest child. In the midst of writing a sermon he might see Hugh "with his tongue protruding from the corner of his mouth (for that is the posture in which you can draw best) and say: 'Dear boy, have you finished your preparation for tomorrow? What are you doing?' Hugh would allow he hadn't quite finished his preparation, not having begun it." Edward would look at his drawing and begin to laugh merrily; or if not amused "a little grave rebuke followed; he returned to his Cyprian and we all sat quiet again." Good study days were rare and cause for rejoicing; small successes brought high praise--Mama wrote letters about it.

Nothing pleased Hugh so much as a hard-played game, a gory tale of dungeons and dragons, a cardboard castle. He built toys and wrote skits like "The Sandy Desert, or, Where is the Archbishop?" for a marionette theater he made. As he never entered the family schoolroom of his own accord, the family safely stored their birthday surprises there, clever hand-made fabrications like a suit of pasteboard armor covered in blue and silver paper, supplied with tunic and sword, daggers and halberd. Games might be quite elaborate as well. There were secret societies like the "Chapter" held in the summer house, complete with secret ciphers, headgear, titles, rituals; and Hugh, being the youngest, always assigned the subordinate role of acolyte for which he was paid a penny. At other times Nellie amused herself by playing the violin, and Maggie painted pictures of her cats. The brood argued incessantly, wrote plays and wrote stories all the time for each other's amusement, and took to publishing their own journal, the "Saturday Magazine," crammed full of imaginative sketches and Hugh's "endless similes for effect," and dotted with caricatures of the family: Edward going to sleep after tea, of Mary "keenly observant above and not through her spectacles, of Hugh falling off Ajax" into a ridiculous posture. "Already we were such savage wielders of the pen that one issue every holiday no longer contented us, but two or three times between term and term my father and mother were regaled of an evening with a flood of prose and poetry. . . ."[7] At rhyming games, Hugh produced decent verses, like this fragment composed at the age of eight about a swarm of gnats--

> And when they see their comrades laid
> In thousands round the garden glade,
> They know they were not really made
> To live forevermore.

Hugh saw little of Arthur who had gone away to school, but took pleasure then as in later years in annoying Fred, older by four years, and easily baited. Once, in Switzerland while on a walk with their father Hugh began stepping on Fred's toes. "Fred poked him with an umbrella and when Papa asked Fred why, he said 'because I chose to,' and Papa thereupon slapped him in the face and said 'I chose to do that!'" As adults Hugh and Fred continued to get on each other's nerves, and were much better off kept apart.[8]

Slight and delicate in physique as a child, Hugh Benson as an adult was anything but delicate. At Cambridge he swam, hiked, rowed the Eight, and exercised vigorously for hours at a time. So it was to be all his life as if driven by a passion to fill every moment of the day with activity. Nothing short of his father's command was permitted to interfere with recreation. Mountain climbing and Alpine walking tours remained a favorite holiday recreation even after a harrowing experience on a peak of the Bernina Alpine range.

Much has been written about Hugh Benson's temperament, that he
was a clever, active, inventive child bent on having his own way, with
a disagreeable tendency to argue over trifles, or what seemed trifling to
others. He was never without an opinion, never wanting in the
independent streak that insisted upon being recognized. But there was
more to him than mere willfulness. There was from childhood a strong
artistic dimension, a love of opulence and an affinity for color and
sensation and detail that was to permeate his life and works, and a
craving even from the beginning to try his hand at every art and every
craft as if the mastery of it were his for the taking. *Hugh*, Arthur
Benson's memoir, rapidly struck in 1915 while the iron was hot (Hugh
having died the previous year), insisted that the artistic dimension was
the root of his spiritual life, insisted that Hugh was attracted by the
splendid ritual of the Catholic Church, its color, pageantry, its
magnificent architecture and adornments; and claimed that Hugh's
"going over to Rome" was a matter more of aesthetics and romance
than genuine conversion. Love of spectacle, he maintained, played a
vital role in Hugh's conversion--it was all a marvelous game to him,
with ceremonies, costumes, processions, secret words, designated roles--
all the toys of childhood revivified.

Mindful of Hugh's legions of admirers, Arthur felt a special
responsibility to keep Hugh's reputation intact but at the same time to
portray him honestly and affectionately as one who went his own way,
knew what he wanted to do, and did it. So the child's antics take center
stage but dressed in such disarming naturalism that the sting goes out
of them. Hugh is mischievous, funny, single-minded and passionate
where his own interests are at stake--and utterly unsentimental. Later,
ardent admirers looking at his life *en couleur de rose* invented a pious
sweet-natured child sitting at his father's knee soaking up sanctity, a
fable that would have sent Hugh into fits of laughter.

The fact is that outside of Hugh's cleverness and spontaneity there
were few redeeming traits to prepare us for one of those edifying
miraculous transformations that are to be found in the Lives of the
Saints. There was no piety, no depth in his early years, merely an
impatient, willful boy. At the same time we learn that in Hugh's adult
life. once the religious crisis had passed and the Catholic Church had
claimed him, his personality changed for the better; he became more
tolerant, mystically inclined to the interior life, yet more practical and
conciliatory in his dealings with others. As spiritual guide and
counselor, he was there always for all who needed to draw upon his
special gifts; but at the same time he was incapable of emotional
attachments (he admitted it), and though the hearts of so many were his
for the taking, it was no good, for profound friendships were beyond his

capacities. No person on earth, friend or otherwise, moved him so powerfully although he had countless acquaintances, enjoyed himself thoroughly in good company, and was to everyone who knew him an excellent and witty conversationalist and a delightful companion. He was fair game to Establishment critics offended by his conversion, yet seemed impervious to their slings and arrows no matter how harsh or unjustified, shrugging off their barbs as one might shake the dust off one's feet, without a trace of bitterness. The truth is that Hugh Benson needed no friend or confidant or lover; in worldly matters he was fearless, emotionally detached, self-sufficient, and immune to lingering joy or sorrow. And even while surrounded by family or friends wherever he went, whether abroad or home at Hare Street, he remained alone and remained content to be so. Is that a defect? Arthur does not grieve, but running through the narrative of his brother's life is distress that Hugh who was loved by so many for his unworldliness, chivalry, and charm was not deeply bound to anyone by ordinary ties of human affection. So be it. As Hugh said of himself, "God has preserved me extraordinarily from intimacies with others. He has done this, not I. I have longed for intimacies and failed to win them."

Notes

[1] Dame Ethel Smith reported that to everyone the Archbishop was a majestic figure. Nellie alone was at ease in his presence. Hugh, whom Dame Ethel did not like, "loved to flit up and down the corridors of Lambeth in coats the skirts of which always swept the floor--a common foible of short men. I never saw him after he became a Roman Catholic, but it was a relief to think of him safe in a cassock." *Impressions That Remained* (London, 1919), p. 191.

[2] Family matters were mined many times by Arthur in *Life of Edward White Benson,* (London, 1899-1900), *Hugh, Memoirs of a Brother* (London, 1915), *Life and Letters of Margaret Benson* (London, 1918); and by E.F. in *Our Family Affairs* (New York, 1920), *Mother* (New York, 1925), *As We Were* (London, 1930), and *Final Edition* (London, 1940).

[3] See David Newsome, *Godliness and Good Learning,* pp. 148ff. for a glimpse of Benson family life to the death of Martin. Martin died peacefully at Wellington with Edward and Mary at his bedside, a blow from which Edward never recovered: "It has changed all my views of God's work as it is to be done in this world and the next, to be compelled to believe God's plan for him really has run on sweetly, and rightly for him and for all--and yet-- he is dead. 'One's views of life change very quickly,' he said to me the last

hour in which he spoke to me. My sweet boy, thou hast changed mine."
Hugh, just 6, wrote of the death, "My dear Arthur, Martain is dead. Nellie
sends you her love. Martin has gone to hefen. Maggie sends you her love. I
am so happy that Martin is gone to Jesus Christ. I hope we shall all come
to HIM very soon. He is Saint Martin now. Your loving brother, Hugh."

[4] Beth is the literary model of Sebastian Flyte's nanny in Evelyn Waugh's
Brideshead Revisited. (For a commentary on Waugh's use of this model, see
Roger Martin, "Robert Hugh Benson and Evelyn Waugh," *Notes and
Queries*, ns 37 (1990), p. 68.) Waugh read Hugh's works, in fact went back
to the historical novels before writing his own book about the life of the
English saint and martyr Edmund Campion. Waugh thought Hugh Benson
an almost faultless novelist.

[5] *Hugh*, pp. 27-9.

[6] *Our Family Affairs*, p. 97.

[7] *Our Family Affairs*, p. 89.

[8] In one of several books written many years after Hugh's death, Fred has
the last word--an advantage denied to Hugh--when he slyly tells his readers
of a friend of Arthur's who disliked Hugh particularly when he was dressed up
in his monsignorial purple writing in a letter to Arthur that Hugh was the
same "sharp insignificant little scug as he had been at Eton" *Final Edition*,
p. 33. The insulting word thereupon found its way into the OED, q.v. Why
Fred repeated this malicious remark in his book is a mystery.

2
To Eton and Onward

"It is not of much use to be entreated to turn over a new leaf, when
you see no kind of reason for doing so."

In 1882 Edward White Benson became Archbishop of Canterbury. The
family settled into Addington Park in Surrey, the Archbishop's country
seat. It was a great white house a mile into the woods with open fields
behind, lovely, busy, not nearly like the home they had loved in
Cornwall. Addington was a short ride to Lambeth Palace, where the
business of running the Church of England was conducted. The
extraordinary activity of the Canterbury See--affairs of church and state
in an atmosphere astir with dignitaries, of official receptions at
Lambeth Palace, and the special glamour attached to that high office
pulling everything into its tide--might have stamped a different character
on the Bensons. It did not, and the children were untouched by self-
importance or self-consciousness.

By this time Hugh had already gone away to the Walton School at
Clevedon in Somerset. He was now 11 and on his own for the first
time. Education at Clevedon followed the High Church line and was
taken seriously; the boys were encouraged to practice their Latin
grammar at mealtime by inventing rhymes and did their learning in
ways that, looking back upon those days years later, he approved.
From Clevedon he went on to Eton.

Neither Eton nor Cambridge has an important place in Hugh
Benson's books. Eton, a breeding ground of snobbishness, he liked not
at all. Ragging and violence that fed on small dreamy boys of
independent mind curbed him for a time, but never stifled his
individualism. If anything, the opposite happened. That inscrutable
detachment from others that in later years left friends who loved him
puzzled and wanting hardened in the unforgiving atmosphere of the
public school. He had a small circle of friends, a lively bunch, full of

pranks and unpleasantly cliquish. And though Hugh was no angel, neither was he beast. An incident of bullying of which he was accused (a charge he fiercely denied) poisoned his Eton days. Hugh recalled how his father having heard about it so paralysed him with his mighty indignation that he was unable to speak in his own defence.[1]

Religion at Eton left him cold; it was too academic, too formalized to affect anyone's religious and moral life interiorly. Apart from the beautiful singing voices, chapel represented "the same kind of official homage to Almighty God as cheering the Queen when she came to see us," a view shared by his brother Arthur. His early training in classics and Latin verse had been strong enough apparently to earn him a scholarship, yet he left Eton a disappointment to everyone, including himself. The school took little account of individual idiosyncrasies, he wrote later in two blistering articles for the weekly *Everyman*. It had killed his love of the classics; only English and history was he able to read with anything like pleasure, and that only because he had never taken a single lesson in either at Eton. A year's study with a tutor taught him more of mathematics, history, and the classics than ever Eton had in four. It was the same for French. This strong criticism uttered years after his schooling conveniently omitted aspects of his own personality, for in these years Hugh simply let slide anything that did not amuse him. He hated being made to learn, and this indignation at Eton's methods (however justified they may have been in some respects) was a latter-day excuse for idleness. "I want to know how you *think* you are doing in school," his father wrote. It was hard for him to develop and hold to a habit. Nothing amused him long enough.

The Archbishop still hoped to make a scholar of him: ". . . *do the work in the first part, and not in the last part* of the time *allowed for it.* You are capital in resolving to get out of bed, and doing it--only be just as resolute about *the right moment* for beginning work. . . ." The tone and substance of letters in 1887 and '88 when he was 17 is unchanged: there is "still *room for improvement.*" His mother warns he is on thin ice: "I hate anything that sounds like a threat--this isn't that--but it *is* a reminder." Each passing day is fixing his fate in no ordinary way: "O Hugh, *do* remember all that was said to you last holidays! . . . We must help you to gain character and purpose and all those things that you need, and it must be by *deeds* now, not words. . . . It came over me so this morning how terribly critical it was--I didn't think you seemed quite to be realizing it--and I thought I must just write one great *plead* to you, and then leave it--but don't *you* leave it. Do take it home to you--sixteen on November 18th." She ends by reminding him that Martin "was only seventeen when he came out head of the school at Winchester." Pleading with the problem-child brought promises to work harder, to read the texts, and to teach himself Italian, if only he is not "*made* to learn it. . . I hate that." Did it happen? Apparently not, for two months later in May, the Archbishop asked anxiously about his studies about which Hugh has been strangely silent: "How are you getting on? Who are you up to? What are your books? Can I send you anything? Mind you tell me all." Alas, he was no scholar then or ever, certainly not a diligent grammarian as the term was understood at the time. "'Our little sheltered boy!' his mother calls him"--so Edward wrote in 1889.

Yet Hugh Benson was capable of a surprise now and then. He had won a competitive scholarship to Eton (which brother Fred, the superior student, had failed to win), and now, quite incredibly, reached First Hundred, an honors program involving heavy reading of classical authors. To this task he applied himself with just about the same diligence as before. While Edward fretted over a falling off in Greek and Latin writers, Hugh was finding diversion in *Truth* and *Police News*, the tabloids of the day. In France he was once again surprised by news that he had captured the prestigious Hervey prize for his poem on Father Damien.

At 18 he left Eton to seek an appointment in the Indian Civil Service. This development was a profound disappointment to his father because Hugh was the one that was supposed to take Martin's place, and India would put two years between Eton and Cambridge. Short of insisting--which the archbishop was disinclined to do, fearful of repeating Martin's tragedy in another child--there was nothing to be done once Hugh's mind was made up. Poor Edward had not ceased to hope: "I always reckoned on this one to be my great friend as I grew old," he wrote in his diary. His letters to Hugh are filled with gentle admonitions to study, to pray, to keep fit in body and soul, to do as Martin had done but not, *not* to over-do; a steady diet of Scripture reading and rest on Sunday made a better scholar. *"Then let the weary body A little while repose: The last thought be of Jesus Before thine eyelids close"* was Martin's translation of a precept from Prudentius, he is reminded. Yet the old careless neglect persisted: "... one word would be so easy to those who love you so."

The grand result was that at Eton he left little behind beyond a name carved into "Gladstone's Door" and a picture of himself in cap and blazer as Steerer of the *St. George*.

Before the Indian Civil Service became a certainty Hugh had to pass an examination. To improve his French and German he sailed to the Continent to the Paris Exhibition and the opening of the Eiffel Tower and afterwards braved Alpine climbing for the first time. He had a grand old time in the Alps (mountaineering became a life-long passion), but neither his French nor German prospered. Returning to London there was a brief flirtation with Theosophy, very much the rage in those years. As for his studies it was business as usual with the result that he failed the examination for the Indian Civil Service. Up to Trinity he

went at last, as his father and uncles had gone before, to read Classics.
While he had put a little effort into Eton, he put nothing into
Cambridge. He was a young man now, slight of build but quite strong,
virtually on his own to follow his whimsy, and so he did giving
himself over to steering for Trinity, entertaining friends, and playing
cards all night. His mother was impressed by his inflated reports of full
days and nights: "The hours of reading make me gasp a little--can you
really possibly fit seven hours reading in the day without lectures or
any exams or helps? O *do* tell me what you are reading. . . . O Hugh,
write to tell me how you bear the life!" Did Mary believe it? A few
months later his father wrote naively that Hugh was hard at work in
"that happiest state of life, a Trinity Freshman."[2] Actually, in this
happiest state of life Hugh did little more than loaf and rack up debts.
     At Cambridge where his individualism was allowed to assert
itself, Hugh's eccentric habits soon brought him fame. He insisted on
two baths a day, smoked a lot of cigarettes, enjoyed "many bibings of
iced liquor and large meals under awnings--at all hours of the day," and
avoided friendships with any man who thought days were for reading
books. On the literary side, he joined the Chit Chat society, from
which members of the secret society Apostles were recruited and also
the elegant Fortnightly (*Twice a Fortnight*) club of Kings described by
Fred in *The Babe B.A.* He wrote for the Trinity literary magazine and
the *Cambridge Review* and produced several poems and stories. His
unsigned lampoon "A Scandal in High Life" greatly irked one of the
"brainless voluptuaries" whom he had satirized, and when one of them,
a "blood," threatened to sue, Hugh went into brief retirement lest a son
of the Archbishop of Canterbury be dragged into court on a charge of
libel. What would the world think? On the bright side, he and Maggie
collaborated on a story that was published in 1891, and for the fun of it
he wrote a bad novel in which the main character dies at the end--for
Hugh practise runs for his later good novels in which the main character
dies at the end.
     Two qualities distinctly stand out: he loved to talk and he seemed to
all to have nerves of steel. His natural gift for controversy made a good
debater of him, both at Eton and at Trinity in the Decemviri, the
debating society where at the least he was an irritating member
"plucking ceaselessly at his chin with fingers stained with (too much)
cigarette-smoking, as he strove with his stammer to break into an
argument which was going against his views, and now and then
exploding into a short laugh." Boyish looks, a mop of fair hair that
never felt a comb, charm, and playfulness attracted everyone. He was
an easy and engaging conversationalist, very bright, with a rapid mind
and love of play, quick of speech despite his stammer. When asked for
an opinion of his brother's novel *Dodo*, he replied, "Well, it's very wo-

wo-wo-worldly." When Fred asked why he was drinking champagne which he disliked, Hugh replied, "B-b-because I couldn't say c-c-claret." He could be hilariously funny as raconteur, parodist, or clown, often throwing friends and family into convulsions of laughter. It was impossible to be angry with him for long.

As a member of the Leander Club he steered third boat for Trinity all four years. Golf he was quite good at; canoeing on the Cam near Kings Chapel was a favored pastime; so was water polo played in Canadian canoes that invariably ended in a dunking for both teams. Boundless energy and zest for life made him game for everything from spending hours at a stretch at grueling exercising to walking the Yorkshire Moors with Arthur in winter. He made at least two trips on foot from Cambridge to London, a distance of 50 miles.[3] He was game for pranks, like playing the robed nun who stood in the Great Court of Trinity smoking a black pipe only to vanish on rubber soles round the kitchen quarters; or flagging down a train with a red handkerchief to see if it could be done; and there was the incident of multiple packages containing buttered bread broken into pieces left everywhere around town addressed to the victim and delivered.

Probably the most revealing glimpse of Hugh Benson's Cambridge days are to be found in Fred's very funny book *The Babe B.A.* Although a real "The Babe" lived and breathed (Arthur mentions such a person several times in his diary), Hugh's arrival and residence at Trinity coincide not only with that of The Babe, but all the favorite activities that divided Hugh from serious work, activites like theatricals, lolling on the Backs near Clare Bridge, lavish entertainments, cards, and the care and feeding of smelly pets--are chronicled in The Babe's hilarious Cambridge career. It is all there in the book in delicious detail, and if The Babe's tale was not a day-by-day replication of Hugh Benson's life, it was very nearly so, at least that was how Benson's American admirers saw it. The Babe was Hugh.[4]

Life had rare pleasures also at Addington Park. There were horses and rabbit shooting, much good talk at the table, long walks and reading in the garden or under the shade of trees. Besides the Bensons, there were two chaplains living at Addington when the Archbishop was in residence, and friends came to visit often, all of them joining in spirited debate over the port. Later, as a curate at the Eton Mission he often brought poor children here for a day of feasting and games.

When the hypnotism craze swept the Quads, Hugh played at it. He managed to hypnotize a couple of local rustics and dabbled in other occultist crazes like crystal-ball gazing and mind reading.[5] When Fred at Kings learned of it, knowing Hugh was not particularly disposed to take his advice, he asked Mary to intervene: "He has struck up a friendship with a person who dabbles in mesmerism: he hasn't been able to mesmerise Hugh, and no harm has been done, but it is a silly thing to meddle with, and wastes time." Mary begged Hugh not to "go playing tricks with hypnotism. (And, I said *Oh, please!*) It is a deadly thing, and ought, I am sure, to be taken up scientifically or not at all." A month later she was more insistent, obliquely threatening to bring the issue to the attention of his father if he persisted in experimenting. He gave it up, fortunately, just in time as other Trinity faddists were found out and sent down. There was also the story of the unfortunate suicide, the man "who shot himself, apparently from overwork at night, and was found dead yesterday morning by someone whom he had asked to breakfast." Hugh irritated the dead man's friends by sleeping that night in the bloodstained room with the intention of communicating with the ghost he firmly expected to appear.

Religion in his Cambridge B.A. days left him flat. One definitely took the middle ground: neither pious nor atheist, chapel from time to time, and music at Kings on a Sunday afternoon. Anything more was rank fanaticism. Hugh could never settle for so little exoticism for very long. There was a fling with Swedenborgism as a little earlier there had been with Theosophy. A Roman Mass attended with a convert friend left no impression beyond mingled contempt and awe, but on another occasion one drop of water falling on his face at the Asperges brought elation. Music alone remained the tie to spirituality, so off he went every evening to services at Kings to hear the choir. Bliss was a gorgeous celebration with copes and candles, with orchestra playing Beethoven and Gounod, and a choir of trained voices rapt in "O Saving Victim."

Then quite suddenly his sister Nellie came down with diphtheria and died. She was 27.

Appealing as it is to turn this sad event into his religious awakening, the fact is he drifted into the idea of taking Orders as the line of least resistance. Like many an Oxford and Cambridge man before him he fancied being a "quiet country gentleman, with a beautiful garden and exquisite choir, and a sober bachelor existence." In 1891 Hugh switched from Classics to Theology, and actually looked forward to reading Hebrew, to the delight of his father. The truth was that little in the way of self-discipline had changed, and examinations found him pacing about his room for days in a panic: "My father, all my uncles, all my brothers--all--all--all got Firsts, and here I am going to get a Third." He was right on the mark, scoring a deplorable Third in Tripos. That nineteen others had failed was something of a consolation.

So ended the less-than-glorious Cambridge days. They had been lovely extravagant days, pleasure-filled, self-indulgent, stimulating; and accidentally he had become decently educated. Now as later, Hugh Benson seemed self-sufficient and was content to be so. No lasting friendships had developed, there were no special affections here to connect him to anything or anyone in particular however, looking back, in retrospect, he may have welcomed them. He stepped unnoticed out of the small circle of friends he had and they out of his so that even when he returned as priest to Cambridge, it was without any nostalgia for the past. Earlier he had written to a friend of having sadly lost sight of everybody he ever knew. "With one consent they have ceased to pay the smallest attention to my existence."

Notes

1 He was cleared of the charge. Hugh had no cruelty in him, not "the faintest touch of the savagery that amuses itself at the sight of another's sufferings" (ACB*Diary*, June 2, 1905). He hated cruelty more than anything in the world, particularly cruelty to animals who could not strike back--"the existence of it is the only thing which reconciles my conscience to the necessity of Hell."

2 The Archbishop's expectations floated sublimely above the head and will power of his lazy boy. Confined to bed with a bad cold, Hugh told Maggie he had nothing to write home about, to which the Archbishop replied by return mail with a lecture on the benefits of a dry room and warm bed, wondering why he said he had nothing to write about simply because he has been in bed unable to get up: "Surely you must have accumulated all sorts of reflective and imaginative stories there." The Archbishop had exhorted young Martin from time to time to work at "concentration of mind and body: to ward off listlessness in attention" (Newsome, p. 175).

3 A hard tramp from Cambridge to London during which Hugh was crippled by his boot and the Archbishop's daunting reaction to it were described by a friend: "After another two hours Hugh was going really lame, but it never occurred to him to give in. Somewhere south of Ware I persuaded him to take my arm, and he stumped along, still perfectly cheerful, buoyed up by the increasing number of houses and gas lamps which deceitfully suggested that we were nearing the outskirts of London. We were only at the tip of one of those tentacle suburbs which fringe the main roads for many miles before real town begins. The pace became slower, and I had to get him some brandy, and then decided that if he attempted more he might make himself really ill. Beaten in body, but still unbroken in spirit, he was persuaded to get into the train at a station called Ponders End, and slept all the way to Liverpool Street. We had sent our bags on to Lambeth, and had a very kind welcome when we arrived there late at night. Hugh was able to dissemble his lameness, and the Archbishop's principal concern was for the levity with which we had passed a series of interesting churches without pausing to study their architecture. . . . That was the first of several visits which showed me something of the bracing atmosphere in which Hugh had grown up" (From a letter from Professor Bosanquet, in M, I, p. 86).

4 A friend informed Mrs. Isabella Stewart Gardner of Boston, a great Benson admirer, of this happy discovery. The full title is *The Babe, B.A. Being the uneventful history of a young gentleman at Bambridge University.*

5 These adventures frequently ended with the group collapsing in laughter. A friend who witnessed Hugh's practical experiments in mesmerism recalled that once "when he was going off after Hall one night with three others to 'read' in the rooms of one (I am afraid on most occasions the reading did not last very long), the conversation happened to turn on crystal-gazing, and nothing would satisfy him but that we should all four stand in different corners of the room gazing into a glass of water (the nearest approach to a crystal that could be improvised) until, greatly to Hugh's disgust, a loud laugh from one of the party put an end to the performance. I also recollect one May afternoon his insisting, after lunch in his room, on darkening the room and our sitting with our hands on the table waiting developments, and his indignation when the inevitable happened, and some of us set to work to get the table going" (M, I, 90).

3
Holy Orders

Hugh's career up to this point had been uneventful and gave no signal for what was about to happen. There was an endearing playfulness to him, but he showed no special talent except for idleness and controversy, both of these perfected in undergraduate days. His brother Arthur's diary which yields so much reflection on Hugh is silent for these years, but the evidence shows there was no precocious religiosity or distinguishing intellectual power. Thus far he had accomplished little. All in all he was something of a disappointment to his family considering the solid achievements of the Archbishop, and even his brother to a lesser extent; but at least by the summer of 1893, he was in his third and last year at Trinity and beginning to think seriously about his future. Doing something useful with one's life became the challenge, and following his father's profession seemed the simplest course. His religious views thus far were entirely and properly conventional: Roman Catholics were corrupt, ritualists tainted, and Evangelicals noisy.

So in September when he was just short of 22 years with his father's permission he went to live with Dean Vaughan of Llandaff in Wales to read for Holy Orders. Vaughan was a saintly charismatic man, a remarkable preacher with a heavy evangelical bias who nevertheless drew students from every compass point of Protestantism to his theological college. The Archbishop had no qualms. Hugh read Greek Testament every morning, wrote a sermon every week (sending them home for correction), got his first dose of parish work, and for recreation played half-back against Cardiff. It was about this time that the mystical quality of John Shorthouse's *John Inglesant* reasserted itself.[1] At 18 he had come under the influence of this powerful book and was able all his life to quote passages by heart. It was Inglesant's

half-mystical, half-emotional devotion to Christ which focused his
vague religious sense, and for a time he envisioned founding a religious
community along the lines of Nicholas Ferrar's Little Gidding, even
walking about from place to place in search of a suitable site.
Romantic fancy it was, an escape without sacrifice, for at the time self-
denial had no part in his plan.[2] Between Llandaff and examinations for
the diaconate, he traveled to Switzerland for Riffelhorn climbing, but
only after delicate maneuvering around his father who worried about his
stamina and his spending habits.[3]

Back at Llandaff Hugh again shocked himself by taking a rare First in
the preliminary examination. On a solitary retreat before ordination for
the diaconate, he passed through what he described as a "dark night of
the soul" when *all* religious sense deserted him. "It seemed to me, after
a day or two, that there was no truth in religion, that Jesus Christ was
not God, that the whole of life was an empty sham." Brooding in the
dark nave of Lincoln Cathedral where his father had been Bishop, he
was a soul in Hell, he said. Hugh's description was more mystical than
was the reality, for in his letters home he talked mostly of walking the
streets of Lincoln, catching glimpses of his happy childhood. His
biographer Martindale hints that Hugh invented the desolation on which
he insists so much in the *Confessions*,[4] but in truth Hugh never
exposed heart and soul publicly, preferring always to explain himself
through the interior struggle of characters in his novels, even to the
persona of his own confession.

He returned to Addington to be ordained a deacon by his father on
Christmas Day, 1894. Mary, writing to Maggie, was ecstatic-- " . . . if
you have been present to us today! O Maggie, it has been very
beautiful. First I must describe Sunday. Hugh came down looking
radiant--quite himself once more--saying he was well and looking
perfectly happy. It was a splendid crisp morning, and a glorious sun.
We were all in Church by 11 o'clock. . . . Hugh was ordained at last,
and then he stepped within the rails, standing side by side with his
father, who just rose from the seat where he had been ordained, his
voice ringing out like a trumpet, sweet and clear and ringing, and then
the choir burst into a fury of "glory be to thee, O God"-- and then his
notes again. 'Let your loins be girded about, and you lights burning'--it
was almost more than one could bear. . . ." Edward whose hopes had
been fulfilled, if not in Martin then in another, wrote in his diary that
night, "I had the wonderful happiness of laying hands on my Hugh . . .
my son whom I love."

Immediately after, Hugh became curate at the Eton Mission in
Hackney Wick. The Mission, supported by Eton as a way to encourage
privileged boys to observe first-hand the problems of the poor, served as

a religious and recreational center for this poor district of east London. At once, Hugh poured himself physically into the task of parish work but his heart was not in it. He had had no previous contact with the poor or with the temperance movement and often fell over his own feet; his nature was artistic and he lacked the rough-and-tumble personality that might appeal to an earthier element: ". . . I have made friends with five or six of them. But there is a class of them who play cards, and apparently have not the slightest wish to pay one any attention."

Of the Eton-sponsored mission, he was critical. It was useless and counterproductive that young rich men made it a practice to set aside an evening or two a week to join in the amusements of the poor. Rather than awakening the conscience of wealthier classes to the fact that the way of the world is not the way of a prosperous home, the visits merely showed the poor how the rich lived. Still, he worked very hard-- preaching, attending social teas, visiting the sick (with trepidation), giving classes in Bible and Prayer Book twice a week, teaching Sunday school which was much harder than preaching "as one sees the boredom of one's audience so much more clearly." Sermons were growing in number (two on Sunday), as he described to Mary his increasing control over that particular strength, preaching extempore: "I first write the sermon word for word--and then analyse it closely, and then preach and I find that it is successful, that is to say I don't stop for more than about half a minute between each word."

He took the boys to football and cricket matches on Saturdays and made friends among the other curates. On the personal side, late hours called for resourcefulness: "I find this a terrible place for sleepiness. One does not get back to the house generally till eleven, and one cannot instantly go to bed; and there is Service every morning at eight at least, sometimes at 7:30. And I am always very sleepy in the morning, and have several devices for waking--an alarum, and a string tied to my finger which is pulled like a bell-rope from outside" (*Letter to MB*, Jan. 1895). He visited the sick, giving the pathetic details in letters home: "There is a boy in my district with a diseased spine. Oh dear me! His mother told me that when he heard I was coming he was very careful to tell her to move a ball off the floor--and a little stick of paper for fear that I should trip over them, and he paints picture frames for his father which he always hides before I come in. I'm going to send him a game of some sort, and am pledged to tell him fairy stories. He saw his father play games in the evening. The worst of the whole thing is that his parents think he is going to recover--and I believe it is really hopeless. He hardly speaks at all but sits and looks with large dark blue eyes. His father is rather odd too. He insists on his family going to church, but entirely refuses to go himself. I have not seen the father yet, but I'm going in a day or two in the evening to see him. I am going to be present at the christening of my first god-child on Nov. 5--a small sister of this boy who has never been christened yet. Her parents think that they will finally have her 'done.' Poor people are dreadfully funny about everything." Again to Mamma-- "Nothing very much has happened. I'm preaching next Sunday for the first time and had my first experience of sick visit yesterday. There were 3 people--two women and a boy. One of the women couldn't speak because she has phthesis of the throat, so I had to be cheerful and reassuring in a kind of monologue for 20 minutes. She was very deaf too, so the monologue had to peal loudly through the house. (I hope this doesn't sound heartless, but she won't die.) The boy was very pathetic--inflammation of the lungs *and* pleurisy--he seems to be very bad--but is perfectly cheerful and yelled with laughter now and then. I lent him the "Green Fairy Book" with "Mary Benson Addington" written in it. That book has done a surprising amount of work: and I expect will do a good deal more before you see it again, if such an unlikely thing every happens. In the evening I nearly fell down a flight of stairs from the top to the bottom at which about 7 children opened their mouths and laughed, including the pleuritic boy. These are rather odious details of diseases I'm afraid. I'm glad I'm not writing to Maggie. . . ."

On the lighter side, he decorated his room and piled his bookcases with novels, made sketches of his surroundings--baseball and football matches, the races, a picture of the soup kitchen, various mission folk. "We can't help being poor, but we can help being honest" he pens under a drawing of a Hackney Wick woman. A silhouette of "A Lady, after Aubrey Beardsley" oddly among the rest and other signs of his literary tastes hint that even if he was not in fact one of them he was attuned to the aesthetic movement then raging.[5] All was perfectly in keeping with his tastes and experience. "His mind was full of mystical and poetical ideas of religion, and his artistic nature was intent upon expressing them," Arthur remembered.

Now and then he went on holiday. From Polperro in August 1896 he wrote to his father, "I'm staying in a most delightful cottage on the cliff. Looking over the harbour and the sea. It's a most ideal life--we bathe every morning and fish every afternoon, in a small anchored boat, sometimes 8 miles out and I'm becoming an excellent sailor. I'm here with Spender, whom I told you of, and his sister, and there are 4 artists staying in the house I went to the celebration here this morning, in a hideous little church on the hill, with horrible appliqué windows, and creaking pine benches. Nearly everybody in this town is a Dissenter, partly because the clergyman is not a good preacher." Still, his mother worried how thin and white he looked.

Though he made friends with the other curates then as always it was with children that he was most comfortable. They loved him because he loved them. He told them stories, entered into their games, coached them in plays and pantomimes (one time with as many as 70 participants), read from that 'great teaching tool' Andrew Lang's fairy books, led children's services, and brought them to Addington Park. It was a singular gift that his own natural childlikeness came out, the innocence, the playfulness, that drew other children to him at once.

Finally about this time there came an event which in retrospect is recognized as a decisive moment. In 1895 he went on retreat with his friend Archibald Marshall to Kemsing in Kent. It was his first visit to the village which he would serve for eighteen months as an Anglican priest. The speaker was Father Basil Maturin of the Cowley Fathers. And as he poured forth High Church doctrines in a frank unvarnished manner, Hugh was captivated, demurring only in the matter of auricular Confession. Breaking the rule of silence more than once (the flesh, with them, being quite too weak for that), he argued against Confession hotly, dogmatically. Hugh was an Anglican holding to Anglican views "and it seemed quite unlikely then that he would ever budge from the *via media* in which his footsteps were so firmly planted."[6] Yet before being ordained he asked and got the Archbishop's consent to make a general Confession, the act that sent him into ecstasy for days.

Ordaining his son just before Christmas 1895 was the last milestone of Archbishop Benson's life. Mary described the moment to Maggie: "Dearest Darling--I must just sit down straightaway and tell you about Hugh's ordination . . . a gorgeous day . . . white frost and glorious sun. . . . They had breakfasted by themselves, but I got a word of good morning with Hugh--he looked very sweet and happy. Then we all went to church . . . In front of me sat the priests--Hugh's dear head just in front and so still. The sermon was good, but too long. Then the ordaining began, and the sun streamed in and the magnificent impressiveness of the priesthood came on me more than ever, the almost audacious promises, and the 'Receive the Holy Ghost . . . whosoever sins ye remit' etc etc, and, as Hugh knelt there encircled with the hands I *knew* his heart was wholly given in dedication and in claim of the mighty power. He has had his sins remitted and he is going, not only to preach and shew forgiveness, but to *remit* when the time comes. We had some dear talk--he can't at present conceive the possibility of giving his heart to a wife, it is so given to God, but he waits the call whatever it is, and is so sweet and kind and so perfectly natural."

Returning with Mary from a visit to Ireland late in 1896, Archbishop Benson stopped at Prime-Minister Gladstone's house and while at prayer

in church, died suddenly. Hugh was summoned at once, and a few days
later followed his father's body to Canterbury Cathedral, where while
storms raged outside, the Archbishop was buried at the western
extremity of the nave, the first priest of the England Church to be
interred in that hallowed ground since the Reformation.[7] The funeral
was attended by practically every state dignitary, including the king of
Norway and future king of England.

What now for Hugh, now that the Archbishop was gone and the
family was faced with changed circumstances? Earlier that year he and
the Archbishop had discussed a country chaplaincy in Kemsing, away
from the city, and it was agreed, to Kemsing he would go. But first, a
tour of Egypt and the Holy Land with his mother and sister, the sojourn
effectively filling the time between Eton Mission and the church in
Kemsing where he was to go directly he came back. He would be deeply
missed at Hackney Wick: "Can you not go away for the winter [a
devoted resident wrote] and come back to us in the spring do not leave
us altogether we are all rough and ignorant but our love is strong if
not shown in the best way, and I feel that I am in some way answerable
for your Trouble I wish I had not spoken to you as I did it worries me
more than I can say and yet I only answered you according to what you
were saying. I am selfish but I know I was one of the first you visited
when you first came and you did not mind my rough way of speaking
to you and there are a great many who think just as much as we do . . .
do not give us up altogether" (M, I, 124). He never returned to
Hackney Wick.

Notes

[1] This quasi-mystical novel in which a young man John Inglesant falls
under the spell of a crafty Jesuit, extricates himself, and later in Rome has a
personal encounter with Jesus Christ, exerted a life-long influence upon
him. The epitaph on Hugh's gravestone is taken from this book.

[2] Plans for this all male community of like-minded contemplatives drew
a smile from Arthur who found it difficult to conceive of Hugh sharing
stewardship with anyone of independent mind. Hugh never lost interest in
the scheme, however, and envisioned establishing a Christian community
patterned after Little Gidding either at Hare Street or on St. Margaret's, an
island close by the monks of Caldey.

[3] Concerned that Hugh's apparently delicate anatomy could not withstand
the rigors of mountain climbing, Edward arranged for Hugh to make a tour of
Switzerland, the last thing Hugh wanted. What he wanted ever since his

first encounter with the Alps was to climb, and he had his way at last after reassuring his father that his body had grown stronger over the past year and that abnormal physical underdevelopment was abating. "As far as health goes," he wrote, "I had last term a great deal of exercise in the war of hare and hounds and the term before any amount of football. . . . I should not of course do the big peak if I found any ill effects to follow after small expeditions." The Riffel had been promised, he reminded Edward--"I heard from Mama his morning that I might go anywhere in Switzerland. I think I should prefer the Riffel to any other place." As for the matter of expense, always to be considered, he promised to be very careful of economy, "and take the cheapest room I could find in the hotel . . . If the Riffelberg is any cheaper, I am thinking of going there--it is higher, for one thing. I am so very grateful to you for allowing me to go to Switzerland--and more especially for allowing me to choose my place. I shall enjoy it enormously."

[4] *Confessions of a Convert* (London, 1913), pp. 25-6. May a writer be pardoned for reconstituting events in a confessional work explaining the drama of conversion? Hugh's struggle was real enough, but without the electrifying moments that make for great theater. Martindale, who makes no comment on Hugh's personal account of his struggle, objected to Hugh's habit of re-inventing himself in his books. Elsewhere, he alludes to Hugh's deficiencies in Latin, wondering for the benefit of readers who had provided the Latin epigrams for *Richard Raynal.* Hugh's language skills though adequate left something to be desired by an accomplished Latinist like Fr. Martindale, yet he gave the impression in his books of being a skilled linguist. Arthur scoffed that after a year in Italy he could not speak a word of Italian. That was untrue, of course, but not by much.

[5] A friend joked about his fondness for Robert Hichens' *The Green Carnation:* "though not the vice." The vice hinted at in Hichens' amusing parody of Oscar Wilde's verbal and literary epigrammatic excesses involves the sensational Lord Alfred Douglas connection.

[6] Archibald Marshall reminiscing in *Cornhill Magazine* 38 (1915), p. 166. Marshall recalled with what delight Hugh came upon the petition "from the Bishop of Rome and all his detestable enormities Good Lord deliver us." Even his views on clothes reflect an anti-Roman sentiment, for he wished to wear a frock-coat, white tie, and a collar buttoned anywhere but in back. His contempt for Rome echoes his father's frequent references to "the Italian Mission" with its subversive unEnglish message. The High-Church party, it should be remembered, regarded their Anglican Catholicism as containing the deposit of faith passed down from the Apostles.

[7] Ancient tradition had it that St. Thomas himself would protest against the burial of an Anglican Archbishop in Canterbury Cathedral. And so he did, if the attendant calamitous consequences of Edward White Benson's interment are taken into account. One newspaper [*The Standard*] wrote ". . . but shortly before two o'clock (the appointed hour [of interment]) rain commenced to fall in torrents, crashes of thunder reverberated through the

crowded aisles of the Cathedral, and then followed a downpour of hailstones of immense size, such as has not been experienced before in the district. The storm passed away, only to return with unabated fury, and the progress of the service was repeatedly interrupted by its tumult. Windows were broken, the city became flooded, with serious damage to roads and orchards. It was not until nine years later that he read Arthur's biography of the Archbishop, which struck some as a curious delay on his part, but that was Hugh. The fact that the biography of the Archbishop existed imposed no mandate to read it.

4
From Egypt to the Resurrection

Outside of some hardening of High Church tendencies, until Egypt Hugh was untroubled by religious difficulties, not for a moment conscious of being called out of one faith and into another. Nevertheless, the sacerdotal die of Rome was cast without his consent or co-operation. But before he took up his post at Kemsing, Egypt, Syria, and the Holy Land waited to be inspected. With the blessing of family physician Ross Todd, Hugh left for Cairo with Mary, Lucy Tait, and Maggie and arrived on the 1st of December, 1896.[1]

Egypt   As expected, the party were joined briefly by amateur archaeologist Fred who stayed a few days, then hurried back to Greece to re-join the team excavating Megalopolis. Maggie traveled with them for a time, then went off to Heloman and Heliopolis with her friend and collaborator Janet ("Nettie") Gourlay. Tourist Hugh let nothing go by untried or untested. He traveled by landau or donkey and an occasional camel to the great Mosques and the great excavation sites, rummaged through mummy heaps for beads and bones, lunched in the shadow of the Pyramid, saw the Sphinx in moonlight, went by steamer up the Nile to Luxor and the Tombs of the Kings. In those years Egypt was the Mecca of English travelers, an exciting place to be at a time when amateur archaeologists could be found digging under every pylon and the great cities bulged with Europeans, Bedouin traders, markets, mosques--the sights and sounds of Arab crowds. Lest Hugh appear too much the scholar, many an afternoon found him at bazaars bargaining for trinkets, though a year later he described Eastern bazaars as terrible . . . dishonest . . . .undignified . . . silly . . . tiresome beyond belief. In the ancient Coptic quarter, beggars ran after him shouting "Christian!"

Twice Hugh met with the elderly Coptic Patriarch, and the entire Benson party were invited to visit Cairo's schools (in a friendly gesture the Patriarch had already given Hugh access to all convents and monasteries).[2] The audience so affected him that impulsively he wrote to the Patriarch asking to be received into the Coptic Church. There was no reply.

Strange sights and curiosities were recorded in his Egypt diary: here Moses was educated, and here also Joseph married the daughter of the priest of On. They saw the "holy ostrich"--the breed that dances, and Bedouin tents and Bedouin camels. They went to the "Virgin's garden" where stood the sycamore and heard three stories, that "(1) She planted it. (2) she slept under it. (3) she hid there with Child: and spiders spin their webs to hide her from Bedouins. We drank from the well in which she washed the Child's clothes and drank from. The only fresh water well, the other salt. We brought back roses with us from garden, and leaves of sycamore tree."

Most days brought new experiences. December 30, for instance, was jammed with novel sights and sounds--"Finally went across the Nile with crowd in ferry, a small canal; was carried over shallow water. W[alrond]. made friends with sketch and he took us to sugar cane. Beat a good deal, but saw nothing--and then to an orange garden. Man with spear guarded it. . . Lunched in veranda of house belonging to omda. Omda's son came, dressed in silk. He drank stout. After we walked around cultivated ground, saw more sugar cane and beat. At last W. fired at fox but missed. We went on, found nothing, and came back to cane. I shot at a fox, and nearly some Arab women--a horrible moment. Beat some more, then went to Omda's great house. All stood except one or two and ourselves. Coffee, then I rode back on horse, W. on donkey. Crossed river, tried to catch train, went across Nile in fisher's boat (like Apostles). Sat in cafe. W. had row with boy and kicked him out. Armenian talked politics. Said England was responsible for Armenian massacres for encouraging them to revolt. [The British had protested Turkish atrocities in Armenia and encouraged other powers to adopt measures against aggression--*Ed.*] Finally caught 6:30. Got back to hotel about 8.30, dined with W. and went to bed early." This leisurely old-world setting included evenings at whist or cards in the hotel, with orchestra playing softly nearby, and string duets after dinner. Much of the following day he relaxed in the bath, a blissful 'recreation', then played a little stump cricket in the afternoon. On New Year's day 1897 he saw the Pyramid inside, spent his afternoon in Cairo, dined at the Juif Club and went on to masked ball at the Continental Hotel. The next was quietly spent on the steamer writing the sermon he would give the following morning.

He went to Denderah--quite wonderful--"an enormous roofed temple with Sanctuary staircase &c, each column head of goddess Hathoc--bees swarming everywhere," and from there to the Temple of Muth at Karnak (Maggie's excavation site)--enormous! spectacular! Hunting for jackals and wolves baited with a donkey carcass provided a few days' excitement. Fred noted that Hugh would join the archaeologists of his family "with the spoils of a day's shooting, two quail and a jackal, and at sunset, the enriched procession returned to Luxor, for there was a statue on a trolley with the spoils of the chase sacrificially disposed at his feet."[3]

Dreams haunted him--there was scarcely a time sleep was untroubled. *"Dreamt at night I was celebrating in Roman Church--no alb--green and blue and velvet sleeves to chasuble. Prayed as I reached the altar that I only knew the English Service. Began in low voice, with prayer for purity. Then began Lord's Prayer, and then awoke. Cardinal was near me."*

Sometimes dreams came one after the other. On January 9th, he recorded four dreams, two of them rather harrowing--*"A nightmare. I was coming into back drive of Kenwyn with a dog. It was very dark. A large wooden door blocked the entrance. As I reached the door I knew something awful was behind. I threw it open and saw the patch of ground beyond empty. The dog said "Oh my God" in a whisper and two creatures stepped forward. Their names somehow rhymed. I think they were dogs. I awoke in horrible fear. (3) I dreamt it was the Resurrection of the dead. I was in a kind of Arab village with wooden doors. I kept running about and opening doors and skeletons ran out of them. At one place there was a crowd of small skeletons pushing their hands through a hole in the door. I opened it by pulling a string and they all ran out. A vast invisible band was playing "My Lady's Coach."*

The strangest dream of all occurred early in February, 1897-- *". . . a most curious dream. One part of it: I was on a seashore, and a figure rose from the sand holding two chalices. The figure was mostly in shadow, but lighted in redlight from the one chalice. The figure lifted a [dark] chalice and poured what looked like red liquid fire from it into the other, and the other glowed red as the liquid fell in; a voice kept on saying "The blood of God." The chalice was held out to me; and I dipped the tip of my finger in and tasted it: and it tasted like sweet fire: and again the voice kept on saying "seventeen years." I know too that I connected that in my mind with my own lifetime--that I should live seventeen years more. Then when I next knew anything I was walking along the cliffs, It was very nearly dark: and I began fishing with a fly."*
Strange how future events may explicate the wildest dreams. Did Hugh

remember later the chalice of sweet fire and the persistent voice allotting 17 years more? Prophetic dream! for Hugh Benson died exactly 17 years later.

From Denderah the Bensons traveled by steamer to Edfoo, to the splendid Ptolemaic temple; then to Aswan, and on to the foot of the Nile cataract. At Philae Hugh went up and down on foot, then journeyed by boat down the cataract to the Colossus of Assonam. In Luxor he assisted at Anglican communion services at the hotel, and in the afternoon slipped quietly into obscure Coptic churches where the piety of worshippers never failed to move him. It was there that he was first struck by the fact that whether in London or Paris--wherever he traveled the Roman Mass was one; the same prayers were being said, the same sacrifice being offered, so that Catholic meant precisely that-- catholic, here and everywhere the same rite, the same liturgy. The Anglican Church on the other hand seemed not to exist, or be taken seriously. As an Anglican he began to feel isolated and provincial. To all but the circle of English tourists he was a clergyman of some recent Protestant sect--a clergyman only and not a true priest, especially since the validity of his office had been unequivocally denied in the papal decree of the year before. He camped out in tents with his friend Molesworth with whom he had struck up a friendship at Luxor, gabbing of unlikely things like ghosts and haunted houses; and spent most of the day in the saddle traveling to holy places from Jerusalem to Damascus. In Jerusalem he preached in the Bishop's chapel (Anglican), celebrated in the Chapel of Abraham on a table (the altar had been removed by the Greeks fearful of desecration). Here he took to wearing his cassock publicly, and recited his office even on horseback.

On the road to Damascus came news came that Father Basil Maturin of the Cowley Fathers had gone over to Rome. Hugh was stunned. Maturin's talks on the sacraments (Confession particularly) had moved him profoundly. He dashed off a letter, a rather harmless shot that the good father wisely did not trouble to answer. Also in Damascus Hugh's waking dream of founding a religious colony revived, with the curious twist that as a way of punishing himself for his love of opulence, worship was to be entirely free of ceremonials. That was as remote from Hugh's real inclinations as bald nonconformism.

Actually the five months between Hackney Wick in 1896 and Kemsing in 1897 were quietly bending him to Rome, with Egypt the crucial milestone; for it was there in Egypt in a mud-and-clay chapel where Mass was being offered, the same Mass as was offered every day in the most magnificent of cathedrals, that he understood for the first time the catholicity of Rome. With Mary and Lucy staying on in Egypt

Hugh left for home alone in late February to take up his new post as curate at Kemsing.

Kemsing Nothing had changed since the day Hugh set his mind on living the quiet life of a country parson with a good income, a robust congregation, and a beautiful garden. St. Mary's Kemsing was it, a dream come true, "pure bliss in every way," and Hugh slipped into a comfortable routine, going at the pastorate with boyish zest.

St. Mary's Church, which the elderly vicar Mr. Skarratt had restored at his own expense, was beautiful in design and detail, just Hugh's cup of tea. Here in 961, St. Edith, daughter of King Edgar, was born and here she became abbess. Typically, the rector's parish calls consisted of a drive in the landau with a pair of high-stepping horses, a word or two to a farmer passed on the road who had not been to church on Sunday. On the return trip, Mr. Skarratt would doze off. Tea later on, a little music provided by Hugh's Christmas playlet towards which the rector, leaving the next day's sermon on the desk, was soon drawn, whist in the evening, a whiskey-and-soda, and then to bed. As the vicar's assistant Hugh would have time for himself, to read, to study, to recover his health, to do as he liked when he liked. Some of the time was passed editing a book of his father's prayers, public and private; some writing. He was given a study in which to hold private conferences with parishioners. Also at Kemsing Hugh made further progress in his preaching skills. He was aware of powerful gifts in that direction, and just as Hackney Wick had convinced him that he was not cut out for parish work, so it was at Kemsing that he decided on a future built on preaching.

The day school with 196 children was given into his care. The children adored him and were very sorry to lose him when the time came for him to go. He was so much like a child himself, playful, innocent, spontaneous, full of fun and mirth, neither petting nor authoritative. He wrote and mounted plays for them, extravagant children's pantomimes with costumes and music that drew crowds from distant towns and villages, even from London. Archibald Marshall, a friend from Trinity who happened to be living in the village, appointed himself church sacristan and became the children's catechist; his brother Frank was already a resident of the vicarage.

For all its perfections, Kemsing with its beautiful tracery and Italian garden and lofty music failed to please him. Restless and unsatisfied, more and more he seemed ill suited for parochial life; he needed more than an occasional project to ward off torpor, he needed greater discipline and systematic prayer life of a monk.

He joined several ritualist societies and took to wearing a cassock with a crucifix thrust under his belt, and at least on one occasion stunned his flock by carrying the Sacrament from the altar to the sick, a controversial practice waiting to be adjudicated by the bishops. Late Communion he disapproved, and when visiting other churches to preach, he sometimes took a seat in the corner in silent protest of communicating after breakfast, at the same time leaving the celebration to the busy vicar. He was "selfish" at the altar, someone charged. Also at Kemsing he heard his first Confession, emerging from the confessional shaken and thrilled by a vague sensation that something extraordinary had just happened. For Low Church Kemsing, it certainly had. Confessions smacked of incense and ritualism, and at Kemsing as well as many places they were heard without episcopal approval. There were limits to how far even a High Churchman like Hugh should engage in a practice frowned upon by the local bishop.

Ever since reading *John Inglesant* Hugh had been captivated by the idea of community life; when his friend Molesworth wrote that he had visited Little Gidding, Hugh wrote back he would "come like a shot, after a little longer time here" if there were any chance of establishing a brotherhood like it. This ideal had been simmering in his head for years, but he agreed he needed more experience and more hard work physically to prepare himself for this type of undertaking. Clearly his Catholic instincts were hardening. If founding his own Little Gidding was not practical for the present, he could do the next best thing, and that was to join a religious community already established and thriving. That turned out to be the House of the Resurrection, a brotherhood of celibate priests bound by a rule of living yet obliged also to go out on missions to gather souls.

Mirfield   At the House of the Resurrection at Mirfield newly founded by Canon Charles Gore (later Bishop of Worcester, Birmingham, and Oxford), Hugh appeared to find the monastic life he was looking for, pious, disciplined, and purposeful. Half the Mirfield year was given over to mission work and the other half spent with the community, which was run more or less along Benedictine lines. Personal property was forbidden. Income from principal was to go to the Community, as well as the copyright of all books written while a member. (At his insistence the Community continued to collect royalties on *The Light Invisible* long after he had gone away.) Obedience to the Superior in all things was expected of the fourteen brothers, except where there was an objection of conscience. Initially

Canon Gore worried that Hugh's impulsiveness and lack of parochial experience had left him unprepared for the life and worried also that his need of a supreme authority might eventually lead him to Rome, but fearing that to refuse him now would have been too devastating, Gore admitted him. A year's probationary period before final vows would tell the tale.

Much about Hugh's character is revealed in the pains he took to get into Mirfield and afterwards the pains that drove him out. Strong objection to his plans streamed in from every quarter. He was warned against cliques, warned against taking a vow of celibacy after so short a novitiate when celibacy involved the philosophy of a whole life, but Hugh was undeterred, insisting that from every conceivable point of view he was not called to the married life, "and to me, therefore, the community life seems normal, not abnormal at all. I do not quite see why it should be regarded as abnormal by everyone." Friends were unconvinced that well-reasoned arguments and a philosophy of life had brought him to this decision. Arthur thought this spiritual call a dream, flimsy and destined to evaporate as Hugh grew older.

Besides these objections from family, Hugh's decision to leave Kemsing had not sat well with Archbishop Temple who had succeeded Edward White Benson as Primate and who now refused to let him resign his curacy at Kemsing. Tempers flared. Hugh was young, impulsive, inexperienced in the world's ways, in short, immature. In this opinion of him the Archbishop had company. His mother thought Hugh was acting hastily, particularly as with the Archbishop against him he was making arrangements to enter a brotherhood in York (Mirfield), thus outside Canterbury's jurisdiction. She feared his actions would strike the Archbishop as that of a "wilful boy thwarted flying out of the diocese to please himself."[4] Soberly Mary begged to be let into his confidence--"I had never thought of there being any difference with the Archbp. Coming so late in the day it is too disappointing. I want to hear about it NOW THIS VERY MOMENT while it is all at boiling point in your life," and urged that he remain with Mr. Skarratt one year more, as he had intended, for if it was his youth the Archbishop objected to, he would be a year older then, and the very fact of obedience would be good training and experience, especially if he entered a Community. He was going from Kemsing, a house with no particular rules for anything in the world, to Mirfield, a place of strict discipline. He agreed Mirfield was a narrowing life, but that was precisely why he wished to go. "You know how strongly I feel about your not committing yourself to anything irrevocable," wrote Mary, "whether any act or undertaking, before the age your father spoke of--30. The fact of his death does not seem to me to alter it and for a lifetime dedication a year or two seems to me a gain, a test." Invoking Edward's memory delayed the inevitable, but Mary could not stop him.

Arthur Benson doubted Hugh could stick to the life and thought Hugh's assumptions about religion and the contemplative life crude. Hugh was self-absorbed, more intent on shining in the pulpit than in winning souls, and painfully ignorant of the human heart--"I don't think I'm unjust: whom does he care for?" To the elder brother every bright virtue slipped into a fault: Hugh was guileless, humorous and extraordinarily undisciplined--that is the flaw that comes up again and echoes in Hugh's own repeated protestation that parish life was not for him. What he needed was the greater discipline of monastic life. He knew himself, Hugh insisted, he could stimulate but not feed the flock. To this Arthur quietly observed in his diary that in refusing hard parochial work Hugh seemed to want *not* the discipline he disliked but the discipline he liked.

For all his imperfections Hugh was genuinely seeking a spiritual life.

He agreed finally to go as a visitor to Mirfield for a few months before he committed. It was an empty if amiable concession, for Hugh's mind was made up, and once made up nothing short of divine intervention could stop him, not Mary, not the sitting Archbishop. In the autumn of 1898, then, he joined the Community of the Resurrection at Mirfield as a probationer--with Archbishop Temple's hard-won consent (Hugh was perfectly willing to bypass Canterbury altogether no matter how fiercely the Archbishop objected). Resigned to the fact that Hugh was distinctly his own master, Mary wrote in her diary "God bless the boy. I think his father would really have liked it."

It was a sharp change from the relaxed days at Kemsing. Prayer and work made up life at Mirfield, with each brother assigned a share of household duties. Some of the brothers like the newly-appointed Superior Walter Frere, a liturgiologist, were scholars; many skillful preachers like Hugh became missioners.[5] Radiant with joy, he threw himself into his new life, dividing his time between the community and mission work in slum neighborhoods, hearing confessions sometimes for eleven hours straight day after day.

Hugh seized upon every opportunity to preach, from small mission church to cathedral, on one occasion in Westminster Abbey. "O you *often* blessed Cathedral character--I am bloated with pride of m'son," Mary wrote. His preaching voice became more resonant in the pulpit or standing on the step. He never worked from prepared sermons, but from notes assembled as lines of argument, summaries, high points--all put into skeletal outline beforehand in a tiny hand; he read them over once or twice until they were fixed in his memory, and once he began to speak, he never referred to them and seemed always to be preaching extemporaneously. No one guessed that from first to last he suffered awfully from nervous attacks. He would fall into a chair in the vestry, pale as chalk, sweating, his heart pounding, sick with nausea; but once in the pulpit, his fear vanished, and his speech became graceful, poetical, moving. He liked being thought eloquent.

When Hugh came home to visit he preached sometimes in the village church in Horstead Keynes (the family were now living in Tremans). His sermons were robust, but sometimes went beyond the needs of his country audience.[6] At Tremans the small room adjoining Arthur's bedroom had been converted into an oratory for his use, with an altar richly draped, and silver vessels on the table. There Hugh often celebrated with members of his family, for his mother would not let him celebrate alone, as he would have liked. For all the disruption caused by his visits, he was missed when he went away to his own place. Mary, who loved him, found the house "horrid" and empty without him, but understood his satisfaction at fitting into his own place at Mirfield again. "Temperamentally you and I are in some ways strangely alike; we want to hold what we hold, and to have what we have, so hot, and so at once."

But was Mirfield his own place, really? Quiet Days to which he returned exhausted from mission work in a day or two found him restless and unsatisfied. Yet there was much to do here. He pored over the mystical *Revelations of Divine Love* of Julian of Norwich, and set about preparing a book of his father's prayers and meditations for publication. Piety proceeded apace: meditations arranged along Ignatian lines, daily Intercessions and prayers to the Blessed Virgin, and for him but not others, daily Rosary.

His days were full: up at 6:15 and lights out by 10, though probationers were permitted to keep lights on in their private rooms. This Hugh did often, smoking and talking well into the night with that same irrepressible energy of mind and body that marked his undergraduate days and would mark the years to come. He did resolve to give up tobacco, and stayed away more or less for a while, chewing on string and seeds when the urge to smoke came upon him. Once a week the brothers assembled at Chapter for public confession made on their knees.

All was not prayer and study. Relaxed time was spent telling ghost-stories, writing letters, making comical sketches of community life, engaging in ordinary conversation with friends. For recreation he played cricket, worked seriously at weeding, cutting steps for a garden path that for a long time afterwards was known as "Hugh's path." His personality can be adduced from these pastime pleasures. He loved animals, he loved going to the zoo; he delighted that Mirfield's Irish Terrier mascot (who ate flies off the window-sill "in a gentlemanly manner") liked sleeping under his bed, though it was a parrot like Maggie's parrot he longed for--"that would put the gilded pinnacle on my hopes." He wrote *Princess Dulcie* and other plays for the Mirfield village children, and recruited musicians from the village to play for his songs and artists to paint scenery and make costumes, and coached the children in acting. These were the happiest of moments. Were he not a clergyman, surely he would be an actor, he declared in a letter about the staging of his play *Beauty and the Beast*--"I was stage-struck again--as I always am, and began to wish I wasn't a clergyman, in order that I might act myself. And I always fall deeply in love with the leading female characters--which is unfortunate for a monk! However, I have torn myself away" (*Letter*, Dec. 19, 1900). He howled when forced to expunge the indecency "Go to blazes!" and when the candles around the Beast's bier of his *Beauty and the Beast* were removed because villagers might think them too Roman Catholic. Here he began *The Light Invisible*, his book of quasi-mystical stories with themes straddling his longing for Rome and filial duty to Anglicanism. Sketching amused him. A sheaf of hilarious caricatures of the brothers engaged in their daily tasks, even to such dangerous dissipations as playing shuttlecock over a clothes line with their cassocks laid to the side, set the home front giggling.

Not much activity stirred the pot his first year as Probationer. There were one or two public lectures. He wrote a little religious poetry. He took up the precious *John Inglesant* again and developed a taste for Georges Sand and Kipling. "I desire to be a pagan," he announced under the spell of *Marius the Epicurean*, and he liked Maeterlink, so odd and so French, and Huysmans even more. *La Cathédrale* and the weirdly baroque *St. Lydwige of Schiedham* became his passion, but he cowered before the satanic *Là-Bas*. He knew *The Picture of Dorian Gray* and Huysmans' *A Rebours*, that had inspired it. The morbid streak in a highly excitable temperament was vented through these bizarre and picturesque novels. Added to these were the commercial "shilling shockers," and sensational tales from the likes of *Police News*, snatched at during days of heavy sermonizing as a sedative for the brain.

The year passed quickly, and when July came round he was able to put off making his profession (essentially, taking the three vows of chastity, humility, obedience), throwing himself instead into heavier mission duties in Lincoln, Cambridge, Sevenoaks, in and around Mirfield, Birmingham--his appointment book swelled for years ahead--

preaching to children, to adults, instructing, giving retreats, talking sometimes in the open in a field; or street-preaching outside a church, followed sometimes by processions through the streets, with cross and lights (to annoy Protestants) and afterwards, filing into the nearby church to preach again to admiring crowds.[7] "We came from our quiet life red-hot with zeal, and found everywhere men and women who seemed to have been waiting for us." He spoke to all types--the pious, the curious, the indifferent, preaching on estimate 70 sermons in a single Lent, "working like two horses." Some who came to sneer stayed to praise. Not every day was a success, however, and apathy remained a major problem. In a little country church he stands and raves three times a day at least to "dull, heavy people who sit and stare and then go away dazed. They need an earthquake" which he cannot give them. Yet often amidst signs of defeat, success was gathering force-- " . . . after a few days of seeming failure, the people began to come up in flocks night by night, quite steady and unexcited, to renew their baptismal vows" (M, I, 165). He was annoyed at being reminded again and again how young he looked.

Physically Hugh was being stretched to the limit, yet, invariably, once back at Mirfield and refreshed in a little while he grew restless to be at it again--"talking and talking" until tired to death, then sleeping heavily in a chair between tasks--"I think I shall bust before I have done." Canon Gore assured Mary Hugh was happy and reasonably healthy, but she wanted assurances from Hugh's lips. What of his diet? Was he wearing warm clothes? Did he sleep well? What about his rheumatism?

Pressure from the Superior to take permanent vows was bearing down heavily at the same time personal doubts about his fitness for community life were intensifying. "I am not yet at all clear as to whether I am called to the life," he wrote to a friend; and shortly after: "I think I have quite made up my mind: Think." To complicate matters, Arthur passed along to him an offer of a well-endowed living as rector at Hungerford. It was an exceptional opportunity that an ambitious man would have seized. To his credit Hugh turned it down, with thanks, in the grounds that at 28 he was too young for such an important position. Under pressure from Arthur who remained skeptical of Hugh's fitness for vocation, and to silence his own disquieting doubts about a life's commitment, Hugh decided he needed yet another year's probation time.

Certainly there were many irritations that set his teeth on edge, unpleasant disagreements about pronouncements of dogma and ritual. There were spells of accedia too, and demands upon his talents that a different personality might have turned to greater advantage. Personality differences, doctrinal disagreements, and the emotional distance Hugh put between himself and others (without his intending it should be so) created difficulties and isolation. "You say you don't know at all what the Community thinks about you," a baffled Mary wrote, "Don't they give you the slightest idea? . . . It seems to me odd that after 1 1/2 years, they've given you no inkling at all." Surely they had, but Hugh had misread the signs, or more likely, absorbed by his own peculiar interests, ignored them. Not then, not ever, was he mentally or emotionally equipped for Community life; and when he comprehended how powerful a voice was his to command, both in speech and writing, a future living under someone else's rule rather than by his own talents became more and more problematic. In reality Mirfield had given him more than an inkling of where he stood, had in fact after several delays reached the end of their patience: make your profession or go. The moment of decision had come, though it was greeted with no enthusiasm. "It is rather terrifying to contemplate, and I am not absolutely determined yet; but if nothing startling happens by the end of July I shall become a fixture." In the greater sense, Mirfield had added whole dimensions to Benson the preacher and writer: as a ritualist he was satisfied, his apostolic work (in Martindale's words) was active "to the point of feverishness," and his literary powers were expanding. For a moment at least, his future appeared settled.

"Are you in any danger of lapse?" Canon Gore asked him at the last moment, still skeptical of Hugh's intentions in light of distinctly Roman tendencies. "No," he answered. There the issue was put to rest for a time, but not for all time. And so it was that in August of 1901, after more than two years as a probationer, with Mary Benson watching from the little chapel, Hugh in brand-new cassock took his vows, for God's glory, "for the honour of Mary, Saints, angels, for my salvation, for all living, and dead . . ."

Notes

[1] Symptoms of rheumatic fever put an end to Hugh's curacy at the Eton Mission. In Egypt it was Maggie who was stricken with a serious heart attack brought on by pleurisy. Fred rushed to her side but before he reached her was himself brought down by typhoid fever.

2 Of Mass at the great Coptic Cathedral, he wrote, "Whole service was sung, incense offered continually. Priest gave his hand to be kissed throughout service. . . . Men prostrated themselves and crossed themselves before altar on entering. . . At end of service about 6 communicated directly in the mouth--and walked around altar and received again till elements were consumed. Elaborate ablutions at end, the water being sprinkled over congregation who crowded forward. A man brought a large linen bag full of bread and distributed. We each received and ate a piece. Some of the water of ablution was distributed in a dish to the Communicants. Each communicant received over a napkin and held the napkin in his mouth afterwards for a minute or two. There the priest prostrated himself before the elements and each communicant received over a napkin and then held the napkin in his mouth afterwards for a minute."

3 *A Mother*, pp. 41-42. The unfortunate aftermath of this last dig was Maggie's near fatal attack of pleurisy. This was the first of her serious illnesses. By 1897 Maggie was an old hand at archaeological digs. In 1895 she had conducted an excavation of the Temple of Muth at Karnak in Egypt, and thus became the first woman to do so. By 1897 she was on her third season and had made several significant finds. The results were published in 1899 as *The Temple of Muth in Asher: An account of the excavation of the temple and of the religious representations and objects found therein, as illustrating the history of Egypt and the main religious ideas of the Egyptians*. See William H. Peck's "Miss Benson & Muth," in *KMT* (1992), pp. 11-19.

4 In a letter of 20 May of that year Mary begged him to reconsider--". . . you know what profound respect I have for Canon Gore and his views and in many ways for his wisdom. But I don't feel happy about your entering on this so speedily considering your father's feelings [that he should not enter into a permanent commitment until he was 30]--let us talk things over. Have you told Canon Gore of your promise to your father? . . But I do *deprecate speed*, partly on its own account, for any hastiness does such danger, partly because it sounds such a defiant answer to your Bishop. When he refuses you at Christmas for mission work, to go off in November from your present post to work of that kind--the tie of a clergyman to his Bishop *is* a real tie, isn't it? and is it well to leave the Diocese and your present work with *such haste as this* and without the slightest reference to him? . . . You know, Dearest Son, *how I should never hold you back from a call*. But never think a call is any the worse for *time*--indeed it is more reverent attitude towards it."

5 Hugh described Frere as "a lean man, a theologian, liturgiologist, hymnologist, scholar, musician, preacher, athlete, and a saint! It is a good list, and he excels in each item, and withal a very pleasant human person." Hugh's enthusiasm at a good first impression often bubbled over into high praise, and in Frere's case, the instincts proved right.

6 "Hugh preached in church--good voice, unembarrassed, an easy flow of clear sentences. Some parts I liked, but it was too polemical and too dogmatic. He made a great point of the hollowness of our lives if Christianity were untrue. But it seemed to me out of place in a little country Church. It must be taken for granted that such a congregation is at least Christian in intentions . . . " [*Diary*, Xmas Day 1901]. On another occasion Hugh preached a sermon on childlikeness of Christian character which Arthur disliked because it urged "complete submission to authority, ending with a tirade against fellow Englishmen for being so independent." Arthur's frustration with Hugh's logic at this time touched all bases from dogma to hymn-singing at school on Sunday evening, to which Hugh (deliciously irritating) objected as utterly profane. Didn't the same profanity attach to singing of hymns thoughtlessly in Church, Arthur asked. No, because there it was an act of worship, and that consecrated it, even though it might be thoughtless. "Je m'y perds!" Arthur groaned.

7 At a mission in Birmingham he made clear that the word "Fathers" in Faber's hymn "Faith of Our Fathers" did not mean "Cranmer, Ridley, Latimer, and that kind of person!"--as if anyone else in the church had ever heard of any of them. His real objection to hymn singing was the evangelical, revivalist fervor of hymns, so different from the plain chant he loved.

5
He Becomes a Roman Catholic

"When a soul reaches a certain pitch of conflict, it ceases to be absolutely logical; it is rather a very tender, raw thing, with all its fibres stretched to agony, shrinking from the lightest touch, desiring to be dealt with only by Hands that have been pierced." *Confessions of a Convert*

Hugh Benson's attachment to ritual was strong, and Mirfield, following High Church practice in many ceremonials, satisfied his need up to a point, but not to the limit. Rooted in him was love of *Stabat Maters* and Palestrina and processions and soaring rood screens. Eye and ear could be fed by the Church of England, the church of his father who had worn the mantle of its highest earthly office, but more was wanted. At Hugh's urging Mirfield adopted colored vestments, and allowed private devotions to Our Lady; but in theology and politics, Mirfield followed a more liberal line. The problem was subjectivism versus dogmatic authority. More and more the Church of England was moving away from Catholicism and towards Protestantism, which in all its forms had affinity with subjectivism that held that spiritual intuition was a necessary part of religious experience.

At Hackney Wick Hugh had clung to the English Church as the "sound core of a rotten tree," but in time came to believe that the majority of Anglican clergy were untrustworthy in matters of doctrine, and that bishops' utterances, often conflicting, made matters worse. Who was right? Who spoke with authority, and by what authority? He demanded a living voice: God speaking through the Church and the Church through a priest. He went to the Book of Common Prayer, but even there found no agreement, as different branches of the Church interpreted the formularies differently. True, the Church safely taught the Fatherhood of God and the importance of the Person of Christ; but once having taught that, the rest was somehow to find its way into the mind and heart by mystical osmosis because priests dared not teach doctrine.

Christianity without dogmas and sacraments, without miracles, was impaired. But the greater problem was the loss of a center in the Church of England itself, a church shaken by one crisis after another of authority, of doctrine, of ceremonial--all of this besetting the High Church (or Anglo-Catholic) wing. Divisions in the rest of the church were ten-fold that, with doctrinal disintegration, undisciplined priests, and Nonconformists in and out of Parliament on the attack. At Westminster Abbey, he admired the raw courage of a Mirfield brother who used the pulpit to denounce the "dead altars" of that hallowed edifice.[1]

From an unexpected quarter now came a dispute that was to make him miserable, and hasten his going over to Rome. The immediate cause was Canon Gore's lecture on Higher Criticism, delivered to the Mirfield Community during Quiet Days, a time to settle back, relax, listen to a lecture or two, and "jaw" into the night.

The issue being raised by Higher Criticism was the reliability of the Bible as an historic document. In his lecture Gore defended those who in conscience were not able to accept parts of the Gospel, specifically, the Virgin Birth. He acknowledged that Christianity could not now rely so heavily on Biblical testimony as had been the case formerly and that the intellect must not be fettered by preconceptions as it sought out facts. Facts, however, were *not* enough, he insisted, and where they failed, instinct and intuition must come into play. "Faith means believing in spite of doubts."[2] Implicit in this approach was the fallibility of the Church in matters of doctrine.

Hugh was shaken to the soles of his feet. Could such issues be raised seriously in the Church entrusted with faith that came down from the Apostles? It was a naive response, and a sign of how uninformed Hugh was of the intellectual and theological battles raging all around him. This controversy was not breaking news and had been around for years. Doubts already gnawing at him began to congregate around these points: where did the Church stand? what, if anything, did it insist upon? When Bishops collided on questions of dogma, who was to be believed? If the Bible was not to be believed, why believe the bishops? He wanted the narrowing life, not one bedeviled by "keeping in touch with current thought."

Where Hugh invested his life he demanded certainty. What should he do? As a way out Hugh decided to be a ritualist in all things that Canterbury did not explicitly pronounce against, so long as it did no violence to conscience. For a time, this compromise settled him, and he resumed his duties. Within six months he was on the rack again.

Haunting him this time was the Roman Catholic denial of the legitimacy of Anglican orders and the larger question of papal infallibility on which it depended. On the English side there was the fact of history and the insistence that it, not Rome, was the true successor of the Ancient Undivided Church. Against this stood the papal claim of apostolic succession through Rome. This conflict could not be brushed aside. If the Roman Church was the true Church and the Pope's claims to infallibility were true, then Hugh, as a priest of the Church of England was a false priest; he was not a priest, and his Communions were false as well. Publicly he claimed to be "serene" in his priesthood, but in his mind the validity of Anglican orders and papal pronouncement could not be reconciled. The anguish this question caused was impossible to describe. He told his predicament to Father Frere the Superior who had seen him through the crisis of the summer before, insisting that he loved the Church of England, bathed in its sacramental Grace, but God was "opening new doors."

Doubts subsided, only to resurface in full force within months, crystallizing in the question of the Teaching Church. The Church may be undecided on purely speculative points, may allow her theologians to argue unchecked as to the modes by which God acts, and speculate about the limits of her own power, but in all things that affect grace and salvation, she must know her own mind, and she must declare it clearly, constantly, and unequivocally.[3] But the Church of England seemed to him not to know its own mind even in matters of salvation. He cited the doctrine of Penance as an example. Practically all the Bishops denied that penance was essential to the forgiveness of mortal sin, but the fact that he was teaching the necessity of penance and absolution unhindered by his superiors meant that mutually exclusive views on the sacrament were tolerated. In other words, he was teaching private opinion. Anglicanism was headed for a crisis.

He needed desperately to resolve difficulties. By October 1902 (just three months after his profession), he was reading Newman's *Essay on the Development of Christian Doctrine* and writing out questions for Jesuit Father George Tyrrell, the controversial Modernist,[4] while Mary, fearing the worst, pleaded with him in all fairness to submit the same questions to the moderate party of the Church of England in which he had been raised: "And no one can say they were without inspiration--people like your father."[5] That point was especially stressed. Hugh could have put before him the whole case, not merely the Roman, and weigh the respective positions: "Dearest, you will just *think* of this won't you?"

Fears about the Jesuit turned out to be groundless, since Tyrrell's Modernist views allied him squarely with liberal Anglicanism. He answered specifically in the matter of papal infallibility that Hugh should wait for a better climate before going over to Rome, that although himself a "minimizer" when it came to the divine authority of the Papacy, he could not receive anyone into the Church except on the terms then prevailing, views that seemed to him impossible to a person of reason. In part Tyrrell's advice to Hugh to remain where he was reassured him for a time although he was stunned when Tyrrell asked to be remembered in his Anglican Mass. Frere was relieved that Hugh was relieved. Could it be the unity he sought was *not* to be found in Rome?

The problem would not go away. Visits home to Tremans did nothing to relieve malaise. It had always been the custom in the Benson home to talk politics and religion robustly and heatedly at the dinner table, with the argument often continuing for hours in other parts of the house. When Hugh visited, talk frequently erupted into argument leaving the brothers "breathing quickly, muttering unheeded phrases, seeking in vain for a loophole or a pause," each accusing the other of intellectual pride. Hugh's visits to Tremans had become disagreeable to him; he could not endure incessant bickering, but the great provocation, Mary reminded him, was his endless shots at Anglicanism. Now, suddenly he had become unusually quiet and self-absorbed; the normally cozy and affectionate setting of Tremans left him cold: there was no humor, no clever arguing of stubbornly held views with Arthur and Fred, none of the old Hugh. In many respects he seemed more mature, improved by his experience at Mirfield, though his views on religion remained contemptible in his brothers' eyes.

The autumn and winter of that year saw him in spiritual turmoil, calmed only in the steadying atmosphere of Mirfield. If the Lord wanted him to be a Roman Catholic, He was certainly taking His time getting him there. By spring 1903 matters had hit bottom.

One afternoon in April he arrived at Tremans from Tunbridge Wells in a dirty cassock, worn-out and looking it. Before the day was out he was engaged again in heated debate over the shrinking of doctrine (the Dean of Ripon had just publicly denied the Virgin Birth): "Here is a Dean saying that the Virgin Birth of our Lord is at all events doubtful, and he is not even rebuked." Hugh wanted at least a pronouncement from the bishops, or even *one* bishop reaffirming doctrine. He spoke of the dissatisfaction of Anglo-Catholics and was markedly scornful of Anglican faults and mannerisms, and "behaved both then and later as if no Anglican could have any real and vital belief in their principles," or any claim on Truth. Challenged by Arthur and Fred in the matter of just who possessed the exact truth, Hugh complained bitterly of being drawn into arguments against his will, a charge hotly denied by Arthur: "I told him that this was very unfair.   That neither Fred nor I talked nor thought much on theological questions--that *he* always started them and argued them in a contemptuous and exasperating way. . . Then he began to say in an infernally Christian kind of way that no doubt he was wrong from beginning to end--could he say more?" (*Diary*, April 15, 1903). Hugh's way of being triumphant and sarcastic behind the cloak of courtesy provoked both brothers beyond endurance, so that when Hugh talked about monastic life Arthur wished "to turn all monks adrift with a horse-whip laid on their backs and to burn down the monasteries."

What Arthur did not know was that behind the contentiousness loomed a crisis.   It had come in the midst of a three-week Lenten mission in Cambridge.   Hugh had finished preaching the Three Hours on Good Friday at St. Giles's Church, tore out of the pulpit and collapsed into a chair with head in hands moaning "I can't go on!" On Easter Day he managed the evening sermon in Tunbridge Wells and knew in his heart as he preached that he stood in an Anglican pulpit for the last time.   He had determined to become a Roman Catholic.

At Father Frere's orders he ceased mission work in order to devote himself to prayer.   He turned again to Julian of Norwich's *Revelations of Divine Love*, and Richard Rolle's meditations on the Passion, which pushed him further towards Rome.   It was during this tumultuous period that he put together a little book of 14th-century devotions later published as *The Book of the Love of Jesus*.   Meanwhile letters went back and forth from Tremans: "You know well enough what a terrible blow any such step would be to me if I looked at it personally--what a sorrow it must be, if it happens," wrote Mary invoking the "vision of the Blessed Dead" to remind him obliquely of the duty owed his father. It was useless.   Her letters are a curious mixture of lamentation and consolation.   She wanted only that he follow God's guidance, even though he was being guided into a different path: " . . . I'm not unmindful--dearest son, how *could* I be, of all your pain and conflict and patience--and all the gentleness and sweetness which have been growing greater every day."[6]

In late May he asked Father Frere for a leave of absence. "I really don't know where I am," he told Mary. "I am afraid things are getting imminent. July, as you know, is the time when we 'renew our pledges': that seems to me a strong reason for getting things settled beforehand. I am perfectly clear that the Community of the Resurrection is my only possible platform in the Church of England. Yet I cannot

deliberately 'renew my pledge', knowing that it is exceedingly possible
that I should break all obligations a month or two later. Yet *not* to
renew the pledge means leaving the Community. . . . Under all these
circumstances I suggested to Fr. Frere that I should go to a R.C.
Convent in June, towards the end: and go into Retreat. Then I should
know where I was. You see this sort of thing depends on the *will* so
much as regards the moment of decision. By an effort of the will, I
might conscientiously put off deciding till August. I don't think I could
put it off beyond that. Everything however seems to point to June.
But Fr. Frere writes this morning that this is impossible. I needn't go
into his reasons. I daresay he will himself. Well, I have written a long
letter to him by this post, which he will find at Tremans; which I hope
he will shew you. But possibly he might prefer not." His letter to
Mary of 30 May described other difficulties: "My dear Mamma, So
very many thanks again for your letter. Briefly, this is how the
situation lies. With Fr. Frere's advice I am applying to the Chapter of
the Community for leave to be absent from Mirfield all June and
August: giving them an understanding, tho' not an absolute promise,
not to be "received" until the end of August: and not to put myself into
formal communication with Roman authorities until the end of July.
This, if they allow it, will give me, I think, every imaginable
opportunity for going into the whole thing dispassionately. The only
further question is, What exactly I should do all that while? I don't like
to inflict myself, under these circumstances, on Tremans for at least
two months. I would see Lord Halifax sometimes in July and anyone
else you wanted: but I shouldn't want to bounce about the country more
than is necessary, and I couldn't with my agreement go and stay with
Romans; and I couldn't bear to go and stay with Anglicans who would
bother. I should be extraordinarily like the schoolboy's "amphi-
biousness". An able-bodied man like myself oughtn't either to loaf at
Tremans all that while. What shall I do? I will let you know what the
Community ultimately says to my proposal: I really haven't an idea.
Fr. Frere is in favour of it, but that doesn't at all necessarily mean that
the rest of them will be. . . . We [Frere] had an immense talk; and I
have been letting the result summer ever since, and this is the
conclusion. Best love."

Part of the "immense talk" accused those who went over to Rome of
being generally willful people who would have their own way, and
Hugh was one of those who need the discipline of *not* going over.
Frere cited his unreasoning dread of reason and intellect and warned him
of the sin of pride in defying God's will, reminding him of Pusey and
Keble, greater men than he, who had struggled and come down for the

Church of England. What Hugh needed was not a shrinking from the risks of faith, but a facing up to them. No! the intellect alone could prove very little, Hugh insisted; the heart and intuitions entered this struggle, and they told him that only as a Roman Catholic could he attain to a complete life joined to Christ.

In June, after accepting Hugh's written *apologia* the suffering Frere yielded, allowing him to depart to the neutral ground of Tremans, but forbidding a retreat in a Roman Catholic convent. In July there came Frere's ultimatum either to return by the end of the month when his pledge was to be renewed or leave the Community for good. Hugh had made it clear that Mirfield was his only possible platform in the Church of England, and now that the moment of decision had come, he chose not to return.

Walking on eggshells describes Mary Benson's approach to her son. From the moment he first broke the news of his discontent at Mirfield to the moment he boarded the boat train Romewards, she had been his mainstay. What choice had she? It was to her Hugh first revealed his intentions to become a Roman Catholic. It was the hardest thing he had ever done in his life. If, once having chosen Rome, he hesitated to act upon it, it was because of Mary, not only because his defection brought her pain, but because as the Archbishop's widow she would hear the public wails condemning his disloyalty. Mary handled him gently, no reproaches--these he was bound to endure from his father's Anglican colleagues to whom his defection was rank betrayal. As painful as his conversion was to her, better to yield to the inevitable than to lose a son entirely. "We know you are ours still, and nothing will ever shake that fundamental blessed reality of love." His heart had found its home, God had led it there, and she begged not to be shut out. He went to the shelter of his new creed as a lover might run to the arms of his beloved.

It was from Mary that Arthur learned of Hugh's intention to "go over" to Rome. In reality, Arthur was not entirely opposed at the philosophical level, for it was but an affirming of doctrines long held by Hugh. But practically, he liked it not at all because this was an all-consuming religion, from which one looked at one's family as from the other side of a high wall. "I am ashamed to say how much I hate it all." What exactly was it Arthur hated? Hugh's submission to iron uniformity at the price of his rational liberty? Yes, but most of all, that his father's son was doing it, and precisely because of his father's name, Hugh's conversion would carry more weight than it deserved, more than an intellectual triumph over a mind won to the Roman cause. And there was unspoken pain of family being ruthlessly divided as a consequence.

"I do not think it is the smallest grief or pain to Hugh; instead of looking like a man who is struggling or wrestling he looks like a person with a comfortable cheerful secret." Hugh, Arthur complained bitterly, had no particular loyalty or affection for those who loved him, "and the ideas of all the old cords snapping, all the old tender associations cut adrift from one are nothing to him by the side of satisfying this childish whim. He was always like that." His idleness at Eton, his abandoning the Indian Civil Service, "then taking his orders and following since every whim of his own mind"--in his own mind Hugh was convinced he was being led by the hand of God, and Arthur conceded perhaps *he was right*.[7]

At this time he was at work on his first Elizabethan novel *By What Authority?* In the protagonists Anthony and Isabel Norris, Hugh was reliving his own spiritual progress towards the Roman Catholic faith. "O Hugh, you are Anthony!" Mary declared. Arthur abhorred the novel's Catholic tone of absolute certainty, but Hugh's literary skill could not be brushed aside. At Tremans, Hugh, now emotionally liberated, used every minute creatively, worked with enormous energy ten hours a day, his room piled with books and papers on which hundreds of facts and phrases were scribbled. "He used to rush into meals with the glow of suspended energy, eat rapidly and with appetite--I have never seen a human being who ate so fast and with so little preference as to the nature of what he ate--then he would sit absorbed for a moment, and ask to be excused. . . . Sometimes he would come speeding out of his room, or to play a few chords on the piano. He would not, as a rule, join in games or in walks--he went out for a short, rapid walk by himself, a little measured round, and flew back to his work."[8] Now that Mirfield was behind him, he returned to the old Hugh: irrepressible, passionate, opinionated, whimsical, energetic. He entered again into the family habit of lively debate, taking up every challenge, whether in the smoking room over the port, at the dinner table, in the garden, or on a walk to Paxhill or to the little railway station at Hayward's Heath where he would range the platform in his cassock, arguing his stubbornly-held views with the tenacity of a pit-bull until the train chugged in.

By September Hugh had met the conditions he set for himself to consult others, and to be absolutely convinced that the Roman Catholic Church was the true Church. He had listened to objections to Rome--its dogmatism, the sinfulness of those in its highest places, its claims to be infallible--and remained convinced and clear-eyed: "I had no kind of emotional attraction towards it, no illusions of any kind about it. I knew perfectly well that it was human as well as divine, that crimes had been committed within its walls; that the ways and customs and language of its citizens would be other than those of the dear homely town which I had left; that I should find hardness there, unfamiliar manners, even suspicion and blame."[9] Father Frere threw up his hands and wished him well. Archbishop Davidson agreed that Hugh could not remain in a faith against his convictions, nor would his father wish it, as perilously false as the doctrines seemed to him, and packed him off to Lord Halifax for a week. The cause was from the first hopeless. Hugh, Halifax agreed, must be allowed to go. He was not quite 32, and had been for nine years an Anglican clergyman.

Hugh arrived at the priory of the Dominican Fathers at Woodchester on the morning of September 8th. Father Reginald Buckler later recalled going down the hill to meet him, "knowing so well the cases of clergy converts from Anglicanism--the loss of friends and position, the sorrow to dear relatives, and the terrific wrench. Here was an Eton and Cambridge man, and the son of an Archbishop. The step would make a stir--and so it did. Coming to the Priory, I said to him: 'We live here far from the madding crowd.' He came in--he was very quiet, and humble as a child. Seeing first to his little needs, as a guest, I then showed him about, that he might feel at home--and took him to the church, where he knelt devoutly."[10] In the afternoons he took long walks with Father Buckler across the Cotswold fields with the purpose of ironing out difficulties. There were none. "But, surely, indulgences!" the good man protested, but Hugh assured him he was completely satisfied on this point, and every point.

One day he wrote out on a single typewritten page the story of his struggle from Anglicanism to Catholicism and the day of his reception was fixed.[11] It was all over rather quickly. On the Friday afternoon, in the Chapter room at Woodchester, he professed the faith, made a confession on his knees and received absolution. The next day he received the tonsure admitting him to minor orders. "I shall have to call you in future, my dear Hugh," said Father Buckler. "I hope you will, Father," Hugh replied as they went into the church. On Sunday, after receiving Holy Communion, he wrote--

"FAIT ACCOMPLI

My dear Mamma--Just a line to say that it has happened. It was extraordinarily simple--so simple that one can hardly believe it. It was like any other confession, only longer and with one or two details. I will tell you more fully when I write again. But this has to go. And it is the first thing I've done after coming out of the church. I want now, at once, to be at Tremans again, to show you that nothing is really different, except--well, what is different. The clergyman was as nice as possible: he might be an old country vicar. He kissed me when it was done.

Arthur thought Hugh's action built of straw, but gave his blessing. Hugh seemed like one "intent on a great adventure, with all the rapture of confidence and excitement about him." On the day of Hugh's reception, however, he lashed out at Rome: "Its arrival doesn't make it any less of a shock and my mistrust of Roman methods, my repugnance to Roman methods, and my enmity to Roman principles is so deep-seated that I cannot face it with indifference . . . He writes to say that he wants to come back here just to show that he is the same as ever; but though he writes and speaks with great propriety and even tenderness, I feel that his absence of suffering, and his indifference to the suffering of others in the matter are horrible. He seems to me to be 'playing a game,' as if he were a child. He has taken a degree without paying the fees; it has cost him nothing to break with the old, I think" (*Diary*, Sept. 11, 1903).

To the end it was not in Hugh's make-up to let others into his struggle; not even his mother, his most intimate friend (insofar as there could exist such a one) ever penetrated those secret places of which it was not possible for him to speak, only write, and then almost exclusively through the created personas of his fiction. "I have nothing more than the deepest possible conviction--no emotionalism or sense of relief or anything of the kind," Hugh wrote, but such conviction as he had was beyond Arthur's comprehending, his own faith being increasingly under assault.

Fearing losing him to this all-consuming religion, Mary wrote of his new life: "We know you are ours still, and nothing will ever shake that fundamental blessed reality of love. . . . only *let us in*, always, wherever you rightly go--my heart cries out for that."[12] Monastic dress was right and proper, she added; it would be a comfort for him to show in his dress exactly what he was, and not to seem like a layman.

Once Hugh's conversion became known to the public, letters poured in to Tremans. Not since 1606 when Tobie Matthew, son of the Archbishop of York, became a Catholic had the Church of England suffered such a loss. Some cynics thought his conversion no more than a literary gambit, an advertisement of himself. Others offered advice to the family, as if some momentous fact lying close at hand had been overlooked.

Lord Halifax assured him it made no difference as far as he was concerned. "Why should it? There is only *one* Church." Remarkably, many Anglican clergy wished him well. Some, deploring the weakened condition of the Church of England and timorous priests failing the people who thirsted for full Catholic doctrine, wished they possessed the courage to do as he had done. Among Roman Catholics there was of course joy at having "snared" the son of an Archbishop of Canterbury--

not since Coventry Patmore had there been such a catch as this. Letters from the Anglican public were mixed. Many were bitter accusing him of being a traitor, of being mad, of being an ungrateful bigot. . . . Hugh answered them all. Father Tyrrell wrote him a cautious welcome, urging patience and tolerance of intolerance (whether he meant Anglicans or Roman Catholic intolerance is not clear). Father Maturin whose preaching had so impressed Hugh at Kemsing also telegraphed congratulations, and urged that he join the Sulpicians in Rome, an order known for sponsoring devotional art.

A scorching rebuke came from the Bishop of Salisbury warning him that he was about to engage in an act of moral and spiritual suicide. "Your father's and your mother's son should not do this," he insisted. It was impossible to imagine how anyone with intelligence could accept Roman claims. Idolatry and superstition, dishonesty, arrogance, coercion that crushed individuality--such was Rome, a religion of lies run by greedy cardinals for profit. Better to cease dreaming and go work in a slum parish. Hugh told Mary that the Bishop's last letter was so unpleasant that he tore it up instantly in order to forget it. With characteristic charity, Hugh forgave the cruelty at once: "I can't think what he means, because I'm sure he intends to be kind and interested. I don't think he knows the meanings and effects of words."

Now that it had happened, now that he was a Roman Catholic, what was he to do? How was he to serve? It was rumored that converts were not trusted by Roman Catholics and seldom made use of. When Father Buckler insisted that Hugh must be a priest, that he could be nothing else, Hugh mumbled a word or two merely for form's sake about a secular vocation, but it was no more than gesture, as his inclination from the start was to join an Order, probably the Dominicans, whom he had consulted even before his reception. He was told by them to come back in two or three years, when he was a bit more seasoned.

In these last feverish days before departing for Rome and Holy Orders, he finished *By What Authority*. On All Soul's Day Mary and Lucy Tait saw him off. For Mary especially it was a bitter day as she watched the train for Dover disappear, sweetened a little by the sudden appearance of Bishop Wilkinson of St. Andrews, an old family friend, who had hurried down from Scotland to give Hugh his blessing but missed him by a few minutes. The house at Tremans was empty now, in a way that Hugh's eventual return could not make up.

Notes

[1] High Church meant Anglo-Catholic, a national "Catholic" church following traditional doctrine and ceremony often indistinguishable from Roman practice. Protestants were the Low Church evangelicals while Nonconformist sects included Baptists, Methodists, Quakers. A serious blow to the High Church party had come in 1899 when, bending to Protestant objections to Romanizing trends, the bishops issued the so-called Lambeth Opinions, suppressing the use of incense and reservation of the Blessed Sacrament for the sick.

[2] The Church of England did not rely on authority exclusively. Scripture and reason both were brought to bear on claims of faith. But in the face of disturbing trends Gore who normally identified with the liberal wing of the High Church insisted upon strict regulation of public worship to conform to the Prayer Book while allowing greater liberty in private devotions. This freedom did not extend to the clergy who had made solemn profession to teach the Articles of Faith and fundamental Christian belief. He criticized the bishops who in their zeal to purge liturgy of Romanism put themselves above Scripture. For instance, when the Bishop of Worcester charged that the Hail Mary being prayed in a diocesan church was "perilously near Roman Catholicism," and that no prayer outside of the Prayer Book was admissible unless taken from Scripture, Gore replied that the Hail Mary came "more perilously" near Luke 1:28.

[3] *Confessions*, pp. 67-68. He feared that drifting church was bound to disintegrate. With inimitable irony, Evelyn Waugh wrote about how easily he lost his faith under the influence of the theologian. "There are, of course, countless Catholics who, for a part of their lives at least, lose their faith, but it is always after a bitter struggle--usually a moral struggle. I shed my inherited faith as light-heartedly as though it had been an outgrown coat. The circumstances were these: During the first World War many university dons patriotically volunteered to release young schoolmasters to serve in the army. Among these there came to my school a leading Oxford theologian, now a bishop. This learned and devout man inadvertently made me an atheist. He explained to his divinity class that none of the books of the Bible were by their supposed authors; he invited us to speculate, in the manner of the fourth century, on the nature of Christ. when he had removed the inherited axioms of my faith I found myself quite unable to follow him into the higher flights of logic by which he reconciled his own scepticism with his position as a clergyman." From *The Road to Damascus* (Garden City, N.Y., 1949).

[4] Tyrrell's books were condemned by Pope Pius X in 1907 and he was excommunicated soon after. He died unreconciled in 1909 in the house of his biographer and companion of many years Maude Petre. Hugh advised others in similar straits that no matter how much Rome was wanted, one "must

not go" until intellectual difficulties (by which he meant Infallibility) were resolved. Once the Divine origin of the Primacy of Peter was granted, papal infallibility ceased to be an obstacle.

5 Mary had in mind Lord Halifax, lay leader of Anglo-Catholics, who had asked to talk with Hugh, whom he had advised when doubts about Mirfield surfaced. "May I say that I *do* strongly desire that you should see him," wrote Mary. "I can't forget how good he was to you in 1901, and I know how sweet and altogether acceptable his atmosphere and way of looking at things is to you. So I'm not asking a hard thing. And not only *He* for your sake, but for your Father's sake and even for mine I know he would do anything. Should you ultimately take the step you will not be forgetting what a blow it will be to the Community I know, but they, like we to whom you are so utterly dear, must long most of all that you should follow God's guidance, *when all has been done.*" Halifax remained a friend until Hugh's death.

6 *Letter from MB*, April 1903. Hugh's letters to Mary rationalizing his problem with the doctrinal positions held by the Church of England are reprinted in the Appendix (2), pp. 201-205.

7 Looking back, Fred admitted that the family were helpless before the force of Hugh's will once he had decided on Rome. "But what would have happened had that conviction taken hold on him before my father's death it is impossible to say. I cannot imagine any human relation; any *pietas* restraining Hugh when he had the firm belief that it was by divine guidance that he so acted: on the other hand I cannot imagine what the effect on my father would have been; whether he would have beaten down his own will in the matter, as my mother did, and have accepted this without reserve at all, or whether it would have been to him, as the death of Martin had been, an event unadjustable, unbridgeable, unintelligible, a blow without reason, to be submitted to in silence which, had it been broken, must have been resolved into bewildered protest" *Our Family Affairs*, p. 319.

8 *Hugh*, p. 119.

9 *Confessions*, p. 93.

10 *The Rosary* (Feb. 1915), p. 35. Hugh was delighted at the unexpected visit the next night of Father Vincent McNabb, and described him to Mary in a letter as "a *charming* person--Vincent McNabb--and he looks about 25, apparently well disposed to the Church of England and Non-Conformism. He spends his time, I hear in writing very brilliant articles and, I think books because he is a real scholar, and in making rosaries--rather a nice combination." They met again in Rome at San Silvestro. Father McNabb wrote a tribute to Hugh upon his death in *The New Witness*, whose distributive philosophy championed by G. K. Chesterton, Hugh disliked.

11 That essay setting forth the differences in religion was later expanded and published by the Catholic Truth Society as *A City Set on a Hill*, a little gem of religious controversy.

^{12} Keeping to her intention not to let him slip away, Mary congratulated him, at the same time reminding him in the warmest terms of their lives passed together--"Dearest dear Son," she wrote on September 2, "I must come if only in writing and be with you in spirit tomorrow. The last Sunday of the old life. It will mean so much to you, and yet probably there will be a curious absence of feeling or realisation at the moment, a sort of numbness in which one is surprised at oneself that it should be so--so it mercifully often is. God bless you through the day and God bless you on the life to which you go on Monday. I know I cannot hear from you for some days but as soon as you can will you write to me? I am very full of you, my dearest boy--and all the past rises up from when you came to us as such a joy and were so intensely welcomed--of your delicious childhood (not but what it had its difficulties!)--school life--your first choice--a London life--College-- Vaughan, to your first ordination--Ah! how that time stands out--and all since. And Egypt when we were together so much. Of course in looking at the immediate future, my one fear personally is that it should come between us. Don't let it. Share with me whatever you can share, write to me and let us keep close to each other as long as I live. In some ways I feel as if I can understand you so well, as I find my own mate in you. In all ways I _long_ to understand, and where I do not agree or disagree so respectfully that it would be no barrier at all and love fills up all interstices. My darling you are so intensely dear to me so dear that I can bear to let you go forward--only this one thing--do for me all you can of letting me share your life. I shall never worry you. I love you too well, but I shall always long, and love--XXX-- your own most devoted mother."

6
In Rome 1904

"I had a strange dream of Truro and papa. Hugh, who appeared as a
little boy, had done something wrong, and papa after luncheon, told
him to walk out first out of the room and to speak to no one, for fear
of contaminating them. I interceded, but was told that his character
must be trained."   A.C. Benson, *Diary, Jan. 1, 1914*

Hugh's heart sank at the prospect of a year in Rome. Fresh out of an
Anglican household, suddenly thrust into the strange environment of
Rome, he became homesick at once and never recovered. Of course he
complained in his letters home. One problem was *pace*. For a man
used to moving at the speed of light, Rome's wheels turned too slowly,
weighted down by bureaucracy and red-tape; but Rome had been around
a lot longer than Hugh Benson and he needed to be patient, particularly
as the seminary training period would likely be waived.   Another
problem was climate. In winter months, Rome was often cold and
damp, and his health suffered.
    San Silvestro-in-Capite provided the perfect setting for Hugh's
temperament. It reeked of history, intrigue, murder, and sanctity.
Several popes had been buried here and here the head of the Baptist had
been kept as a relic (thus the *in capite*) before being moved to the
Vatican. Here also Pope St. Leo III suffered mutilation. Other students
stayed at the Beda, or the English College, or St. Sulpice. Sulpician
devotional art and ritual suited him temperamentally, but their Roman
college was already filled to capacity. It was a disappointment that
turned out to be a blessing. Had he entered St. Sulpice or the English
College he would not have been ordained for a full three years, an
intolerable delay from his point of view. On the day he arrived in
Rome, Hugh was taken to a tailor to be fitted, treated himself to a
ferrida (a furry hat with tassels) and a pair of buckled shoes which he
thought hilariously funny. He arranged to attend two or three daily
lectures in elementary Theology delivered in Latin that pronounced like

Italian and was introduced to Professor Lauri, a popular preacher, well-connected, who agreed to be his coach. Improving his Latin was essential as that was the language of the lecture hall and of the confessional. To his amazement he managed to stumble through.

Hugh's room at the convent was elegant and spacious with a wide window six feet by five feet looking onto a court and fountain. Food and drink were excellent and plentiful. He and a friend Evans, a popular ex-Anglican priest from London whose conversion had made headlines, were the only Englishmen among the fifteen men in residence; the rest were drawn from places all over the map.

At San Silvestro there were no rules beyond a 10 p.m. curfew--"Work here seems a secondary matter: but, after all, the point of Rome is Rome." The day was mapped out precisely: roused at 6 or 6.30 by a friend hammering on the wall, to church until 7:30, breakfast, then off to lecture in Moral Theology in the College of Propaganda. He wrote letters, read a little until 12.30 lunch. In the afternoon he was lectured across a table in Latin by Lauri, and was off to afternoon lectures in Theology.[1] Then "a walk or something: tea in my room about 5--then, presumably, work till 7.30 with Benediction sometimes 1/4 hr. after the Angelus: then music in [Father] Holly's room--or prayers and beads or reading: and bed 9.30-10. . . ." There were two or three masses a day to be heard, prayers, meditation, and communion three times a week.

At various times to lighten his loneliness, he took in a dog, a couple of parrots, and cats. He was particularly fond of cats and had often noted with amusement how they liked to trot across the altar rail in church, even as Mass was being said. It was in fact the Church's position on the souls of animals--or absence thereof--that had delayed his conversion.

Hugh's situation was not typical. For a seminarian preparing for Holy Orders from 5:30 wake-up (not 6:30) to lights out at 10 there was little dawdling possible in a day packed with four lectures, study, and spiritual exercises. Hugh was not ordinary by any stretch; he was in his thirties and already an ordained clergyman. The same was true of his friend Evans. Ex-Anglicans preparing for the priesthood were not bound by the same regulations imposed upon young seminarians. They lived in a religious house (like San Silvestro) not a dormitory, and were expected to finish their studies conscientiously without supervision. A few activities--bicycling, theater, going out without cassock--were frowned upon as unedifying, but not absolutely forbidden. Unrestricted freedom, however, invited dissatisfaction and ennui, as he told Mary: "It all does seem to me a most astounding waste of time: all that I want to do is to say Mass and make sermons and books and 'deal' with people: and all that I am allowed to do is to come out here and read Theology that I know already, and learn colloquial Latin and go through a number of social acts and ecclesiastical functions!"

Hugh had no sooner stretched his legs than he set about seeing to his future. He went with Evans to see English-born Cardinal Merry del Val, the newly appointed Secretary of State known to be sympathetic to Anglican converts. They chatted amiably about Arthur's biography of the late Archbishop (Hugh never mentioned he had not read it), and at one point the Cardinal hinted that he could be counted on for a favor. Before the first week was out Hugh had seen the Pope, Pius X. Not in a formal audience yet, but the dramatic effect on him was no less: "We went this afternoon to one of the courtyards of the Vatican, by ticket--a huge place, *crammed* with a garlicky crowd, and all the roofs and windows filled. A huge red canopy was at the wall at the end, with Swiss halberdiers, all on a platform, and a blaring band below. . . . At last we saw halberds going along behind, in the cloister; and the crowd began to sway and roar, and a woman fainted next to me. . . ." (*Diary* Nov. 7, 1903). Descriptions of plenipotentiaries abound. The Pope's secretary was "a little man, like a fox-terrier, with his head on one side, in purple silk." And at Mass, the Pope appeared with "ruddy-brown face, white cassock and cap, and gave his blessing in the doorway, then vested at the altar, with three officials helping him, in a purple jewelled chasuble." Mass at St. Peter's was overwhelming, the whole church "cobbled with heads, and over that pavement came the huge canopy, with the great jeweled figure below it, and the solemn fans waving behind. In front came an almost endless row of mitres moving along. And then, of course, the final great moment was the Elevation, in dead silence, and only broken by the silver trumpets exulting up in the dome." Hugh was deeply impressed with the Pope's simplicity and humility, without "the suspicion of an air of a great prelate except in his supreme naturalness." In the English audience with Pius X a week later, Hugh thought the Pope looked tired and depressed.

The sheer catholicity of Rome was overwhelming: "English, dressed like Roman priests, in cassock hat and ferrida. German in black with scarlet cinctures. Greeks in blue and orange. Italians, Canadians, French--all gathered to listen to the one language! The first mass I heard, on Thursday, illustrated the same point. It was said by a German, served by an African boy, heard by Italians and myself. Nationalism is a poor thing after this!" It fixed the impression made upon him years before in Egypt that the Roman Church was truly catholic and universal. That is not to say he felt at home in this atmosphere. Everything was different, language, temperament, customs,

a hard adjustment for an Englishman who had worshipped all his life in
a national church. Hugh said of himself that he lacked the sort of mind
that would ever take easily to this religion. He had never dined out on a
Friday in Lent, for instance, but did so for the first time in his life here
in Rome, being reassured all was proper when brought to a private
dining room "where two Cardinals and an Archbishop were bowing and
murmuring to one another and to 4 or 5 magnificent ladies." Different
beginnings had given him one cast of mind and the excitable Italians
another. "At present," he wrote Arthur in November, "I feel nothing
but discomfort, and am finding more every day how hopelessly insular I
am, because of course, under the circumstances, this is the proper place
for me to be: but it is a kind of dentist's chair."

Self-discipline had always eluded him, and once Hugh's eyes had
become accustomed to Rome's visual splendors, he relaxed into a kind
of lassitude of the luncheon set, at the same time complaining about
these wasted days as if he were being drawn into the endless teas and
socializing against his will. For the Englishman of means Rome was
very much the place to visit. He was pointed out as Hugh Benson the
Archbishop's son and invited everywhere that important Englishmen
with their "swarms of doubtful counts" showed up. Many days were
spent away from San Silvestro taking supper with this or that hostess,
meeting rich Americans, making dozens of friends like Father Bernard
Vaughan and Abbot Gasquet--"*so* nice, and English, and sensible"
(rumors were circulating that Gasquet was going to replace Archbishop
Bourne of Westminster)--and visiting the salons of titled women where
in his words he 'jawed' with clerics and laity alike over the burning
issues on the Roman political calendar. Before long he was much
sought after as a lively *raconteur* of ghost stories or simply funny
stories: he was Hugh Benson, literary savant tossing out learned
opinions about writers he had barely heard of; Hugh Benson engaged in
'High Talk,' by which he meant lively excursions into the Meaning of
Life--all of it immense fun.

He went off to meet hordes of people with whom "one sits and
quacks about small ecclesiastical details until one never wants to see a
chasuble or a relic again. Bah!" But in truth ecclesiastical small talk
interested him when he could choose the time and details. Anti-
Anglicanism encountered among English Catholics annoyed him, and
Roman indifference positively infuriated him. "But poor England! No
one understands or cares for her," he wrote in his diary. "How incredibly
stupid the authorities are! They have their little formulas and set
pieces, and just wag along, hopelessly outside the life of England! If
they only knew the power, the refinement, the learning, the meanest
cathedral town contains, they would be astonished: but no! Protestants

must be stupid and insincere! because they are not Catholics!" Never in his Catholic life did he cease to defend Anglicans as individuals against detractors or suffer their being maligned.

On the official side "functions" annoyed him. These were ceremonial events for every occasion, a Cardinal's Mass or Papal procession, at which everyone in Orders (or soon to be) was expected to turn up. "I don't really like functions: I wish I did, because it is the chief occupation of everyone to go to them. Yesterday, as I had a little cold, I stayed indoors all day and worked in the library and wrote letters and saw nobody--and loved it" (*Letter to MB*, Nov. 2, 1903).

In reality there was a great deal for the conscientious aspirant to Holy Orders to do--read, study, at the least learn Italian, but after nine months in Rome Hugh had learned only enough Italian to get by, and done rather little to perfect his Theology. In lecture hall his faulty Latin disabled him; he often became confused and a little foolish, bringing fellow students to laughter. Theology never was his strong suit, either as an Anglican or as a Roman Catholic, and he wisely avoided doctrinal disputes where he might slip into serious error. His devotional life went on, however, with venerating relics, saying the Office, going regularly to confession at St. Alphonso's, and hearing Mass. One morning he received communion from the Pope's hands: "We went to his Mass in his private chapel . . . A little room opened on to the one where we knelt, with the altar in full view. He said Mass with such simplicity and humility, like a country priest. I needn't try to tell you," he wrote in December to a friend Miss Kyle, "how touching it was . . . Imagine an immensely high room, hung with red damask and tapestry; folding doors, and a great gold altar just beyond, with a communion rain in front of it, and a holy, simple old priest with a ruddy-brown face, in a purple jewelled chasuble and white cap; and three officials in white and scarlet serving him: and a *dead* silence, except for the very soft murmur of a rather pathetic voice."

Fascinating Rome, paganized Rome, gorgeous in gold and jewels, idolatrous, musical, beautiful and ghastly beyond words, teeming with life--the colors and flavors of crowds. He immediately wrote home for his *Marius the Epicurean*. That and *John Inglesant*--Christianity and paganism in strong doses--made up his literary pleasures. Hugh's antiquarianism was fully fed by Rome--and he paid her back by making her come alive in his letters. He went everywhere and absorbed the flavors. He disliked Oriental rites "with chorus howling like dervishes and tinkling long poles with balls on them and beating tom-toms." More to his taste were the Catacombs where he went often to hear Mass, once on St. Cecilia's eve: "Below the High Altar is her body: the tomb blazing with lights, and a crowd fighting to get near it; the crypt of the church is her house, with all the mosaics left that she trod upon. She was half-beheaded, you know, and lived three days, and then 'fell asleep'; and her body was found in the catacomb, her head on her hand, lying on her side, as if in a natural deep sleep. The stone where it was found forms an altar-slab in the crypt; and people were kneeling there and kissing it and laying their rosaries on it today; while that glorious choir was pealing away overhead. My word! The Communion of Saints means something here; there were bishops, and peasants, and bald-headed men, and children all crowding everywhere; every chair taken; hundreds standing, and walking, and kneeling as they liked. Really this religion is alive" (*Letter to MB*, Nov. 7, 1903). Even more striking was Mass in St. Callixtus' Catacomb, sixty feet down: "High Mass in the chapel where her body was found . . . the whole place full of red and white chrysanthemums and altars with hundreds of candles. One went straight back 1800 years when the same words and language were used in the same place. It has touched me far more than anything in Rome." The knowledge (and even deeper, the sense) of continuity, of succession, of growth and natural accretions overwhelmed him in Rome, the center of the universe.

Extravagance, splendor--every day brought a dramatic event to allay his loneliness. In December John the Baptist's head came home to St. John Lateran after being away for 33 years. "It's in a gorgeous reliquary with pearls and amethysts, all together about 7 feet high. We met it at the door with torches and cottas and pealing bells; it came in a wagon drawn by mules." It was to remain in the private chapel until a niche for it was built. "It is crammed with gold and jewels. Very grim. Parts of it are elsewhere; as there is a hole in the skull too." Does Hugh accept it as an authentic relic? "One can't say whether one 'believes' it to be the head or not--one's imagination cannot grasp what it means; one can only paw it. But here it is; brown and shrivelled and without the lower jaw" (*Letter to MB*, Dec. 6, 1903). Six months later the holy relic would sit unveiled near the altar of a tiny chapel in the Lateran overseeing Hugh Benson's ordination to the diaconate.

Nothing perfected Roman worship like music; and finding an exquisite choir united to a solemn Mass was worth writing home about. Music was either glorious or wretched, but in all places the atmosphere of faith and worship overwhelming, even in a church physically unattractive from every point of view. Hugh went wherever his feet took him. He joined processions, Cardinals' Masses, attended ordinations that took four hours to complete: "There is a tremendous moment when the choir is filled with men in albs, flat on their faces,

until you are aware that the entire Court of Heaven is assisting."
Popular singing of a robust *Te Deum* thrilled him. And the crowds!--
50,000 at St. Peter's for Thursday Tenebrae, 100,000 on that same day
at San Silvestro. "The sense of worship is beyond anything I have ever
dreamt of out of heaven." He sought out small churches to pray in,
like St. Teodoro's on Good Friday morning where a choir of Roman
nobles of a guild, barefoot in sackcloth and ropes and hoods, kissed the
Crucifix; and at Easter morn St. John Lateran packed to the walls for
the lighting of candles and the roaring of "Deo Gratias," followed by
the "Exultet," and all the rest: Mass in white vestments, with the
Cardinal in an enormous gold mitre "then the organ and ALL bells
roared and jangled for the first time in a sort of frenzied voluntary . . .
MY GOODNESS ME! What a religion it is! You feel that the entire
creation has part in it, and that nothing is common or unclean after
Christianity has taken it in charge." Amidst religious pageants when all
the bells in Rome were ringing, he was carried away, reaching over
heads and outstretched hands to touch his rosary to Our Lady's veil,
leaping to his feet at the blast of trumpets, transported by sounds and
sights and the sweep of ecstatic crowds. Twice during Holy Week he
climbed the Scala Santa on his knees. "Then I walked to the Scala
Santa, and ascended the wrong stairs on my knees--stone!--with a
Cardinal in front. At the top was a chapel or two. In one a relic of the
True Cross was being shewn and kissed. I kissed it, among a mob of
poor who were roaring "Viva La Croce, la Croce, la Croce!" and I
buzzed too. It was very touching. Then I looked into St. John's . . .
Then I went to St. Croce . . .Then back to the Scala Santa, which I
went up on my knees, and kissed the Dead Figure at the top" (*Diary*,
April 1, 1904).

No period of Hugh's life better illustrates his tremendous power of
observation than this. On the one hand he is the breathless tourist,
relishing the great personalities glimpsed here and there, drinking in
holy minutia, and jotting down every step of his way in a diary and in
letters. Nothing escaped his eye--everything from papal galas to the
piety of simple folk, from sojourns to Pompeii to the naming of guests
at this or that tea party, was stored away in his diary to be made use of
later. The diary became a source book of several novels, *Initiation*, *The
Coward*, *The Dawn of All*, *Lord of the World*, in which contemporary
people and places were scrupulously depicted, so that even today the
novels offer a wealth of detail of what this world was like before World
War I cut it off forever. Often Hugh's was overwhelmed by the visible,
palpable faith, as when a visit to a favorite chapel revealed the piety of

simple souls at devotion. At the Church of San Claudio, a mere
two minutes walk from San Silvestro, a dozen or so people besides
himself would kneel silently before the Monstrance, their eyes cast
down, "floating in grace." At times his happiness seemed heaven-sent:
"I woke this morning under heavenly circumstances. The first thing I
saw was a luminous delicate blue sky, deepening to green above the
dawn, an atmosphere like clear water, that tasted like champagne, room
beautifully fresh and cold; the larch branches almost black against the
sky, and no sound but the fountain splashing below. The bath was a
sort of dream, like the whole morning made tangible: and I went to
mass and communion in great joy. I am beginning to meditate every
day on attributes of God: and for the present I am doing His
Tranquillity: there is no other word for it: and this morning was an
incarnation of it; deep, cool, luminous, still. It was splendid too on
coming into the church to see the gilding and marbles and gesso-work
brightening steadily" (*Letter to MB*, Dec. 27, 1903).

II

Rome was stupendous, the atmosphere volatile, rumor-crammed, with
controversy in the air and on everybody's nerves on edge. There were
revolts like Tyrrell's, and defections like the Abbé Loisy's to keep the
Vatican occupied, violent anticlericalism on the rise in France, with
radical factions calling for suppression of religious orders and
secularization of education. Yet despite unrest, the Catholic center held--
a truth never lost on him. Hugh's attitude towards such controversies
as were rife at this time shows a naiveté destined to get him into
trouble in the future. He was not a good judge of men or causes.
When he arrived in Rome the Abbé Loisy fever was at the boiling
point. Loisy, a renowned Biblical scholar, had scandalized Rome by
rejecting claims for the historicity of the Bible. All Scripture was
allegory to him. Hugh quickly (albeit timidly) joined the small clique
of Loisy admirers. Considering that Canon Gore's mild lecture at
Mirfield on the admissibility of science into Biblical study had plunged
Hugh into a depression, hastening his flight to Rome, his admiration of
the abbé seems queer at best. Mary was quite surprised at his reaction to
the French cleric she described as outHeroding Herod, but the fact was
that for some time before his conversion, Hugh had been reading and
recommending Modernist texts to Mary, intending to prove how open
he was to all points of view. At all events, it had been the equivocating
bishops he had deplored as an Anglican. Now safely in Rome and
protected by dogma and authority that could not be stormed, he was
more free-wheeling, eager to be seen among the progressive Whites.

With typical hyperbole he claimed for Loisy what the heterodox Abbé dared not claim for himself, that he was the only man in all of France who knew the Bible. What Hugh misjudged was Loisy's actual position; he had long ago given up being a Catholic and had joined the rationalists.

Loisy's cause had not been fueled by any intellectual depth on Hugh's part. Fine points of doctrine lay in terrain mapped out by men of superior learning. He was still unlearned in the permutations of Biblical criticism as before when at Mirfield, Father Frere and Canon Gore, distressed by how little he knew of Theology, urged him to read New Testament Commentaries, including several written by his own sister Maggie. In his eagerness to defend the independent minds of Roman Catholics who welcomed the infusing of contemporary thought, he also hailed Father Tyrrell's Modernist ideas, heresies about to be condemned by Pius X.[2]

Politically, Hugh aligned himself with the Whites, the liberal faction, rather than the staunchly Roman Blacks (Ultramontanes), but the alliance was timid and rather short-lived. These factions had made their appearance fifty years earlier when the Pope's temporal sovereignty was the explosive issue, but by 1903 the battlefield had shrunk to the usual contention between the more liberal and the more conservative practice of the Faith. The Whites considered themselves "modern" Catholics who recognized that the world had moved on and that exclusiveness was bad policy. They were sympathetic to Tyrrell and Loisy. The Blacks were aligned with the "Old Catholics" who still remembered the Penal Laws, distrusted the government, and insisted their priests live simply as priests. "I have also been meeting some dangerously White people," he declared, "and like them *very much more* than the Blacks; they are really sensible." He had also been meeting "horrid" Blacks "with their minds about as big as *o*," always suspecting every convert of being a wolf in sheep's clothing, ready to offer up all their suffering to one saint or another. He and Evans made friends on both sides, Blacks and Whites, acknowledging that healthy growth had to include both wings though neither man was latitudinarian. Once he became a priest, however, he dropped Tyrrell and Loisy altogether, obedient to the Church's decision in this matter and in all matters of faith and doctrine. Henceforth his job would be to defend the Church against her foes, not meddle in ecclesiastical politics or doctrine. In any event, he had good friends from both sides, among them many Blacks like Reginald Balfour, editor of *Dublin Review*, the Wilfred Wards, and Lady Kenmare (with whom he lunched every day and dined twice on Sundays!).

Of priests as a group he had a poor opinion. Many of them who had come through the seminary system seemed narrow-minded, lacking in culture and initiative and originality. Good priests there were of course, and these were "nicer and broader than anyone in the world," men like Dominican Vincent McNabb whom he first met at Woodchester and again in Rome and the two Irish priest "with flaming red faces and a brogue that leaves stains behind," and Father O'Connor, the best-educated man in the house, to whom he gave a copy of *John Inglesant*. Whatever their faults, priests carried weight. Whenever he put forward an unpopular view (he told Mary) he had merely to say, "a priest said to me the other day . . ." It was like the coinage, if one had the stamp, it was all right. In a December 6th letter, he expressed an opinion of clergy: "One is slowly sorting impressions now; and they are instructive. Does it bore you to hear them? (1) Everyone, priests and all, first of all have an intense faith and realisation of the supernatural; and express it perfectly frankly in words and behaviour--quite naturally and devoutly. (2) There are also however, flippant very often. It is the seamy side of faith: They make jokes that make one's hair stand on end. (3) They are rather stupid. That is the fault of the seminary-system: It teaches them their business and their faith admirably, but it teaches them nothing else at all. But when, as in the case of great directors, they *do* know human nature, they know it far better than any one else in the world. If I had the training of a boy for the priesthood, I would first shelter him entirely with a great deal of *attractive* religion, appealing to his heart, and dogmatic religion appealing to his intellect, till he was 14: then I would send him to Eton or Winchester till he was 18: then to a seminary for a year or two: then to a university Oxford or Cambridge, till he was 24: then to a seminary again for 3 years. And I believe he would be a splendid priest after all that. If I had to cut anything out of the course, I would cut out the Public School. . . ."

As the months dragged by, his fear that the authorities were not eager to rush converts into the field were rekindled. When was he to take Holy Orders? Who would arrange it? Vatican bureaucracy and indifference to the English converts loomed like an insurmountable wall. Hugh shrank at the prospect of a two-year wait at least, despairing that no one in Rome seemed to have the foggiest idea what to do with clerical converts. "Most of them seem to think we know nothing at all, and tell uwith gloomy pride how trying the confessional is!" He deplored Rome's handling of other ex-Anglicans as if they were children who had to be protected from controversy: "Really, the way they are treated is abominable--supposed to know nothing at all. The other day a Franciscan scholar came into the Beda and was asked by one

one of them to come up to his room to talk about Loisy; and the Rector of the Beda, overhearing, rushed up there first in order to prevent their hearing what they ought not hear, and that to men who have lived for years in the Church of England, and have read and thought themselves over the border. It's incredible" (*Letter to MB*, Feb. 6, 1904).

That week he went to see Archbishop Bourne at the English College about an appointment to Westminster. An unimpressive man distrustful of converts, Bourne heard him out, then advised patience. Hugh went away satisfied at least that Bourne did not seem to think him quite so ignorant of Theology as everyone else did, but Bourne's advice to Hugh that he make good use of his time apparently went unheeded. Early on, Hugh had become convinced that the one thing at Rome was to get hold of the right people "and then you get everything." On the official side, he cultivated Bourne (whom he came to dislike) and Archbishop Stonor, an important link to Vatican officials but a man known to make promises without carrying them out, and kept up with latest rumors. Merry del Val, who had the Pope's ear, assured him that the time of ordination was drawing near, that delay was merely a formality. Hugh should consider him a friend.

In December the weather had turned brilliantly blue and crisp. He planned to spend a week in and around Naples as the guest of Francis Spender, an ex-patriate English friend, but first relished Rome as it prepared for Christmas. "The whole church is hung with large tinkling chandeliers, and red damask is beginning to come out, and the Cribs to be made." At the Ara Coeli two brown friars were making a whole chapel into a stable, with the Bambino covered with rings and bracelets and shepherds all along the side "life-size and *hideous*, and cardboard angels descending; but it was heavenly, with a crowd of children moving up and down the steps into it." Midnight Mass with orchestra and harp was very beautiful, the church blazing with candles and in the little room over the high altar the Child lying on a bed of straw; and on Christmas night, an enormous revel with a huge meal of turkey and wild boar and hours at the piano afterwards. His letters about this time are "newsy" and descriptive, and rather blunt in expressing opinions of the endless formal "functions" and the priests whom he had met. Meanwhile, elated by favorable reviews of *The Light Invisible*, he allowed himself the amusing fancy, "I like to think of S. Augustine and Newman and myself, arm-in-arm." But when after a month he had not heard from his publisher Isbister about revisions to his first novel *By What Authority?* his confidence faded. "Oh! I hope Isbister will take my book! I dream about it now--that they have accepted it unwillingly and have insisted on expurgations. Your sentence alarms me about

'Even if they don't take it'--as if you had heard?" Mary had not heard, but he would soon hear from Isbister that they would publish.

In Naples he was overwhelmed by Spender's exquisite house, and was bursting with details: "First, the rooms are almost the most lovely I have ever seen, with exquisite furniture, all old, and damasky and brocady and gilded, with embroideries and pot pourri and cabinets and little Renaissance temples with Christian and pagan images, and peacock curtains and tiled floors, and all very large and breezy with balconies, and a sheer drop of 100 feet into the town, and the bay beyond. It's a lovely day too, and all the windows wide open, and venetian shutters drawn, and the sun lying in streaks all over the tiles. There are books everywhere too, bound in vellum and brown leather. It's really all beyond words, lovely" (*Letter to MB*, Dec. 1903). He was expressly given the haunted room, and was wakened twice during the night by violent blows on the door.[3] At Mass the next morning he was moved by the devotion of the people: "audible praying during communion and quite remarkable reverence. The priest was perfectly rapt in prayer, but interrupted himself twice, to spit." He was deeply moved by the piety of the people towards their priests and nuns--Mr. Spender's cook, for instance, who came to say a word or two of good-bye, and then kissed his hand. In the street one day two children came up to him and also kissed his hand. That sort of thing went on all the time.

From Naples he wrote poetically of crowded narrow streets, white and yellow houses, and the bay beyond, "with Capri like a blue cloud across it, and Vesuvius, looking as if it was made of purple velvet, slowly smoking." In Pompeii he went up Vesuvius and looked over the edge of the crater at volumes of white sulfurous smoke; in Ostia and Anzio he sat and mused on the ruins of Nero's villa.

Good news from his publisher Isbister lifted his spirits and he threw himself vigorously into the next project, laid in the reign of Charles II. His heart sank before the labor of the project, but once immersed, he did nothing but write. In the Victor Emmanuel and English College libraries (among others), he read everything in sight as plot and setting slowly began developing in his head. "But I don't want to petrify anything till I know more history. I went to see some Jesuits about it, and one of them began, just a little superciliously: "'The book for you to read is--let's see, what is his name; he died in the 50's, I think.' I said, 'Yes--Lingard--I've read him.' 'Oh, well--then you ought to read one of our Father's books--Father Morris.' 'Yes: Works of our Catholic Forefathers. I've read it.' 'Oh-h-well, there is a very interesting, but very big book by another of our Society. Foley's 'Records of the S.J.'

'Yes, I know that well.' Then he took me seriously, and was perfectly charming; and took me all over the place; and to another library; and helped me to search for books, and told me to come again. And I giggled stupidly all down the street when I left him."

Already something of a celebrity, he was often pointed out while walking to a morning lecture, his arms loaded with books--Hooker . . . John Evelyn . . . Pepys. The novel in his head absorbed him as he mapped out plot and setting, consulting by post with Mary on fine points, speaking of his characters to her as if they were old friends dropping in to chat: "And I am getting really sorry for Gertrude. She is so very nice that I hardly have the heart to make her end so drearily; but she *will* do it, and I can't stop her," waking in the middle of the night and scribbling on the wall a phrase or word that had come during sleep, throwing himself mind and body into the conception until he had done the first draft.

When it came down to finding pleasure in his own work, he was unembarrassed. For *The Book of the Love of Jesus*, a collection of ancient English devotions almost entirely drawn from the 14th century mystic Richard Rolle (first discovered at Mirfield), he designed a cover of vellum with pierced red hearts and roses alternately, with a frontispiece showing the Five Wounds. "It is heavenly!" And the Charles II novel! "Good gracious, I am excited about that; and I hope to begin another instantly. But at present I've started on short stories, told by priests in a Roman palazzo--it is really an idealised S. Silvestro, very much idealised clergymen." And he was amused to report that an Anglo-American Hugh Benson *culte* based largely on the popularity of *The Light Invisible* had already sprouted and was growing. The hotter the flame the shorter the life, and soon, caught up in the ceremonials, his mind flew to other matters and he put the book away. When the novel appeared as *Oddsfish!* ten years later it was in its sixth version and was a different book entirely, even to the title. Only the Charles II setting remained the same.

Hugh loved always to talk about a book in progress and to watch faces as friends became engrossed in his imaginative flights. Of a priest to whom he read sections he remarked, "He sat, the other night, trembling with excitement, with his mouth and eyes open, as we skirted along the very brink of what was possible, and he panted with relief like a whale when it was over. I *am* pleased with myself" (M, I, 312). At the same time, he was polishing up *A City Set on a Hill*, the tract presented at Woodchester on the eve of his reception into the Church. With days and nights given up to his books, was there time for study? Finally, frustrated by endless processions, endless waiting (he and Evans seemed to be fading out of mind), he proposed becoming a lay oblate of a religious house where he could spend his time writing. This was desperate chafing at his uncertain position, made all the worse by a rumor that Anglican clergy converts were to be trained for *three years instead of two.* The oblate notion faded quickly when Maggie wrote that she did not think that even as a family there was enough profundity collectively to do that and only that, and implored him to be a priest. He talked of taking a doctorate, but Mary remembering his study habits discouraged it. His thoughts turned again to joining the Benedictines of Downside, literary men, or going to Woodchester with the Dominicans, or starting an "oratory" on the style of Mirfield, a simple affair with a tin chapel, where he could write and preach and evangelize without interference by a bishop. That at least would be a step in the direction of the community he had dreamed of founding in the days at Kemsing.

January and February came and went. Months were dragging by with nothing more than a vague promise of taking Holy Orders in the summer.

For a while there was strong talk of Hugh and Evans going to America. Both powerful speakers, they would form the nucleus of an American mission-society with a free hand to do what they liked without interference. "The priest who has asked us to come is continually saying 'We want men like you. We know you know your faith, and we want people who can deal with Protestants; we haven't got any: you would simply sweep them into the Church.'"4 They were flattered, particularly when the Archbishop in Oregon personally endorsed the invitation and gave assurances of ordination by Christmas. "*If* I go, I shall probably live at the Cathedral at the Archbishop's house, take over the newspaper at once, and go travelling all over the place, preaching," though he would be appallingly homesick.

A disquieting rumor that Archbishop Bourne was on the verge of appointing an Italian to be Bishop of Southwark moved Hugh closer to decision: "a fearful snub to the English clergy and it means, I expect, America for me." To provoke Bourne to action, Hugh let it be known that an offer from America had been made. "I hear that Bourne thinks that our mention of America is a threat--which indeed it is, but one that we mean." Bourne disapproved of priests who did not live simply as priests, and with one celebrated convert (Basil Maturin) already on his hands, he was not inclined to take on more ex-Anglicans not content to do parochial work to which he routinely relegated them. Hugh and Evans were nuisances, but he could not let them slip through his fingers.

For the moment Hugh's immediate problem remained what to do about America. He liked Americans, and they liked him too. "Not that

I have anything but horror at the thought of leaving England, but exactly the two things that I can do less inefficiently than other things--mission-preaching and literary work--are what are offered me." What did she think? Whatever she advised he would interpret as a "leading": "I am perfectly willing to be pushed about by Divine Providence; and the thing that pushes hardest will win; and I shall be perfectly content." Mary approved of the scheme, for it was only a three-year obligation with long summer holidays to spend back in England. Nevertheless, fearful he would be incapacitated by homesickness, he put off the decision.

America faded when friend and supporter Father Whitmee petitioned Cardinal Respighi for a waiver of the ordinary two-year waiting period. Hugh's Anglican priesthood and his tract *A City Set on a Hill* were offered as evidence of readiness.[5] Respighi agreed and a date for Holy Orders was set at last, provided the Pope approved of it. He did, on condition that Hugh agree to do more reading in Moral and Dogmatic Theology either in Rome or London. It would not be in Rome. In April Hugh took the examination for the diaconate, an unthreatening ten-minute round of questions by three examiners, one of them his own coach Professor Lauri. They sat around a sofa while Lauri asked questions in English, and Hugh answered in English. A difficult second examination a few weeks later left him shaken; overconfidence and social calls had taken their toll. Nevertheless, he passed although narrowly.

Hugh was bursting with pride that everybody else had needed at least two years' preparation, and he not even one. To a young man not usually bothered by appearances, what the world thought of this preferential treatment scarcely mattered; seldom had the Church landed such a fine catch as the son of an Archbishop of Canterbury and a trained priest to boot. "This is simply a unique event in the entire history of Holy Church," he wrote blissfully but inaccurately, "and I tremble to think of the row that will ensue." It needed to be kept quiet until Archbishop Bourne accepted him for Westminster, which the Archbishop did, reluctantly, at the specific urging of the Pope. Sensing that a clash of temperaments between Hugh and his bishop was inevitable, Mary advised he take a different course--a religious house would be better suited for him than the Cardinal's house at Westminster, at least at first. There he would have real time for writing, while at Westminster he might find himself frittered away without being given real work.

May opened uneventfully without news, and he resigned himself to waiting upon the unhurried Italians. Then word came down suddenly that on Ascension Day he would receive both tonsure and minor orders (exorcist, lector, acolyte) with major orders to follow soon after. To prepare for major orders he went into a ten-day retreat with Benedictines of San Anselmo, and soon after in a "wonderfully beautiful ceremony at St. John Lateran" he was ordained sub-deacon by Cardinal Respighi. The diaconate followed on June 5th quietly in a private chapel of Lateran with the head of St. John the Baptist, unveiled, looking on.

On Sunday morning the 13th of June, St. Anthony's day, dressed in new second-hand clothes ablaze with gold and flowers bought in the market, Hugh became a Roman Catholic priest. The simple ceremony was performed by Archbishop Seton, Titular of Heliopolis, replacing the ailing Stonor. Hugh, who thought Seton quite mad, noted that two priests stood behind him watching "like dogs at the mouth of a rabbit hole, to see he did nothing wrong." Outside a storm provided drama with a thrilling peal of thunder at the Elevation.

He was ecstatic: "We have had prosperity beyond all belief. Everything we have touched has succeeded! I am a priest within 9 months of reception! and within one month of tonsure. The whole thing is like an incredible dream." On the day his letter came informing her "it had happened," Mary wrote back warmly--

> Dearest Son--You will know your letter has possessed me. It's difficult always to know exactly why some days one holds a thought or a feeling, and other days it holds us. So it is with this last letter. We were all very full of you last Sunday. The Rector had been carrying you in his heart and preached on Holy Orders. There is a notice in the Times today of yours and Mr. Evans' ordination. Well, my darling, I shall pray for you just this--the words you will be hearing on Sunday "Grant that his teaching may be a spiritual remedy for God's people and the fragrance of his life a delight to the Church of God" . . . Your descriptions are so *acute* that I always see everything you describe--the chapel laid out, the Reliquary (surely the one that was brought home a few months ago?) Oh my Dear, I don't believe whatever the service on Sunday is that it will be disturbing. You will be out of all that. The thought of your masses in S. Peter's (the Altar of the throne?), the Catacomb! S. Gregory's for England, all is so strong and wonderful. But it's the same Hugh, and the same God. I get confused at times, but try to go just steadily on . . . Yes indeed I DO realise what an exceptional thing your ordination is. Someone said the other day that Manning had been, and Newman I think, ordained within the year but no one else as far as they knew--I *longed* to keep you with us as you know, but you saw otherwise, and I long for your future happiness and it is *A Priest* in the Church of God, both here and there. . . Child of my heart.

In a private audience with Pope Pius X, Hugh received permission to say Mass in the oratory at Tremans: "Si, si, si," replied the Pope, on condition that he have his mother's consent. Then, smiling broadly, the Pope took off his scull-cap, lifted Hugh's, and exchanged them. Hugh knelt down for the Pope's blessing, the cap fell off, both reached for it and knocked heads. Flustered, Hugh genuflected twice again and mightily pleased with his trophy and with himself trotted happily through room after room of patiently waiting people.[6] (He was probably the first person then or since to go to the Pope in pajamas under a cassock.) Later, at the altar of St. Gregory on the Ara Coeli, Hugh said his first Mass. Nothing now remained but to come home to England.

To draw to a close, reading through Hugh Benson's Rome diary presents two portraits, Rome and the man. Rome is clear enough; nothing in the physical world escaped Hugh's eye or his power to recreate setting. 1903-4 is a mere year out of his life, not even that. It looks superficial, an extension of the underactive scholar and overactive imagination, with Hugh doing just enough to satisfy authorities; making his way about this incredibly opulent world, but never joining it, put upon by needless delays in an official milieu that barely knew he existed, so it seemed. Protestant claims he had grown up with, that Rome was wild to convert England were untrue; he was merely another impatient English convert forced to wade through a vast bureaucracy, and had he not promoted himself and his cause he might well have been shunted aside for two more years.

The difference between Hugh's diary of a single year and Arthur Benson's of any single year reflects how differently the brothers saw the world--Hugh committing little of his interior life to paper beyond impressions and sensations--carried away by an angelic schola, intoxicated by physical beauty--*gorgeous this! gorgeous that!*--by curious despiritualized details, but beyond that giving little of himself. Hugh's diary is truly a daily chronicle, a daily log in which people populate a landscape shaping it without defining themselves Experience is defined entirely in physical detail. Asked years afterwards what Pope Pius X was like, he replied, "Oh! he has a warty face." Missing in his diary unfortunately is what we demand of this particular priest: introspection, self-examination, a sense of unworthiness, in other words, the bared soul of a holy man deserving of the legion of admirers already gathering about him. No, he is too busy and far too private to satisfy that need. His letters as well, though enormously interesting, were little more than colored photographs, detailed mementos of where he had been, what he had seen, whom he had lunched with. Mary was desperate to have an inner photograph, however small: "DO, but, never, never, never unless you want to." Hugh kept his interior struggles to himself except in those rare moments he confided a detail or two to her, and then only after the fact. "May I say one thing in return about myself?" he wrote cautiously to Mary, "that the deadness which has been upon me without a break since Easter, has gone at last: only a day or two ago, suddenly. It is a blessing! And I know myself well enough to know that it won't come back for the present." What simmered inside his heart remained hidden from every other living soul including Mary, his only confidante. Because his English temperament did not take easily to Roman ways, he fled to the company of ex-Anglicans, who welcomed him (he was already something of a celebrity). In their midst he made his contacts, did what others converts like him did--but more so, because he was already in Anglican Orders and thus he merited early ordination. In Rome everything depended on "who you know," quite demoralizing if you come to her from another Faith. The circle he inhabited was small but influential, including minor royalty and one or two dubious barons, American millionaires, Irish priests and Cardinals who might be players in arranging for an early ordination. Tea with a fellow Englishman or woman, Roman or Anglican, was like a summer breeze to him, but he would not tolerate insult to the Church of England. His humor and charm made him many friends, probably too many, for he found himself agreeing wildly with everybody on every subject, of "putting on too much fuel," a habit he vowed to curb even though boyish enthusiasm was as natural to him as breathing. Behind the charm and courtesy, the truth was he hated it all, hated Italy, the mad pace, shuttling from one function to the next, the empty chatter across the claret, needing to be always brilliant, always correct, the endless audiences, the waiting, waiting--so many hours squandered with so much work to be done. Had his Charles II novel not absorbed much of his time, the eight months would not have been supportable.

During these months he spent very many hours talking to "inquirers," potential converts whom he eventually brought into the Church. He worked earnestly at this and had great success. What Hugh Benson lacked as a moral theologian he made up as apologist and proselytizer. This had been proved at Kemsing, at Mirfield, and now in Rome. "My people are slowly arriving: one was received at York a fortnight ago, and another who went to stay at Woodchester has settled to be received at the Epiphany, and two others are coming nearer every day," he wrote Mary in December, a mere month after his arrival in Rome. Remembering his own spiritual agonies, he was genuinely devoted to easing "his people" into the Faith. In February he asked Mary to be kind to a girl coming to Hayward's Heath Convent, who "is really in a bad way, and she wants generally comforting and cheering up. I know you could do this, and give her rest from controversy."

His health was less than robust much of the time. He often came down with the flu, and suffered from the suffocating summer heat. Sleep was too often plagued by strange dreams of brutality and coffins and beheadings and harrowing escapes; and one night a "dreadful dream about telling Papa that I had become a R.C. Nellie finally told him." So the stormy journey to Rome was over at last--even Papa had been told. What remained was going home to England and creating a sensation beyond his wildest dream, or wish.

Notes

[1] Hugh started off well, and was soon talking back in Latin at a very moderate pace. A month later he was weary of being instructed in basics.

[2] In 1908 Tyrrell and Loisy were excommunicated; five of Loisy's books were put on the Index, and Modernism condemned in two papal documents. In the 1907 decree *Lamentabili* and later that year the encyclical *Pascendi*, Pius X laid out in the strongest terms measures to be taken against Modernism and its promoters, but it was not until 1910 that all clerics were called upon to take an oath affirming the condemnation. Hugh spoke no more of Loisy, but remained sympathetic to Tyrrell.

[3] Hugh allowed for being influenced by the power of suggestion, having just been told that a "phantom cat had been seen by Mr. Spender, that his brother who is a seer, had been in great terror of a woman, whom he knew instinctively was haunting the place, and that a family had previously left the rooms "because Aunt saw things" (*Letter to MB*, Jan. 10, 1904).

[4] The Jesuit magazine *America* called him a "leader of religious thought" in England, quoting Anglicans to the effect that he was the greatest loss since Newman. "What *incredible* stuff!" he laughed.

[5] That Father Whitmee intended to ask Hugh to preach the Lent in Rome the following year added weight. Evans discouraged it as an impossible position, bound to stir up hostility (some priests whom they considered supporters actually protested the ordinations to the Vatican). Archbishop Bourne distrusted Anglican convert-priests who by converting had already disobeyed their bishops and set obstacles to discourage them from seeking higher office. So it had been for Maturin, and so it would have been for Hugh. Evans escaped from Westminster by flying across the Thames into the arms of the rival bishopric of Southwark, where Tyrrell had gone to live

after being booted out by the Jesuits. When Bourne wanted Southwark added to Westminster's jurisdiction, Evans helped defeat it.

6 As an Anglican he had said Mass in it when he came to Tremans from Mirfield. Mary could not have been pleased, but Hugh argued here was an oratory already consecrated for Protestant services and no Catholic Church nearby. "The oratory--what is right will happen . . ." she replied and was understood as giving her consent. A newspaper clipping for June 24 designed to stir indignation among readers reported that "Rev. Mr. Benson, who was recently ordained priest in Rome, has left for England, after having had an audience with the Pope" *and has received permission to say Mass in a Protestant house in England*, where he will stay during the summer."

7
He Makes a Name for Himself, Again

1. At Llandaff House

From Rome Hugh came home for a last visit before he took up his work. The family were living at Tremans, the house Mary had rented near Horsted Keynes in Sussex, that very house that Hugh fondly described as Isabel and Anthony Norris' house in *By What Authority?* The house of red brick was a lovely thing surrounded by lawns and gardens and a cherry orchard with a small movable shelter erected for Maggie's pleasure. Here she did her reading. It was in this orchard that Hugh proposed Mary should build him a cottage. From the garden one had a view of the beautiful South Downs. Tremans was run on schedule: Mass at 8 for Hugh when he visited, breakfast before 10; tea at 5 and dinner at 8, with the gong sounding an alert at half-past seven. After dinner, the men smoked, or played cards or sang at the piano or organ until compline--about 9:30 or 10.

Hugh was in a queer state of suspension. He had been ordered not to preach or begin active ministry for a year when, presumably, he would have made up deficiencies in Theology. And what then, when the year was up? Archbishop Bourne showed no interest in using him; parochial work was not to his liking--how often had he said he could feed the flock, but not lead them--and while joining the Benedictines remained an attractive possibility, he was not ready to commit himself to an Order. It was not in his nature then or ever to be bound down by a rule of living except of his own making. Nevertheless, a religious house was to him preferable to the Cardinal's House in Westminster. That he wanted least of all. So he settled back and waited.

Now that he had got Mary's permission to say Mass in the upstairs oratory, he set about fitting it out properly. He laid a stone slab on the

floor, cast a statue of the Virgin and painted it, and then painted saints
on the leaded window panes. A large oak chest with a stone upon it
served for altar. In this little chapel Hugh prayed the Office and said
Mass every morning in full vestments. Arthur lying in bed late in
order to avoid morning prayer downstairs, often heard the tinkling of the
sacring bell and the murmur of voices through the wall and he pictured
Hugh on the other side moving about in his alb and chasuble "playing
conjuring tricks with white wafers," while his server, the porter's son,
knelt in the corner wishing to be home in his own bed. One day Hugh
took Arthur to the chapel to show him his chasuble and the altar stone
incised with crosses. Hugh opened the silver casket and took out "a
white thing," as Arthur put it. "'This has been shut up a long time.
I wonder if it is all right.' He broke it, ate, and handed me a piece. I
ate it too. . . I thought it was odd to hand it to me thus: but I accepted
it as a kind of brotherly sacrament." Hugh perhaps hoped to infuse the
Spirit digestively. One morning at breakfast a package came for him
containing Mass wafers: "Hurrah, they've come," he cried, ate one or
two, and passed the rest to Fred.

These were carefree days indeed. He was free to do what in Rome he
had promised to do, "immerse himself in lawns and trees and puddely
roads and villages." The sole restrictions were he was not to go to the
theater, or wear dress clothes. No matter!--he loved dressing up in
cassock and tippet for all occasions, even for a game of billiards played
with great zest. On the lawn directly under the chapel where the
peacock strutted Hugh and Fred played croquet, one of Hugh's passions.
Nothing except his Office interfered with his game. In September, he
was Lady Kenmare's guest in Ireland to hunt and fish. The trophy of
his "great stalk" would adorn his sitting room at the Cambridge Rectory
the following year.[1] Back at Tremans, he began work on a new Tudor
novel *The King's Achievement*, set in the time of Henry VIII, and
continued his habit from younger days of dashing into his mother's
room waving sheets of inky paper continued. "Mamma, I must read
you this," he would say excitedly of the newly finished chapter, "It's g-
g-gorgeous. May I have a cigarette here?"

To his family he seemed to be very happy, and much easier to live
with, "really a very delightful creature," Arthur agreed, with his change
of faith adding to his charm. The opposing parties were no closer on
creeds, but at least they were more amiable at the dinner-table.

At last, in October 1904, four months after his return from Rome, he
had his assignment: Llandaff House in Cambridge, to assist Monsignor
Barnes, the versatile Catholic chaplain who looked after undergraduates.
At 43, Monsignor Barnes, also an Eton and Cambridge man, was ten
years older than Hugh, and like Hugh had taken Anglican orders. When

Pope Leo XIII declared Anglican Orders invalid, Barnes lapsed to Rome, took Holy Orders and was eventually promoted by Cardinal Merry del Val over the objections of Bourne. (Bourne would also oppose Hugh's promotion to monsignor in 1911.) Barnes's detective work led him to conclude that Anglican Bishops all the way back to the first under Henry VIII had not been properly consecrated, thus making all Anglican orders since that time invalid. Antiquarian and amateur archaeologist, Barnes was a fascinating fellow who claimed to know the identity of the Man in the Iron Mask and better than that, to have discovered the actual site of St. Peter's tomb. Not since Charlemagne laid a silver cross upon it had the tomb been seen, but with the rebuilding of St. Peter's the exact site was lost, or misplaced. Accompanied by his friend Cardinal Merry del Val, Barnes located a hollow corner spot under St. Peter's where he was certain the Apostle's body lay buried. Unfortunately, the site could not be proved because Pius X refused permission to pull down the wall.

An assignment to Cambridge had been rumored in Rome, so Hugh cannot have been taken by surprise when it happened. Of course, returning as a Catholic priest to his father's university might create awkward moments, but so be it. At Llandaff House he gave up his mornings to the study of Theology, but with what diligence one may speculate. Theology was not his strong suit. His one public venture into a theological sermon at the Catholic Church in Cambridge failed and as long as he lived he steered clear of that minefield, at least in public. Afternoons were spent writing ghost stories. Caught up in the terrors of his tale, he emerged from his room pale and quivering--"I can't b-b-bear to be alone," he gasped, and launched into a reading of his creative labors aloud to anyone within hearing distance, either the disapproving Mgr. Barnes or an unsuspecting undergraduate he had managed to collar. "I can see him sitting in the firelight of my room at Kings," Shane Leslie recalled, "unravelling a weird story about demoniac substitution, his eyeballs staring into the flame, and his nervous fingers twitching to baptise the next undergraduate he could thrill or mystify into the fold of Rome."[2] Ghosts and martyred heroes of the English Reformation always made for lively conversation.

To Llandaff House on Sunday evening came Catholics and Anglicans, shy undergraduates and bold ones, college dons, eccentrics, and aspiring mystics. Among distinguished visitors was Baron Friedrich von Hügel, the promoter of Modernist causes who (as Shane Leslie put it) "had pushed Father Tyrrell off the giddy edge." Why Tyrrell had been excommunicated and not Von Hügel remained a mystery. Von Hügel piously received Holy Communion every morning of his life lest, as Hugh was heard to remark, he should return to find his excommunication waiting with The Times on the breakfast table. How Hugh had managed to become a Roman Catholic priest in nine months instead of the normal three years intrigued everybody. A story began to circulate that Pope Pius X had sent for Hugh and Evans, examined them in Moral Theology, and decided that within the year they should be entrusted with the conversion of England. When at Easter the Pope inquired about their diaconate and was told Archbishop Bourne had delayed it, he demanded 'Who is Pope, myself or the Archbishop of Westminster?' To this, of course, the Theologians could find only one answer. Benson and Evans were immediately raised to the diaconate and priesthood, critics said by the backstairs, but it was by the backstairs that lead into the Vatican."[3]

Once Hugh got back into the pulse of university life he lost no time in renewing his contact with the Pitt Club and with the debating Decemviri. His vitality and charm actually put the younger men at ease; they liked him, they trusted him, even when he was busy capturing a "type" as often happened. People, he insisted, divided up into a few types, and when you had spotted what type a man belonged to, "you know all about him that there was to know." A Cambridge friend remembered being called upon early on by this nervous "grey-clad figure, with untidy hair" who flung himself into a huge chair and glared at him beneath his brows. "How I felt myself being ticketed: how I resisted!" "Sizing up" a person by the shape of his hands was another of Hugh's eccentricities; he insisted if the hands were right, if they were a good fit with the face, all would be well. He relied perhaps too much on first impressions.

At Kings, bastion of free thought and free speech, where one found many High Churchmen, a handful of Catholics, and enough agnostics to spice up controversy, debates seldom flagged. At the Roman Catholic Society for St. Thomas of Canterbury Hugh's lively speeches were roundly cheered by Anglicans. Sometimes he read papers at Oxford, sometimes to the Westminster Dining Club. He was making quite a reputation at Cambridge and beyond.

Creations and inspirations   Life was so fully packed there was hardly enough time to write books; life was ever percolating, "a delightful life, heavenly!" He heard that *The Book of the Love of Jesus* was to appear within the week, very attractively got up with a limp leather binding decked with gold, and *By What Authority?* the week following. *The King's Achievement*, finished with lightning speed, was the next historical novel to fall from his pen. It had been rushed, and although packed with historical color and detail, lacked the passion and conviction of *By What Authority?*, written during Hugh's spiritual struggles. Still, there were numerous artistic touches everywhere including a detailed if idealized picture of monastic life and a Thames procession featuring the revoltingly amorous King Henry and Anne Boleyn.

Trifles distracted him--a monsignor's dress with purple buttons, a papal procession, sketches for a religious tract, another pantomime for the family's amusement when he visited Tremans--all of these lovely toys lured him away from hard work, but gave healthy breathing space after intense and furious writing spells. Gladly he put away the tiresome Charles II novel (the project launched in Rome and now in its fourth version), and embarked on his "Mary book," determined to make Queen Mary Tudor human. It was undertaken on a dare, for reviewers of *The King's Achievement* had challenged him: now that he had shown up Henry VIII as an obnoxious tyrant, could make Bloody Mary a sympathetic figure to a largely Protestant audience who hated her very name? By March 1905 research for *The Queen's Tragedy* was underway. It would be the best thing he'd ever done, he said, full of little touches of fact: "I have already found out she ate quantities of meat for breakfast." With typical fury, he threw himself into his work, struggling with every scene as if independent of its creator: ". . . for the last day or two I have stuck in a furious brawl, and my people wait hour after hour with uplifted weapons, and I can't let them put them down. At this moment someone is pausing with clenched fists and a savage expression." His approach to characters was summed up in a letter to a friend--

When I write for the first time my characters do their own business and say their own words entirely. Then I have to select them in rewriting, and have an eye on the readers, and it is just exactly this that I HATE. E.g. in my present book two people have a long technical interview. Now they did have it, and they said just those things. But the public would be bored by listening; I can't utter a word. So I have to refuse to be in the room with them, and the result is that pages of labour disappear, and we are left waiting outside with a dull clergyman until they have done. Now, how heartbreaking! Because it is really very interesting indeed, and all perfectly true. (M, I, 385)

For Mary Tudor, he composed one of the most inspired death scenes ever put on paper. He wrote as if he had lived her hallucinatory spells, as if Mary had breathed her last breath through his lungs. One day promptly at the sound of the luncheon bell he appeared in the dining room to announce "Queen Mary's d-d-dead. She has been dying all the morning. Such a death-bed--really, it's too moving--quite tremendous-- but I am completely done up."

Surely never had fiction handled this sadly maligned queen so gently, but as for technique *The Queen's Tragedy* is short on plot but rich in vivid sketches stitched together by interesting characterizations and details. There was no denying his power to establish a remarkable intimacy between reader and character--Mary's thoughts are dictated from within, as if he'd got inside her brain and heart in the last hours of life--but had he taken greater pains with plot construction, his work would have been stunning throughout rather than in isolated scenes, and more durable. Asked why he did not trouble more about his novels because a thing worth doing was worth doing well, he disagreed, explaining that he wrote to make a point, all the rest was mere literature. This worn path he traveled too often, and he has paid the price. Father Martindale thought him a good storyteller, with an eye for pageant; with a wasted talent like "treasure tossed about by a millionaire, too rich to care, adequately, for his own beautiful gift."

No sooner had he put Mary into her grave than he launched into another book that was to be his personal favorite *Richard Raynal, Solitary*--all this during residence at Llandaff House. That done, he managed a complete change of setting and purpose for *The Sentimentalists*, a modern psychological novel about Christopher Dell, an aesthete with a seamy past, who is salvaged by Mr. Rolls, the no-nonsense physician of souls. Boldly declaring "the man must be broken to pieces," Rolls proceeds to make it happen. In Mr. Rolls readers saw Hugh's own methods operating. He was like Hugh, he was Hugh, with Hugh's relentless drive to strip away the sham of the "poseur." The novel became a big hit, and for a time there was talk of adapting it for the stage. Here and in the sequel *The Conventionalists*, into which he dared put himself as a character (not a felicitous device), the intriguing question Who is the real Chris Bell? fueled Cambridge gossip for months, causing consternation to Hugh who needed to defend himself in letter after letter against the charge that in his revelations of Bell's questionable past he had stepped over the line. He thought of taking an advertisement to put an end to the mystery once and for all. Laughing off the whole affair the real "Chris Bell" assured him good-naturedly that the notoriety was no bother, the storm would soon blow over. Actually, Chris Bell was not one man but three, a composite of the paganized dandy Ronald Firbank, an undergraduate whom Hugh brought into the Church; the notorious Frederick Rolfe; and Eustace Virgo, the strange, pathetic convert and sometimes-tutor whom Hugh had met in Rome. Like the fictional Chris Bell, Virgo had drifted about the Continent, eking out a small living as a part-time journalist, and most recently as a tutor. He was to write two novels using the pen-name E.V. de Fontmell, one autobiographical (in which Hugh appears under the alias of Father Mason), and the other about a fated sensualist, obviously Virgo himself. He was a small, high-strung man with a colorful past, a sad case with pain of past addiction and present confusion written across his life.[4]

Cambridge charactery   Fascinating types abounded in Cambridge in those days. Among them was Jack Collins, a staunchly Catholic undergraduate who usually served at Mass, and practically ran Llandaff chaplaincy. Everyone liked him. Like Waugh's Sebastian Flyte he should have been a monk, but was too humorous. He loved Continental religion and conceived the excellent idea to make the Catholic church more picturesque by hiring an old Italian peddler woman to sit on the steps selling fruit under an umbrella. Another scheme of his in the Catholic cause was to arrange for lectures by noted clergy, invite the Masters of various colleges, and plant a hand-picked band of "atheist" hecklers in the stands until the good priest silenced them with shows of irrefutable logic (to the consternation of the Anglican dons).

Cambridge eccentrics provided the characters for Hugh's modern stories. The most interesting of the "colony of Cranks" at Llandaff House probably was Arthur (Ronald) Firbank, purportedly Hugh's model for "Christopher Dell" of *The Sentimentalists*.[5] Firbank was a rarefied bloom at Trinity, who Shane Leslie tells us painted his nails red long before women dared to. It was still the fashion for undergraduates to follow the aesthete's cult preached by Walter Pater, and Firbank played the part up to the hilt. He lived extravagantly in a room stocked with fresh flowers, had his portrait painted by Jasper John, pranced about like an exotic, and "invented the novel in which the wholly unconnected passes for conversation." Hugh brought Firbank into the Church in 1907, and laid penance for outrageous excesses by making him row in hot and cold conditions that nearly killed him. Once he became a Catholic Firbank lived his Faith to the hilt, and died in Rome a Papal Guard in 1926 at the age of 40.[6]

By far the most sinister figure to enter Hugh's life in 1905 was Frederick Rolfe, self-styled Baron Corvo. Hugh had been bowled over by Rolfe's novel *Hadrian the Seventh*, which Eustace Virgo had given him to read, and instantly dashed off a letter: magnificent, the greatest work to ever see light, etc. etc. Out of the stream of letters a friendship akin to discipleship on Hugh's part developed, followed by a disastrous literary collaboration that caused both men much grief. Now, Frederick Rolfe was a disreputable fellow with a monstrous ego, a convert from

Protestantism, who had yearned to become a priest but had been booted out of seminary. He retaliated by reviling all Catholic priests as apes, slanderers, and liars, and founding the Grand Order of Sanctissima Sophia, complete with heraldry, a freemasonic society complete with secret words and ceremonies. He wore a ring fitted with a sharp spur with which to scar the faces of priests out to kidnap him and imprint themselves with his personality. His was a brilliant but paranoid mind, crammed full of fascinating incunabula. Rolfe's pretensions to aristocratic blood (hence, *Baron Corvo*), and dandyish manner were part of his magnetism apparently. Imagination filled up the rest. He was frequently penniless, begging favors of friends and insulting them afterwards, making a career of making enemies. He had written a history of poisons after discovering the secret of the Borgias, from whom he claimed descent though no Italian blood ran in his veins. Kaiser Wilhelm was his godfather, he said. Hugh liked Rolfe's paganism ("all sound Catholics are that"), and used him in constructing the character of Christopher Dell. For a while, thanks to Hugh, Rolfe became all the rage among Cambridge undergraduates, and a small cult gathered about him which, when they raised themselves from their knees, set about imitating his style. Rolfe could be charming when it suited him, and Hugh of course was utterly enchanted, to the extent that he sang Rolfe's praises to everyone within shouting distance, kept his *Hadrian the Seventh* and *In His Own Image* on the night table by his bed, promised to ordain him as soon as he (Hugh) became a bishop, consulted him when decorating his rooms in the Cambridge Rectory, and even took to imitating his handwriting.[7] Under Rolfe's influence too, bathing took on a sacramental dimension. It had never been so exquisitely enjoyed, nor had so much prose lavished upon it as was lavished in Hugh's novels, never, that is, until Leopold Bloom took the plunge years later. For Hugh bathing every afternoon became ritual, but bathing outdoors on a warm night with "wreaths of mist coming off the water, and the stars and moon, and dead silence" was exquisite joy . . . mysterious.

If Rolfe who delighted in corrupting others had intentions towards Hugh, he was disappointed. Hugh was celibate, and though he preferred always the company of men and shrank from women, he was not homosexual, or sexual in any way. All friendships were ascetic to him; he could be fervid, but the heat passed quickly and when it did, he let go the friendship without regret or great sense of loss. What Rolfe demanded of a friend--"eternal unflinching fidelity"--Hugh could never deliver. "People come to me and pass on," he admitted to Arthur. With Rolfe, the fatal infatuation ended bitterly in 1908. Hugh was to learn a hard lesson from putting on too much fuel in this friendship.

After corresponding for a few months, they went on a rigorous walking tour together, at the conclusion of which Hugh asked Mary if he might bring Rolfe to Tremans. Arthur took an instant dislike to him. Here is the diary entry for Sept. 1, 1905: "And then Hugh is going to bring a Roman priest [Rolfe was not a priest], whom I call the infernal exorcist, to stay here. He doesn't seem to know much about him--and all that we know is that he wrote a quite appalling book (which Hugh thinks clever) called Hadrian VII. I do not want this man intruded. He will probably be a gentleman, and though I shan't see much of him, I shall see nothing of Hugh." Rolfe arrived that evening, "a very trim, grey-haired priest; neat, long nosed, short upper lip, badly dressed, large silver spectacles, enormous rings. Very silent and deep at dinner, but not in the least shy or humble, or conciliatory. I discovered, by his talk in the chair-room, while we smoked, that he was a great egotist, and fancied himself a great writer. He regaled us with long accounts of how he wrote, how he punctuated, how he conceived his books, how he re-wrote them (Adrian [sic] VII was done eleven times). But when one thinks a book thoroughly bad it is depressing to hear how much pains have been spent."

Rolfe the exorcist lay like a lead on Arthur's spirit. He was pretentious, mysterious, incoherent, conscious of his genius and of being scrutinized, when all they were thinking was "to wish a dull man away." Arthur noted the stark contrast between Hugh and the "exorcist," Hugh a delightful talker, full of ease, humor, and fractiousness, as usual, while Rolfe played the patronizing egoist. "I realised that he thought of himself as a great author, bringing light and interest into a rather hide-bound dull home, and being eagerly speculative about and curiously regarded by the inmates." As Rolfe discovered that the family was nearer his intellectual level than he had thought and had even written books, his pose diminished. All in all the family wished to be rid of him as soon as possible.

To ingratiate himself with Arthur, Rolfe claimed to admire his work (Rolfe's baroque tastes and Arthur's meditative habit were worlds apart) and drew up an elaborate horoscope.[8] Arthur, ever the gentleman, treated Rolfe politely, but Mary suggested to Hugh privately that Rolfe might like to come another time, preferably when Arthur was away.

Hugh was not everybody's favorite priest; he was excitable, wildly throwing himself into the passion of the moment and sweeping his friends into orbit with him. He could be hard and thick-skinned and was often oblivious to the pain a careless word or neglect caused others. Dissembling was not in his nature; and while a more diplomatic man might have made excuses for peevishness or rages or temperamental outbursts, Hugh, having passed quickly through a mood, moved on to the next piece of business, without a thought for hurt feelings. An unfriendly Cambridge acquaintance citing a passage about Guy Manton, the hero in *The Queen's Tragedy*, summed up Hugh Benson: "[Hugh] was a strange creature; they could understand neither his tenderness nor his spasms of rage. He had made himself ridiculous more than once in his friendships by showing a passion for queer persons they could not comprehend; and he had made himself a little terrible, too, half a dozen times in his furies against disloyalty, and his contempt of what they considered academic finesse" (M, I, 388). His friendship with eccentrics like Frederick Rolfe and Ronald Firbank did make him ridiculous sometimes.

11. At Cambridge Rectory

In June of 1905, after three terms at Llandaff House, Hugh was now ready to take up full duties of a priest at the Church of Our Lady and the English Martyrs, with assurances that he would have greater freedom to do as he liked. Remarkably few parish duties were entailed upon him, with Canon Scott carrying the lion's share; but there were the usual social calls and sick calls, luncheons and outings to attend, all the little duties he disliked. "I have started visiting, hard, and go round on a bicycle in the afternoons. Rather dreary work. I cannot do it; but I suppose it is necessary to make everyone's acquaintance, at any rate. . ." (M, II, 9). That was an old story with Hugh, clear from early days at the Eton Mission when he discovered that he had no pastoral gift, that he could "kindle but not support." In point of fact, judged by his extraordinary success as a preacher and spiritual director he might have been an immensely effective pastor, but this individualist had no patience for making sick calls or keeping parish records. Nevertheless, he never complained publicly and faithfully discharged the few duties assigned to him, attending this parish function or that, enjoying himself despite himself and always giving delight to others.

He was no sooner settled into the Catholic Rectory than he went about the joyful business of decorating his rooms. They were modest enough, a very small bedroom and sitting room which, to his delight, overlooked a tangled garden within a stone wall of devils and angels. But the artistic decor of his sitting room which he labored to perfect caused a small sensation. Rumors flew that it was too elegant, rankly aesthetic, and many who did not like him for one reason or another, found his taste bold, suggestive, self-indulgent. The sitting-room was done in garden colors, hung with jungle green canvas, rumored to be Gobelins. Everywhere were bowls of lilies and roses and poppies and walls covered with art-nouveau and photographs of friends; tall wooden candlesticks and Madonnas dripping with Rosaries and moonstones; a mahogany writing desk with piles of letters fallen over as if left in haste, and a big oak chest he tried but failed to cover with scarlet leopard skin, which now lay in a heap at its side. The floor he laboriously stained making the boards look like oak. He was proud of the results, and said so. This shockingly unsacerdotal setting raised more than a few eyebrows, though to Hugh it was all innocent fun with none of the decadent excess about it that aestheticism gave rise to.[9] When a disapproving friend expressed the opinion that as Hugh was neither religious nor apostolic, why shouldn't he have pretty things? he flew into a rage, but instantly regretted it--it was usually the case with his quick temper--though he made no apologies for his taste for "things." Mind your own business! he shot back. "For the first time in my life I am content with my rooms."

He was hearing confessions regularly and preaching the Sunday evening sermon. In June 1905 he sang his first High Mass; and on July 4, 1905, on the Feast of Relics "mad with nerves" preached his first sermon as a Catholic priest on 1 Thessalonians, 4:3: "Hic est enim voluntas Dei, sanctificatio vestra."

One of the vivid memories long held by Cambridge undergraduates in those days was of Father Hugh Benson preaching in the Roman Catholic Church filled to overflowing, the crowd held spellbound as that fund of nervous energy--head, hands, body, arms, all thrown this way and that, pleading, exhorting, demanding--took the audience by storm. At first glance, he was not at all commanding, like a young boy about to wade into water over his head. He had none of the orator's skills: his speech was fast, his gestures theatrical, the voice often raucous: "But the man's personality gets him over these defects. He acts, he lives, he sees every word he speaks. His enthusiasm never flags, his energy is unwearied. . . . You must follow him, must give him your undivided attention . . . He arouses anger, hope, love, pride, pity, faith at will. . . . "

That agile voice some found too shrill. With excruciating tact Mary told him that she and a friend one day went to hear him at Cambridge, liked what she heard, but not how she heard it: his pitch (too high) and his tone (too shrill): ". . . and a Mother's 'ART felt the strain, and when you dropped it, [pitch] all was lovely." She offered to send him the address of Lady Radnor's Roman Catholic physician, "who has dropped his practice to become a 'VOICE PRODUCER'--isn't it interesting?" She thinks she can get the address if any friend of his wanted it. Complaints like this were rare and even critics opposed to him on religious grounds conceded him this great strength, that he excelled in preaching more than novel writing, for his spoken word, torrential in power, reached people directly and forcefully without the interference of allegorical constructions necessary to the writer's art.

Two things Hugh loved about Cambridge were the river where he could do bathing, and the friendship of his brother Arthur, who had left Eton to edit Queen Victoria's papers and was now a Fellow of Magdalene College. His presence meant long chats to look forward to, and Sunday rambles through the lovely countryside beyond. This was early in 1905. Before this moment, Arthur's age and the fact that he was away at Eton most of the time Hugh was growing up had prevented a real friendship from developing. Apart from Arthur, there was little else about Cambridge Hugh liked, and although he stayed a full three years until 1908--three terms at Llandaff House and two years at the Catholic Rectory--he never got used to the frosty atmosphere that spilled over from university. He was looked upon with suspicion even by those College dons who received him warmly at their dinner parties; they remembered with bitterness that during a mission at Cambridge, when Hugh was still an Anglican, several undergraduates who came to hear him preach went away Roman Catholics. Things were worse now that he was a priest. Thirty young undergraduates whom he had instructed threatened to go over to Rome. The authorities who up to now had not cared a whit about religion outside of the debating societies began to make noises to Arthur about the harm Hugh was doing, accusing him of treachery and deliberate proselytizing, all of it the more painful because his father's son was doing it in his own university! Arthur rallied to Hugh's defense. If the authorities were so worried about Hugh's influence over undergraduates, then it was their job to counter it by finding an Anglican preacher of equal eloquence. For his part Hugh was stunned to hear it; he was not aware that he was being talked about in that light. "It is a perplexing business, and I don't see what to do," Arthur wrote unhappily; there was much bitterness of feeling surging but it would not come between them. Hugh was just being Hugh.[10]

In the arena   With a growing reputation as a Catholic apologist came the burden of meeting objections of eminent critics, even to locking horns with historian G. G. Coulton. The battle began when in consecutive issues of *Contemporary Review*.[11] Coulton accused Abbot Gasquet, the head of English Benedictines, of suppressing the truth in an article he had written, "Henry VIII and the English Monasteries." Helping to spread Gasquet's falsifications about English monasteries were Catholic and non-Catholic journals, including the *Athenaeum* and the (Anglican) *Church Times*, whom Coulton accused of being tools of the Catholic Truth Society, the arch Romanist propaganda mill. He lashed out against "the best-known Roman Catholic controversialists in England," alluding to the moral bankruptcy of their position in defending the corruption of monasteries which every schoolboy knew had been justly purged. At length he turned his attention to Hugh's *The King's Achievement*, deriding the novel as full of gross historical errors betraying "scarcely an inkling of what Tudor manners were even at their best." Furthermore (he went on), Father Benson, a romantic convert, had falsified history for purposes of anti-Reformation propaganda. In a personal slash, he reminded readers that Father Benson had relinquished an atmosphere of "pure and noble ideals" in the household of an Anglican divine for the company of Papists. For several reasons, then, Hugh was compelled to reply, if only to defend himself against so able a mud-slinger, as he called him. It was a task not to his liking, for Coulton was an eminent historian, vehemently anti-Catholic, writing in a journal where the No-Popery champion was sure to have all the applause. "Mr. Coulton has honoured me by an attack upon my novel," began Hugh's reply. It was an impressive reply, countering Coulton's charge that the novel swarmed with anachronisms amidst a cheap profusion of carved oak and stained glass. This reply in turn prompted a nasty rejoinder from Coulton. It turned out to be an acrimonious debate without the usual surface courtesies and Hugh was glad to put an end to it. More disturbing than Coulton's jabs were charges by Catholic reviewers in Catholic journals that the novel had drawn Thomas Cromwell too sympathetically while monks were made out to be cowardls, caving in at the first show of force to save their own skins. Criticism of this kind was not idle, for the tendency to portray priests in an unfavorable light particularly in his modern novels had caused much irritation in priests who did not speak out publicly, and reviewers who did.

Another Benson controversy sparked followed the publication in late 1907 of *Lord of the World*, a futuristic tale of the Antichrist, begun early in 1906 and finished by June of that year. In it the people have long since thrown off the yoke of Christianity in favor of pantheistic positivism. Only Ireland remains Christian. The priests have defected and now serve the religion of Humanity under the socialist Freemason Julian Felsburgh, who rules the world. It is a dark novel thin in plot about civilization or what is left of it charging full gallop to Apocalypse. So chilling was the effect upon the public, that one disillusioned admirer admitted to Hugh that for him the book had struck heaven out of the sky, he was at a loss how to get it back: "Only when I found you, a guardian of the faith, forsaking hope, except in a cataclysm, did my frail shield break down" (M, II, 75). This from a non-Catholic! He never intended that his fiction present anything other

than a Catholic solution to the problem at hand; but to many thousands
of Catholic and Protestant readers, what he said and wrote carried the
weight of authority. The public, weary of uncertainty, were leaning on
Hugh. At the semi-official level, the Church was annoyed on several
points--how nimbly Hugh had described the apostasy of Catholic clergy
as the natural religion sweeps the world, the treatment of suicide in a
godless society, and the defection of Catholics but for a few faithful
hold-outs in Ireland. Reviewers ridiculed fantastic futuristic toys like
suicide machines and hovering aircraft while Protestant readers resented
the assumption that without Catholicism the world would revert to
paganism. The official Church too bristled at the suggestion that
materialism could succeed in doing what faith had failed to do. Hugh
never expected the book to be taken as denying the primacy of God over
Man. To console those who found *Lord of the World* too gloomy
Hugh came up with *The Dawn of All,* in which the opposite happens:
it is the year 2000 and Christianity under the Pope has triumphed
throughout the world. This anodyne succeeded only in disturbing
Protestants further; even Catholics recoiled at the unscriptural concept
of the Church Triumphant on earth. Visiting Rome shortly after
publication, Hugh was told of the harm such books were doing, and
ceased using the theme. Later on he called *The Dawn of All* deplorable
and wondered what had possessed him to write it.

Say what he liked about cold Cambridge, life there was good for his
art. Not counting *City Set on a Hill, The Book of the Love of Jesus,*
and *By What Authority?* (all predating his Cambridge curacy), he had
written *The King's Achievement, The Queen's Tragedy,* worked on the
fourth revision of *Oddsfish!,* finished the ghost collection *The Mirror of
Shalott,* done up two books of apologetics *Papers of a Pariah* and *The
Religion of a Plain Man,* and set to work on *Richard Raynal, Solitary.*
In addition to these, *The Sentimentalists,* written during his residency at
Llandaff House, initiated the second branch of his fiction, narratives of
modern Catholic life. *The Conventionalists* was soon followed by *Lord
of the World.* Also that year he wrote the chapter on the Dissolution of
the English Monasteries for the *Cambridge History of English
Literature.* And there were many pamphlets for the Catholic Truth
Society, and lectures reshaped afterwards into essays for *Dublin Review,
The Month* and the American journal *Ave Maria,* among others; and
sermons collected into books. A paper on "Mysticism" made the
rounds, first read with spectacular success to a gathering of 250
enthusiastic Theosophists and Christian Scientists (sects he personally
deplored as dangerously misguided). Stretching his work the full length
of the religious circuit gave his ideas extraordinarily wide exposure, but
also laid upon him the burden of being looked upon by the public as

spokesman for the Faith, a responsibility for which he was not equipped temperamentally or doctrinally.

Were six or seven novels not enough? In these years too began the massive correspondence with inquirers and penitents that occupied him every day for the rest of his life, at the cost of his health. "Be a Mr. Rolls to me!" they pleaded.

How did Hugh do it, how did he move so swiftly and determinedly from one project to the next, how collect and sift and transform ideas and impressions into orthodox commercial fiction? how manage his new role as spiritual advisor to so many who came to his door or sent letters, expecting a reply, and getting it? Motivating him by now was the real possibility that the independent life he had always craved was attainable if only he could be sure of a steady income. Writing books for money, and writing lots of them, suddenly made the dream of owning his own house closer than it had every been.[12]

Addendum
Benson and Rolfe

When Hugh and Rolfe made plans in 1907 to collaborate on a book about St. Thomas Becket, with Rolfe providing medieval lore but Hugh doing the actual writing, Arthur and Mgr. Barnes stepped in. Rolfe was a dangerous man with a lurid reputation; the venture was bound to cause scandal. They begged him not to proceed. On the other side, a book carrying the weight of Hugh Benson's name was just what Rolfe wanted. Not only would it bring him a third of the profits, but it would go far to raise his stock as a marketable writer. Here was a most painful dilemma for Hugh, going back on an agreement with a friend, or doing incalculable damage to himself as a priest.

All this time Hugh had been begging Rolfe in Venice to send the required material for the Beckett. As writers they crafted differently, Hugh writing at the speed of sound until exhausted, Rolfe painstaking in research and detail. Acting on advice from Arthur and Mgr. Barnes, he proposed to Rolfe that the book appear under his name alone, while Rolfe's contribution would be acknowledged in the preface, offering him £100. Rolfe refused. Finally, Hugh offered to send him the entire manuscript and all rights to it with the stipulation that Hugh's name be omitted entirely. Rolfe felt betrayed. He denounced the "scorpion" in a stream of letters to friends and publishers, mocked him as a "banausic fire-insurance agent" (fire-insurance because he was a priest), and ridiculed him in *Desire and Pursuit of the Whole* in the diabolical figure of Bobugo [i.e. Bob for Robert, Ugo for Hugh] Bonsen," a stuttering

little Chrysostom of a priest, with the Cambridge manners of a
Vaughan's Dove, the face of the Mad Hatter out of Alice in
Wonderland, and the figure of an Etonian who insanely neglects to take
any pains at all the his temple of the Holy Ghost, but wears paper
collars and a black straw alpine hat."[13] For months obscene letters and
post cards addressed to Hugh accusing him of various crimes and
misdemeanors arrived daily from Italy. While the friendship lasted,
however, in Hugh's eyes Rolfe could do no wrong. No other person
had captivated him so completely. He admired him, emulated him, but
abandoned him when it became necessary to protect his own reputation.
That, Rolfe's devoted admirers have never forgiven. In 1908 Hugh's
own little book on the life of St. Thomas appeared.

Little remains of the Benson-Rolfe correspondence beyond a single
angry post-card from Hugh dated July 10, 1908: "I'm returning your
letters unopened to the postman: so do not send me more. I shall
probably have to communicate your name and address to the Postal
authorities if any more arrive. I haven't read either of them, except the
first two sentences of the first. I'm keeping that one." As a gesture of
contempt Hugh put the cards with their obscene drawings on the mantle
of Hare Street, and what other letters he did not dispose of himself,
Arthur destroyed after his death. In a surviving letter written at Llandaff
House in 1905, before they had met face to face, Hugh expressed delight
that Rolfe had answered his letter of praise for *Hadrian*. It is stiff and
rambling and pedantic, quite unlike Hugh's normal style--

> My dear sir--It is so good of you to have written again. To tell the
> truth, I was not perfectly certain whether you wished me to write or
> not: and I thought I would wait. I also have a message to give you
> from a man here, Eustace Virgo, who first gave me your book: and
> who wishes me to tell you how greatly he admires it, and how much
> he would like to write to you and make your acquaintance. He says
> that he goes wholly with you, and would like to see you Pope instead
> of even Hadrian VII. . . No: wormwood is not 'sweet,' but it may well
> be medicinal if it is mixed with other things. . . . I'm afraid I cannot
> agree with the distinction you make between a thing and one's idea of
> it. At least not in the case to which you apply it. (But--probably
> you have forgotten what you said)--But, for practical purposes one
> may be pretty sure that one's idea of the Church is to be found in its
> contents: and that the contents are a great deal more, and not less,
> than one's idea. This seems involved, but my own brain is involved
> at this moment, and I cannot attempt to straighten it. But that
> principle seems to me to run through everything. Even the "fatuists"
> of whom you speak appear to me to have got hold of a piece of truth--
> certainly you will say this is fatuist nonsense--That piece of truth is
> false when isolated from the rest, --I know all that-- I wonder if there

is any possibility of our meeting some time--I should like to so immensely. Just at present I'm up here living with Mgr. Barnes who is chaplain to the Catholic undergraduates: until June at least, and "pursuing my studies," (which I think is the proper phrase) and after that, I have no particular plans. Are you not near here? Please excuse the extreme stupidity of this letter and the abominable paper it is written on.[14]

Notes

[1] Lady Kenmare joined Hugh Benson 'culte' in Rome in 1904. He became a frequent guest of Lord and Lady Kenmare in Ireland until the house was destroyed by fire.

[2] *The Film of Memory* (London, 1938), p. 341. The ghost stories were published in 1905 as *The Mirror of Shalott*. Leslie in *The Cantab*, a humorous autobiographical work with Leslie lightly disguised as the hero Edward Stornington, described Father Rolle (Hugh Benson) in his familiar haunt at Llandaff House: "They made their way into the clergy-house, a red-brick bungalow, bran-new, but pleasantly shaded by a big bottle-green cedar. The priest's room was filled with signs of canonical vesture, dilettante sport and unfinished fiction. Huge rosaries hung out of deers' antlers. In the midst stood a real Roman priest! His atmosphere was not oily nor foreign, and he looked more deluded than deluding. His eyes were a smoky blue, courageous in the goggle-glare. Like his nose they were, if not more prominent, more arresting than his brow and chin. His chin was shaved in more ways than one. The aquiline nose sniffed or snorted contempt or complacence. His mouth was tender without being well shaped, rather like the mouth of a horse desensitized by a bit. Over his skull strayed wispy hair the colour of stale honey. The general effect was winsome and winning. Father Rolle spoke with the same keenness about the Pope that Englishmen feel about hunting. Religion was more than a Sunday game to him. It was God's sport revealed to men!" *The Cantab* (London, 1924), p. 168.

[3] Shane Leslie, *End of the Chapter* (London, 1916), p. 89. Hugh repaid the kindness by writing five articles about the Pope following his death.

[4] Hugh introduced Virgo to his literary agent James Pinker and tried in other ways to help him. Arthur's diary entry in February, 1917 described him as "a Catholic, a friend of Hugh's (whom Hugh caricatured in *Conventionalists*). He is a frail, feverish. ambitious, artistic, creative, transparently honest and fine--not much gift for writing but with good taste." Virgo traveled with Princess Rispoli as her children's tutor and kept them out of her way. He is mentioned often in Hugh's Rome diary. Virgo, past 50, attached himself for a while to Mary Benson after Hugh's death,

then to Arthur who gave him the task of sorting his eight volumes of essays. Whatever was done for him came to nothing, however. He was pathetic, the sort of man it is impossible to turn away, but who eventually fades leaving few traces. Among his distinctions were membership in the Knights of the Saviours of Greece and work as a sometime special correspondent for newspapers. Two of his novels were published, but he claimed to have written others.

5 In November he mentioned he was reading *The King's Achievement* to "Christopher Dell," whom some critics have taken to be Ronald Firbank, others Frederick Rolfe; but more likely Dell is a composite of Eustace Virgo and Firbank, with a hefty dose of Rolfe thrown in.

6 Miriam Benkovitz quoting Shane Leslie writes that Firbank went to the Catholic Church rather than Llandaff House because he required vast spaces for his "uprisings of mysticism." Irony aside, Firbank (like Hugh) has been accused of mere submission to the aesthetic aspects of the mass, but the decisive verity for Firbank was Hugh's "fierce faith and willing acceptance of the authority of the Church" In that authority was expressed the highest moral order by which human behavior could be judged. So Firbank argued in two publications, "The Wavering Disciple" and "A Study in Opal." See *Ronald Firbank* (New York, 1969), pp. 93-95.

7 It was while writing *Richard Raynal, Solitary* that Hugh noticed that his handwriting was becoming pointed and 'fifteenth-century.' Rolfe, not Richard Raynal, provided that tracery. Perhaps Rolfe was right after all, priests *were* out to steal his personality.

8 On Feb. 2, 1904, Arthur wrote in his diary: "I learn from a donkey called Rolfe . . . that my stone is moss agate or emerald; that my metal is copper and that my Angel is Azrael." After Hugh's death Arthur came upon Hugh's correspondence with Rolfe. Hugh was not very good about seeing inside people, Arthur thought, or he would have detected that Rolfe was corrupt, caddish. Mary went the length to please Hugh. *Hadrian the Seventh* , read at Hugh's insistence, Mary found "virile," struggling to find those "clever shrewd tasty thoughts on morals and character" that had escaped first impression. Shane Leslie in *The Cantab* drew a very funny parody of Rolfe the "clerk in Divine Orders, acolyte and exorcist" (as he did of several controversial characters who came regularly to Llandaff House) when Edward was "introduced to a short, baldish figure lying on the sofa. 'Mr. Stornington of King's--Baron Falco.' Edward smelt something of a Chinese curio shop and something of decaying fish but not quite decayed fish. Perhaps it was imaginary, for odours vanished in the strangeness of his personality. Cold bluish eyes were focused between huge antique silver-rimmed spectacles. Thin nervous hands, one with a Bishop's amethyst, played with some sheets written in garish inks. 'The Baron promises a paper on the Borgia,' somebody mentioned. The Baron leaned back and sighed. "Oh for the rosy criminal rapture of a Caesar Borgia! or the unscrupulous and magnificent sublimity of an Alexander the Sixth these days!" The Baron

soon spoke of rooting out Americanisms by Inquisition and publicly decreeing words of true beauty. "He offered to supply a number of neologisms from a private lexicon, which he had compiled for himself out of Greek and Latin. 'I shall leave my most exquisite coinages to my friends. The Baron, for a foreigner, spoke perfect English, though with the suspicion of a cheap boarding house. But Edward could not doubt the Baron's titles and quarterings, especially as he showed the armorial tracings for his own book-plate" (pp. 109ff).

9 Aestheticism was still all the rage, even among the dons, particularly the egoist Oscar Browning of Kings, who wallowed in sensational gossip. Arthur wrote in his diary for January 31, "I had been telling Hugh about O. B. and the aesthetic movement--how, last night, as he warmed to his work, he got more and more horrible, leering, salty and the like and splashed mud on many honoured names. . . . Well, the moment we got up to O.B. [on a bike], he began his 'aesthetic movement' once again for Hugh's benefit, after first asking whether I was being "converted." Hugh's aestheticism was the ritualist in him speaking, and little more than that. The aesthetes' argument that to be beautiful is to be good was a delusion, as he pointed out to Fr. Watt: "I am sorrier than I can say, and without a TOUCH of superiority, for the man who is led wrong by beauty. He is like leaves--I cannot bear to see such a whirling fall; and how many there are! They fly so exquisitely on rosy wings so far above me; and then without warning they are in the mud flats. If only they will understand that they are in the mud, and that they are ugly and shattered . . . . But I despair when they insist on looking at their broken wings and saying how lovely they are; when they declare there is no mud, and that the mud itself is lovely too and that it is better to fly and fall than not to fly."

10 Mary advised Arthur not to approach Hugh lest their beautiful relations be disturbed. The issue surfaced by itself a couple of days later and Arthur was able to broach the matter tactfully. "Drove comfortably back with Hugh. He was very full of all he was doing, and followed up the young men who came to see him. This was by chance, and I said that Cambridge was strongly Protestant, and that there would be an outburst of feeling if a lot of men went over, which would be very painful both for him and me. He laughed and said that the men who came to see him were nowhere near taking the step. I could not condemn his actions. He is only doing what a simple, sincere and fearless person would do who had taken a like step." Hugh's attitude, described by Arthur in *Hugh* for public consumption is sober, reflective, not at all dismissive of the commotion he was causing. In point of fact, Hugh was undeterred by such complaints; his tone was triumphant if anything. "He said that he was going to read a paper before a Jesuit society on the Conversion of England. 'Is it a practical position?' I said. 'Not an immediate possibility,' he said, 'but an ultimate certainty of course.'"(*Diary*, Nov. 22, 1905). On another occasion, when Arthur cautioned that he ought not buy a house in a place where his presence might offend the local parson, Hugh said defiantly, in such cases if he were challenged he "would give them

something to be disagreeable about.   That meant reprisal by active proselytising, making converts under the parson's very nose."

[11] Dec. 1905, pp. 808-17; and Apr. 1906, pp. 529-38.

[12] Like an Abbot Suger designing his masterpiece, he filled the empty hours at Llandaff constructing the perfect house of the imagination, complete with chapel and chantry. No seigniorial manor inhabited by his characters was more elaborate or more meticulously spun. His English Perpendicular chapel would have a carved altar with white stone reredos and a Tabernacle with "iron door, black, with gilded iron over it in relief"--or perhaps a triptych instead of the stone (shall he inquire after a triptych in Belgium? No! he will carve it himself. . .) Or, instead of Perpendicular, solid Tudor, roughed-out on the outside and plaster and tapestry within, with stone altar and triptych behind. Not a hint of brass, but in essentials of worship "only stone and iron must be used." These plans change, reverse, revert, augment even to the smallest detail--from a wooden footpave on one stone step to foliations in east and west windows, and there must be statues with plenty of paint, and hundreds of small touches in between. And the organ? How is it possible to put the rood-screen anywhere but at the ante-chapel, but then what to do about the organ-loft? And what gorgeous vestments for Hugh to wear, sewn with pomegranates and a mother-of-pearl Host emerging from the embroidered chalice, gold crusted with amber and carnelian, all vestments sewn with ivory-tinted Christ, instruments of the Passion, and six-winged seraphs in shades of blue and peacock and green with cloth-of gold halo and stole, gold fillet and girdle. And a chalice of moonstones and turquoise . . . Here was the aesthete in him treated to a vision of heaven. Martindale gives Hugh's complete account of these stunning designs conceived in the house of imagination in II, pp. 113-15.

[13] As the book was published after his death Hugh was spared the embarrassment of the caricature. In 1913, Arthur commented, "Had a very interesting talk after dinner about the wretched Rolfe who is now dead. He must have been mad: he accused Hugh of all and sundry of nameless crimes and misdemeanours. Hugh does not seem to mind this. . . ."   Only a few days before Rolfe's death Hugh told Father Reginald Watt, "The man's a genius, and I love him. If he'll only apologise I'll ask him to come and live with me. He's quite destitute now, but he is welcome to everything I've got."

[14] *Letter,* Benson Papers, New Bodleian. See Donald Weeks's introduction to his privately printed edition of *Saint Thomas* (Edinburgh, 1979), pp. 5-13, for the circumstances of the collaboration and rift. It is highly partial to Rolfe. Rolfe's handwritten account of the terms of the agreement and the unfortunate aftermath is held by the New Bodleian.

8
Cambridge Frost

Hugh had little reason to be unhappy at Cambridge Rectory where he had been given relatively few responsibilities. Canon Scott wisely recognized that such gifts as Hugh possessed needed to be exploited rather than buried under duties easily performed by others. In June he received faculties to preach and to hear confessions. His success at both was immediate and lasting. On the lighter side he was able to write and mount a Nativity play, complete with sets and costumes for the children of St. Mary's Convent, Cambridge, a task he threw himself into with relish, as he had at Kemsing. Plays always brought out the child in him. When it came to children, Hugh was the good Pied Piper: they loved him and he felt entirely at home in their company, in playfulness and simplicity very much one with them. All in all, he made quite a hit in Cambridge. Curiosity and a little awe accounted for the attention paid him, but also genuine warmth, for Hugh was then and ever a delightful conversationalist, sparkling and witty at the dinner table, without a trace of self-importance, and was often sought out by many who liked him but did not like his religion.

Despite his many successes, he was not happy. Cambridge left him flat. "There is something the matter with this place," he told Mary. "I think the University generates a coldness. The congregation are as good as gold, but they're oddly cold." Perhaps what he sensed was intellectualism lying like a frost over that "capitol of East Anglican Puritanism" (as he put it) and general academic Anglicanism that disapproved of Roman Catholics. It surprised and bothered him that the University suspected he had designs on their undergraduates; and he was annoyed too that his perceived worldliness had become a conversation piece in many a drawing room.

Certainly the most demanding duty Hugh took upon himself was that of spiritual advisor for ever-increasing numbers of penitents and inquirers. To the long lines of converts and potential converts from High Anglicanism, he offered comfort and encouragement. Letters were stacked in piles all over his desk, costing him hours of work every morning. As his popularity as a writer and preacher grew so did the flock, and he never failed them, giving them guidance and advice remarkable for honesty and practicality. Many inquirers came to the door, others he saw by appointment for all sorts of causes--a case in point, an exhausting morning spent with a clergyman, his wife, and three Bibles--"Douay, A.V., and R.V.--discussing twenty-nine Petrine texts. And I am DEAD and BURIED today."

First impressions were very important; he trusted his instincts when it came to "sizing up" a person by a facial expression or by the shape of the hands; he insisted if the hands were right, if they were a good fit with the face, all would be well. And he managed the eccentrics and fanatics patiently and firmly, but with kindness. To the man who interrupted Benediction with a cry for brotherhood, Father Benson gave the "Pax" and pronounced him suffering from suppressed vocation to the Carmelites (M, II, 128); another time, Arthur noted, when a lunatic came into the church and "rose in his place after the sermon and began to address them, 'Fellow Christians, I am called upon by God, etc. etc.' Hugh, just coming down from the pulpit, went up to him, 'You mustn't do this here,' he said. 'He looked at me in silence and then said 'Well then, I won't' and left the church. Afterwards Hugh spent two hours talking to him, and found him reasonable and easy to talk to." He had something of the prophetic spirit that Hugh admired. From there the man went to the varsity church, and cursed the heads of Houses as they went out.

This was 1906, as Hugh was about to launch into top form when writing, preaching, lecturing filled every moment. Tastes changed rapidly, he knew it, but while his vogue lasted, there was work to be done and money to be made.

As early as 1904 when in Rome he had begun to think seriously of settling somewhere away from towns. One afternoon, he suggested to Mary that they should buy Tremans and she should build a cottage for him in the orchard. There he would live alone with one Catholic manservant to look after him and serve him at Mass in the oratory of the main house. While Mary was thinking it over, other Roman Catholics began to wander in from the countryside for his Masses, to the consternation of the family. Making matters worse in this Anglican-of-all-Anglican household, he happened to mention one morning just before his departure for Cambridge that his friend Father Richards, a young convert whom he had sent to the Woodchester Dominicans, wished to offer Mass at the chapel by himself the next day. Lucy and Maggie recoiled in horror.[1] The oratory had been turned over to Hugh for his personal convenience; it was not going to be used as a public chapel in his absence. Well, said Hugh as a veiled threat, this obstacle would probably oblige him to go elsewhere in the future rather than Tremans; but Mary would not allow it. "It makes my blood boil to think of it," Arthur fumed, accusing Hugh of a step-by-step Romanizing of the oratory. Yet Hugh appeared unbothered by having disturbed his family in any way, especially when, on the heels of this outrageous proposal, he carried off a chalice-veil and altar linen, and had them blessed so that, he declared triumphantly, the family could not use them again.

Now that Mary had refused to build him his cottage, he began to look for a house in earnest. Any number of picturesque, romantic places would do, like the old palace of King James I, a piece of which was on the market. "A heavenly little place," he sighed but smack in the middle of the town. Ideally, the house ought to be a little cottage in the clean Cornish atmosphere by the Atlantic, or perhaps deep in the Cotswolds with plenty of land. There he would say Mass and the Office, and write books. Heavenly! At Llandaff House he had told Rolfe that in a year or two he hoped to retire from Cambridge to a sweet and secret place, and be perfectly happy for the rest of his days. Rolfe must join him there. They would live in two cottages and not speak until 2:30, the earliest hour at which he was fit for conversation. A true contemplative life was impossible. He wanted friends, and he wanted solitude--solitude for prayer and friends for conversation, games, and ears to listen to his Catholic schemes. Practically, the house must be an affordable house, in reasonably good condition. (A ghost or two would be lovely.) A few months later he looked over his bankbook, in "bitterness with both hands," because he hadn't the money.

One evening Arthur told him of a house he had seen for sale near Buntingford, about 30 miles from London, and the next day they went to see it together. It was perfect--spacious, private, sitting on two acres "with not even a Church of England church in the village," and because it had been vacant so long the owners were willing to let it go for £800. A small price indeed for such a house, but where was the money to come from? Why, why had he ever set eyes on it! he cried. Of course, with the small income inherited at the Archbishop's death he could not hope to support himself outside of a parish, but he was now earning enough money from his novels and lectures so that the kind of independence he craved was within reach. He already had a decent yield from £4,000 invested, but by itself that was not enough to buy the house and live a life apart from a parish. For that kind of independence he needed an annual income of at least £150 ("without that one is not really free"), but in fact he was making only half that, which meant observing the strictest economies, and devoting all his energy to preaching and writing, particularly writing, for no other activity brought in so much money so fast. But what if the talent ran dry, or he fell ill, or his sales fell off, what then? How would he live? "Oh, why am I not a wealthy man!" he moaned.

"Hugh has bought the house and garden and done up the house," Arthur wrote in March, 1908. And so he had. The place was too much of a bargain to let go though no one denied it would be costly to repair and maintain. Happily, furniture posed no problem because Mary had stuffed her possessions from Addington and Lambeth into Tremans, with the happy result that Hugh was able to furnish Hare Street House with the excess; but a host of other expenses faced him--sinking a well and repairing the roof, and installing a heating system, and hundreds more spent fixing, restoring, creating, until every detail was stamped with his personality. Best of all was the excellent chapel he set about making out of the brew-house: "I'm looking forward to saying my prayers in it. It is extremely dark, which I like, and has an earth and brick floor, and is mysterious and TIMBERY."

In June 1908 with the consent of the Archbishop he left pastoral work in Cambridge "to settle down in my own house in the depths of the country--if that can be called 'settling' which involves being away every Sunday for at least the next year. But it will be heavenly to have a little time in the week" to do the 50,000 things needing to be done. There were no immediate financial worries--his engagement book was filled for this year into the next, including preaching the Lent in Rome in 1909. In the meantime, it was a mere hour's journey from London's Liverpool Street Station to Buntingford, where Reeman his manservant waited in the dog-cart for the short ride to Hare Street. Hugh was 37 and on his own at last. The best was yet to come.

Notes

[1] Lucy particularly was annoyed. Her father Archbishop Tait in 1874 described the Roman Canon with its invocation of the Virgin and the Saints as composed of "the worst errors of one branch of the Christian Church," a desecration of Holy Communion, and forthwith proposed the Public Worship Regulation Act against the silent use of the prayer. R. T. Davidson, *Life of Archibald Campbell Tait* (London, 1891), II, p. 201.

9
Family Matters

The doors of Tremans in Horstead Keynes were flung open to guests, and many took advantage of Mary Benson's hospitality, often staying on for days at a time. She was delighted to receive the attention of many dignitaries who came to call, including bishops and prime ministers, in every way relishing her role as Archbishop's widow, the mother of three famous sons, and the sister of three Cambridge dons, one of them philosopher Henry Sidgwick. Fred had established himself with a couple of best-selling novels *Dodo* and *The Challoners,* and was busy in London living up to his reputation as an important talent. Arthur had already achieved fame as editor of Queen Victoria's letters and biographer of dignitaries from Disraeli to Ruskin to Archbishop Benson, his father, and had written many books of meditative essays. He had established a following among the public.

Mary Benson's life at Tremans was a crowded and satisfying one, more so after thre Archbishop died than while he lived. She was known to be a good companion and witty conversationalist, intellectual by mental habit but warm and passionate by nature. She kept up with the latest developments in politics and religion, conversed easily on any topic, and was emphatically conscious of being adored by her sons (if not by her daughter) and admired by the rest of the world. Under her management, Tremans came alive with good port and good conversation; and when thrown together, her children soon showed their mettle. "You *couldn't* play the fool in that house--you may be brilliant and chaff people and make epigrams and be intense, of course; but even serenity there has to be rather like that of an Archangel off duty."[1]

She was a child of 12 when Edward White Benson came to live with the Sidgwicks and decided practically at first sight that at the suitable time this intelligent, vivacious girl must be his wife. Five years later they married, and Martin was born a year later. Edward's masterful personality was so different from hers that while she waited to come of marriageable age she was haunted by misgivings--perhaps she was not clever enough, or mature enough to run the household of a rising star in the Anglican establishment--in a hundred ways afraid of disappointing Edward by not living up to the very high ideals he had set for himself and for his wife. Love would grow, but after his death Mary admitted that happiness had eluded her; probably she had never loved Edward, but had come to admire him in all respects, which was a kind of love. She was a child when she and Edward met, and practically a child when they married, without her having had the opportunity to meet other young men more suitable in age and temperament, or make friendships with other girls her age, which she deeply missed. Nevertheless, there was within her great sympathy for others though she would not suffer fools. Her natural high-spirits, long suppressed, were rekindled in the company of her children in the delightful hours spent in story-telling and make-believe when for a little while she became a child again. That gaiety and playfulness certainly passed down to her youngest son Hugh.

She lived comfortably at Tremans and kept a cook, maids, a gardener, and a coachman, often outspending her considerable £2000 income so that it became necessary to trench the principal (Arthur's phrase), an act tantamount to sacrilege in this family. Neither she nor Lucy Tait (now firmly a member of the household) could manage finances properly-- laundry alone amounted to £120 per annum--causing much consternation to her sons who needed to make up the deficit. She enjoyed frequent visits from her sons who adored her, and from his first novel to last had the pleasure of hearing Hugh's books read aloud to her even as the ink was drying.

In defense of Benson Mariolatry is the fact that Mary was always on hand for her sons when needed--absolutely and unequivocally. Her letters, effusions of warmth and sympathy, do not dispute the image of Perfect Mother drawn by Fred and Arthur in their books. It was to Mary that Hugh first made known his intentions to become a Roman Catholic, to Mary and no other he opened his soul, a fact that gave her pain and pleasure. Her tenderness during these anguished days was genuine. But Mary, once informed of it, could do nothing more than scatter a little dust, and resign herself to the inevitable; for once Hugh was determined on a path no power on earth could stop him. "I feel now I have a rope round my waist, and I can no anywhere," he told her on the day he came home a Catholic from Woodchester Priory. With Hugh's ordination to the priesthood her influence waned, and when life at Hare Street House commenced, she ceased to be an important factor in his life though he continued to read his books aloud to her, valued her advice without following it always.

However painful a blow had been her husband's death, Edward's passing had brought something of relief, for while he lived it was impossible to move out of his shadow. Her longing for a harmonious life free of stress Edward thought unworthy of a great lady, and now that she was growing old with only "remnants" left to her, peace was slipping away again because her daughter Maggie whom she had nursed and cared for through years of illness, had begun to hate and distrust her.

Arthur   Arthur loved Hugh but fought him vigorously on points of religious faith. Brisk debate pushed to the point of mutual exasperation was a commonplace among Benson men, and though they huffed and fulminated, they remained unbudged in both their opinions and loyalty to each other. Long ago they had agreed that in the matter of Liberty and Authority their positions were staked out. Hugh often pushed Arthur to the brink with his habit of dismissing a verbal challenge with an absolutist "but I belong to a Church that happens to know." Ever the rationalist, Arthur was shocked that Hugh's explanation of Transubstantiation was based on unscientific conceptions of matter, reinforcing his opinion that Romanism was a good religion for entirely unreasoning and unintellectual people. One time when Arthur made a little joke about the Virgin, Hugh turned pale--"Don't say that. I feel as if you had said something cynical about someone very dear to me, and far more than that. Please promise not to speak of it again." Such pleading drove Arthur to distraction for there was no replying to it. Hugh's "Isn't it perhaps simpler to believe it happened as recorded?" was not acceptable.

Hugh religious zeal was not altogether genuine, he suspected; it was a kind of game, particularly at Tremans where in his clerical dress, his devotions, his gesturing at Mass, the drama of ritual took center stage. Arthur understood Hugh's love of the Beautiful, but laying too much stress on the aesthetic emotion in religion had the smell of idolatry about it. It was especially evident in Hugh's attachment to beautiful trappings which often brought scorn-- "Hugh's horror of going to see the sick man yesterday was much abated by his having such nice embroidered bags to carry the Pyx &c in, and such a pretty little stole to hear his confession" (*Diary*, Dec. 27, 1904). He accused Hugh of "sheltering himself under the Roman belief that the mere devotions of the Church and the daily Mass are the priest's real work" when this world of men is still "a sadly dirty place with much dust to sweep up before the coming of the Lord." Here Arthur was speaking for the Protestant conscience that preferred practical solutions and had little sympathy for high ritual, yet looking out at the world from his mullioned window day after day, he was far more out of touch with the cruder forms of reality than was the priest whose daily contacts with suffering had to be met face to face.

He was angered by Hugh's propaganda pamphlets, particularly those like one comparing the deaths of Mary Tudor and Good Queen Bess, calling it "so smug, so unjust, so one-sided, so complacent, so simply damnable!" Yet, in spite of complaints he envied Hugh's faith, the more so as he felt his own tepid faith eroded by doubt into a cold Christianity inhabited by a remote God. Perhaps inadvertently, Hugh pushed him to the edge, because the more Arthur insisted upon a rationalist religion against Hugh's mysticism the further he was driven from creeds and ritual, leaving him unsatisfied. "I find myself filled with a ghastly envy, not of his success but of his power of worship and enjoying work" (*Diary*, May 26, 1908). Contradictions in Hugh's character were puzzling. He was unworldly, hated rudeness and inconsiderateness above everything, yet was he not himself inconsiderate of the feelings of others? One evening while Arthur accompanied Lucy at the piano and Hugh on the organ, "he changed the harmonies so that I had to stop. Then he proposed something that I couldn't play--so that after sitting unemployed at the piano through two songs, I went softly and sadly away and Hugh continued in possession." At Tremans "table and ledge, all over the house, are heaped with books he has torn out of the shelves and thrown down. The litter in the little smoking room is fearful. Last night he would not leave dear Beth in peace till she had found him a box, and she trotted about for more than was good for her." As for Christian poverty, Arthur knew no one who took greater pleasure than Hugh in his possessions, buying himself a comfortable house and furnishing it with beautiful things, saving up all his money to insure an income, while at the same time selfishly insisting that he could not give money for Maggie's hospitalization without giving up his own house. Bitterness like this was uncharacteristic of Arthur and usually followed hard on the heels of an argument.

Yet there was no doubt that Hugh had changed for the better, that religion had improved Hugh's character. He was less combative, kinder, deeper, and wonderfully colorful too with "youthful sunburnt face, over his tippeted cassock, with a rose pinned on his breast."

Hugh loved Arthur with a deep and genuine love; in locking horns over religious questions their independent minds and fixed loyalties were merely asserting themselves. It had always been the so. Their friendship stands out as the precious harvest of Hugh's middle life. They often went on holidays together, to the seaside or to the Cotswolds or the Lake District. In spite of himself, Arthur was a little jealous of Hugh the celebrity. In 1905, his neighbor Charles Kempe (the artist and church designer) asked him to his house, but the note betrayed "a pathetic anxiety to see *Hugh*--and all his guests want that. It is odd if I, after having spent the earlier part of my literary life as the brother of Fred, should now be known as the brother of Hugh!" On hearing that a large edition of 3000 of *The King's Achievement* sold out on the day of publication, he wondered that his brothers should be such successful authors, sheltering himself in the knowledge of his superior refinement. That he envied Hugh's popularity he admitted, as when on a hot and sultry August Sunday afternoon he "found Miss Bickersteth in a tent on the lawn, shawl over feet, two nice girls and Cyril B. rather tired and faint. They were all engrossed in Hugh. Hooray, new in love. I felt inclined to say, 'I also am a man.' So I sate sweltering like a toad swollen with its own venom, trying unmercifully to engage jauntily in talk" (*Diary*, Aug. 15, 1909). At such moments he regretted the direction his writing career had taken: an undistinguished history, he thought, with limited appeal even to the middle-aged spinsters who comprised his audience.

Arthur was plagued by fits of depression that might go on for days or for months; so had Edward been; and Mary, too, soon after giving birth to Hugh had suffered a nervous breakdown. It was in the Benson blood. His worst fear was that he would follow the tragic Maggie into madness. To draw his mind away from his mental state, he threw himself into even more work, but depression pressed in upon him and he was at its mercy entirely until it passed off of its own accord. And in fact late in 1907 when poor Maggie was moved to a sanitarium for serious cases, he became so debilitated that at the advice of several specialists he entered a nursing-home. In that oppressive atmosphere, so different from the world he knew, the darkest spells of despair all but overwhelmed him. He thought of killing himself, but lacked the courage. A journey to Rome, a totally different atmosphere, proved useless, so it was back home to Tremans to wait for the depression to lift. There, both Hugh and Fred faithfully stayed by his side while medicine worked what little relief it could. Of Hugh Arthur said, "he has done his best these dreadful days to beguile and entertain me--he's a delightful companion--so easy and sympathetic." It was not until 1909, two terrible years later, that Arthur was himself again, a glorious awakening from nightmare.

Fred   Normally, Fred liked to joke and be thought funny, but when Hugh was around his genius was rebuked. Contentiousness became the order of the day. Fred felt that Hugh was deeply opposed to him, but it was Fred, not Hugh, who delighted in provoking debates that usually ended with the whole household ranged against Hugh because of his religious views. When Fred did not get the upper hand, he sulked and wished himself back in London. They each got under the other's skin and Fred's frustration often amused him: "Poor Fred is having a hard time of it--snow, and nobody and no golf. But he is less depressed when I'm not there I gather. Poor fellow! I'm sorry for him. I cannot conceive what to do." Hugh thought him snobbish and combative, and despaired of their getting on for any length of time. In earlier days Fred had lived at Tremans, but, feeling cramped by so many women took a flat in Chelsea. He liked London, liked smart friends with smart repartee, all of whom leaped nimbly into his Society novels. There came a point when Fred's conversation was made up entirely of titled people, and little else.[2] In one small respect Fred and Hugh were alike, they both wrote modern novels. Of course, Hugh's literary fixation was Catholic life shot through with idealism and sacrifice; Fred's was highlighting the manners and foibles of the social set.

When all three were together they talked too much, each bottling up the other, each inclined to cry out "Time!" At Tremans, Christmas 1913, the three brothers went at it with gusto, with Fred extremely combative--a thing which he himself greatly resented in Hugh. "I, Fred, Hugh--didn't show up well," Arthur wrote in his diary. "We talked too much and too fast and too long and too loud--argued, made jokes, paid no attention to anyone else. I think Fred is the worst, because he does not attempt to listen to a story or a joke--even goes away in the middle--nor does he attempt to include anyone else in the talk, while he is really irritable and peevish and cannot bear any statement to be questioned." All three brothers were like that from time to time, but Fred lately had got used to being deferred to and applauded by the smart set of ardent but uncritical admirers gathering about him. He was rather selfish and conceited and could be as fractious as Hugh at his worst. "But I felt today that there was a strain of real caddishness in us all . . . greediness, loudness, claiming and clutching at happiness . . . a Benson fault. At dinner we were ruder and louder than ever." Everyone agreed Fred's snobbery had become insufferable, and after gloomy days and nights at Tremans he longed to escape. Arguing was a way of life to the Bensons. There is not a trace of disloyalty in it. The family were critical and contentious, fully equipped for the exhausting give-and-take of brisk debate. So it had always been, when even as children playing at games they were critical of one another and every command was challenged. The Archbishop was alive then, and the children were very close, bound by strong but unsentimental affection. In those days Fred and Hugh got on much better than was to be the case later.

Yet it was Fred who recalled the most charming incidents of Hugh as a child, for instance, a holiday in the Lake District, when five children, two parents and Beth all managed to stuff themselves into a tiny rectory for the summer: "In these holidays, Hugh, owing to inveterate idleness at Eton (where, beating me, he had got a scholarship) had a tutor to whom he paid only the very slightest attention, and on these evenings he would have some piece of Horace to prepare for next day, and would work at it for a little, and then drop his dictionary with a loud slap to the floor. Soon he would begin to fidget, and then catch sight of Arthur reading, and something in his expression would amuse him. He drew nearer him a piece of sermon paper which Nellie's pen was busy devouring on behalf of the next Saturday Magazine, and began making a caricature. At the same moment perhaps I would observe below lowered eyelids that Arthur was drawing me."[3] On the sober side, Fred related this harrowing experience of making a difficult descent down the Piz Palù in the Alps, the notorious ridge swept by bone-chilling winds and whirling snow. It is worth repeating--"Once as we halted, I noticed that Hugh shut his eyes, and seemed sleepy, but he said that he was all right and on we went. He was on the rope just in front of me behind the leading guide, and suddenly, without stumbling, he fell down in a heap. He was just conscious when we picked him up and said, 'I'm only rather sleepy; let me go to sleep,' and collapsed again. Raw brandy stimulated him for a moment, "and soon, after another and another dose, our brandy was gone. It was not possible to go back over the summit, and so to get into more sheltered conditions again; the best chance, and that a poor one, was to convey him down somehow along the rest of this bitter ridge, till we could find shelter from the wind. Very soon he became completely unconscious, he could move no more at all, and the guide and the porter whom we had with us simply carried him along the rest of the ridge." Was Hugh was alive or dead? Fred was unsure. His only thought was of the telegram he would be sending his father, that Hugh had died--that is, if he himself were left alive to send it. At last, with the dangerous ridge behind them, Fred who had lost sight of the others turned a corner and found the two guides roaring with laughter at Hugh who was trying to sit on the point of his ice-axe. He was drunk. "The moment, apparently, that they had got out of that icy blast, his heart-action must have reasserted itself, and there was a half-pint of raw brandy poured into an empty stomach to render accounts. With thick and stumbling speech, he staggered along, assuring us that he had only been rather sleepy." Hugh was 22.[4] This perilous slope remained to be described as the climb over the Riffelhorn in the early part of his novel *The Coward.*

Maggie   She had studied at Lady Margaret's Hall, Oxford, taken a first in Moral Philosophy, and afterwards gone off to Egypt with Nettie Gourlay to excavate the Temple of Mut in Egypt (a stature of Rameses dug up at Karnak stood sentinel outside the dining room at Tremans). In 1901 she wrote *The Soul of a Cat*, followed by the scholarly *A Venture of Rational Faith.* For years Maggie's health had been fragile. Pleurisy, heart problems, depression had made her a virtual invalid, but now in the country air and pleasures of Tremans she seemed to be thriving. When she was well, she was high-spirited and happy; she had been gifted with brains and talent for writing and painting and was eager to use them. But once in the grip of a black mood she became morose, accusatory, and violent, unable to care for herself.

It was in 1907 while she was editing her father's papers that a black depression came down full force upon her. In this morbid condition, she became subject to dark brooding, convinced that her mother was plotting against her, plotting to steal the little inheritance left to her by her father, plotting to get rid of her. In better times, Maggie and Mary talked things over, made up their little differences, but these peaceful intervals were short-lived because however deeply disturbed she was, the immediate and deep-rooted cause of the depression was Lucy Tait who shared their home. Maggie was jealous, jealous of Mary's friendship and affection for another, a stranger, whom her mother trusted and relied on more than on Maggie herself.

Lucy Tait had lived with the Bensons for ten years as Mary's companion, traveling with her, helping her with her correspondence, and paying a share of household expenses, without which Mary could not have remained at Tremans. Lucy was liked well enough by the men of the family, but what Maggie saw and felt profoundly was that Lucy had taken her place in her mother's affections and her father's place in her bed. In that bed Mary's six children had been born. The daughter felt betrayed and abandoned, her place and her father's place usurped by a stranger, and when kindling was thrown upon this anger, the demons took possession.

Lucy Tait had strong opinions and made them known, but opinion may be construed as interference, and often Lucy injected an opinion where one was not wanted. On one occasion, when Maggie proposed to plant a hedge in the garden, Lucy objected that it would obstruct the view of the South Downs; and when Maggie proposed to sit outside in the July evening when a nightingale was just then singing, Lucy objected that the evening dew was heavy and Maggie ought to stay inside. And again when she talked of stocking a weedy pond with ducks, Lucy on the verge of interfering caught a glance from Mary and said nothing. That afternoon after tea, Fred recalled, "Maggie lingered on, wanting to talk to my mother, but Lucy lingered too, and so she left them together." So ended a day, with Maggie unsatisfied not once but many times and Mary knowing it but not knowing what to do about it.

Then there came a fatal moment one night when Maggie poured out her loneliness to Mary in a "terrible" talk that at some point got near the delicate subject of her likeness to her father coming to the surface partly through depression and partly because, in poring over his papers, she had fallen in love with him (so Mary suspected), was becoming dominated by his personality and thus taking his place as guardian of the home--with the implication that in choosing Lucy over Maggie Mary was betraying not only Maggie, but Edward as well. Maggie spoke resentfully of Lucy Tait's influence in the house, how over the last few years Mary had become dependent upon her--mother and dear friend, practically inseparable, sleeping in the same bed--being with her *day and night*, seeing her "first thing in the morning, last thing at night." Mary tried to make her understand that the last few years had been difficult and Lucy had helped her cope, but Maggie countered that the bond between Mary and Lucy had changed over recent years, and with it Lucy's influence over her. Maggie dismissed jealousy as the motive behind her anger, and accused Mary of not trusting her or her brothers, for that matter. Later that evening she came to Mary's room to speak of how she (Mary) "had kissed her unlike any other time in her life today twice and she could not bear it. I told her how despairing I had felt and was feeling. She said she was sure it was all nerves and health if I felt like that, and she was sure I wanted *my own kin*--and that was what she had felt when she wanted Fred and me and her to be at Brighton together, without Lucy." Here is the daughter, unhappy and unstable, watching helplessly while her mother's affection was being stolen by a stranger, and hating it to the point of madness. It was a pathetic scene in Mary's bedroom that night, Maggie offering herself to Mary, to be wholly reunited with her *without* Lucy, and Mary terrified how Maggie intended that this should happen. These long years devoted to Maggie's care when (as Mary wrote into her diary) her only desire was to soothe and please her, "and make her sad ill life as sweet and cherished as possible" were hidden from Maggie--they did not exist in Maggie's mind. All the years a stranger was stealing her mother's affection and taking her place at Tremans, Maggie had looked on and said nothing.[5]

This dark spell passed over, and Maggie appeared to get better. But how long would it last? She loved animals and took delight in stocking Tremans with hens, and ducks in a pond, turkeys, a pair of peacocks, and piglets. And there was her own Welsh collie, and her cats, and a pet parrot Mathilda. She and Hugh planned to collaborate on a collection of tales, but in the end it was left for Hugh to write them. They appeared as *The Mirror of Shalott*. For three years she seemed her old delightful self, despite an occasional bout with the old demons--ill omen of things to come. She worked on Edward's papers in the orchard, or in winter in the parlor above her bedroom. Sometimes her friend Nettie Gourlay came to visit staying on for weeks on end, but Nettie did akmost no talking and their time was spent reading novels silently at the window or in the orchard shelter erected for Maggie's comfort. From time to time an old school friend from Lady Margaret Hall would appear at the door.

Ominous signs began to reappear--sleepless nights and miserable days; once again she needed to be nursed by Mary as in the past, to be shielded from the ghosts that haunted her. Her suspicions of treachery fell again on Lucy, but in a more menacing way. She suspected strangers of having predatory designs, "caught glimpses in the faces of passers-by, of brutish instincts and lusts lurking below a smile or casual glance." To exorcise these demons she beat herself with Roddy's whip, "trying to see what pain could do." These fits passed over, and she returned to her former self, but the memory of her behavior while in their grip could not be erased. Then, on the night before Mary and Lucy were to leave for Venice together, Maggie took a knife to Mary. The next gray morning, while the household staff turned their eyes to the wall, Maggie was bundled up andtaken down the stairs quietly and driven away to a sanitarium[6] For a long time she reviled Mary in reproachful letters and refused to see her, convinced her mother had arranged her confinement to get rid of her. "You didn't treat me well often did you?" she remarked under her breath one afternoon. Mary pretended not to hear.

A few days later, Arthur and Hugh visited her and after a little coaxing by the nuns she agreed to see them. "Maggie covered her face with the sheet and would not let me kiss her," Arthur wrote, "I did not press it. But she was all right in a minute. . . . She was entirely herself, asked for everyone, glad to be reassured that we cared about her." Arthur assured her that she looked very much herself. and she brightened up at this. She had been very bad in her mind, she said, and reminded them it might come back (*Diary,* May 9, 1907). At a point she asked to see Hugh alone, and the visit ended with a kiss. On the ride back to Cambridge Hugh spoke of how Maggie had talked of her soul and the terrible despair. He had done his best to give her hope, comforting her and laughing at her fears. Arthur's helplessness that he could bring her nothing, that his "own dim religious philosophy was a poor thing to ask anyone to hold on to in a state like this" was dispelled by his happiness that Maggie seemed better and had kissed them as they left. Hugh in bringing her comfort had given her the kind of religion that she wanted, which meant other people's prayers, and the personal touch of Christ. He assumed from this that Maggie would be inclined to join the Roman Church, anything to get her back to her old self. It had been a wonderful experience, and chased his horror of such places, for which he was infinitely grateful.

Not all visits to the hospital ended well. In August when Hugh came into Maggie's room she stared at him, refused to speak, hinting with gestures that the convent tea was poisoned. Another time she became badly agitated and begged Hugh to exorcise the demon in her. Maggie's good days were rare, but every good day raised hope that the corner had been turned, particularly in her feelings towards Mary: "She's ever so much better, thank God. She wrote to Hugh lately asking him to help her; saw MB, had a good talk, asked her to come again and has written asking for several things and photographs of us all." These recoveries were short-lived, and the lapses more terrible for the dashed hopes. Mary's visits fell to a trickle in the face of Maggie's outbursts, but letters found their mark. "To me she has written dreadful things . . . and then she surpassed anything she has ever said before in bitterness and dislike and reproach and fulminations--so I have passed into silence again. Oh how I wish one could find the source of this poisonous hatred!" By now it was too late for Maggie, but the source of discontent Mary sought to discover was not so dark or malignant because a good deal of the blame lay with herself, for by choosing Lucy she hastened her daughter's destruction.

On Christmas Day in 1913, Hugh's last, Maggie went off to Hare Street to keep her best Christmas with Hugh. It was a day full of laughter and cheerfulness and kindness, the happiest Christmas she had ever had, and he himself was the mainspring of it. As encouraged as everyone was that she was recovering at last, it was not to be, for by the New Year Maggie was sending menacing threats about Mary, who, she said, had stripped her of all her property and ruined her soul.

Maggie's illness was the cause of a terrible row between brothers, in which Hugh came off shabbily. Two problems came together, Maggie's mounting hospital bills and Mary's unthrift. She and Lucy were spending a lot of money, more than was coming in. "No one has control of the expenses here," Arthur moaned. Money had to be found. Maggie's own money had been used up, so it was left to the brothers to make up the deficit. Arthur put in the lion's share, Fred offered £100, but Hugh when asked for £50 became indignant and said that he would have to give up Hare Street and become a monk. Hugh's refusal was selfish: he had bought Hare Street House and a cottage, was building another, and was making repairs all the while managing to save £1000 a year. When Arthur insisted he must give something, Hugh stalked out of the room, intensely irritated. A day later, Hugh sent a check and an apology. Conflicts like this pushed Arthur found extremely painful, pushing him further into depression.

By early 1914 costs for Maggie had mounted to £3800 with no end in sight. Paying a fair share again caused an angry row between brothers when Hugh was told that he would have to pay more towards Maggie's care than he had done for the last year. "He said 'Oh, good Lord!' and began to talk about the 'bottomless pit' and the 'constant anxiety'--he said he lay awake at night, thinking about money. He admitted that he had saved since 1908, about £9000, but his needs have increased--he used to say he wanted to save enough to bring him in £300 now--it's grown to £500--he said 'My hoped-for motor car recedes into the distance.'" Hugh then drew a pathetic picture of himself--he felt he might be ill at any time, or might be made a Bishop, and then he should be done in, for he couldn't write more novels. "I said that if this happened, *we* might help: but he said with a noble pride that he could not bear the idea of being dependent on anyone. At one point I rather lost my temper, and reminded him that he hadn't even paid the miserable sums he had undertaken to pay--'Very well then,' he said. 'I have a very good mind to give you a cheque for it--of course I know it's very generous and all that, but you needn't keep reminding me of it.' There was something rather audacious about his using, as a *threat*, to cause me pain, a promise to pay his just debts, dishonestly withheld by a man with an income of nearly £2000 a year! He went on about the necessity that lay upon him to save money--the simplicity of his life-- his tremendous work--the danger of his work to his health. When I said that if he felt *that*, he need not put on *quite* so much--"Ah, a priest cannot *choose* like ordinary people!"--but a moment later he saw that "the *one* thing" he was slaving for, night and day, was to make money. He was rather down on the luxury in which I lived--yet he has bought his big house, bought land, put in hot water, electric light, spent a lot on his chapel" (*Diary*, Jan. 2, 1914). On he went hotly, venting his frustration, but to Arthur the problem was simple avarice.

After passing a bad night, Arthur came down to breakfast to find Hugh gone. The rupture was healed when Hugh sent a message that he had spoken unadvisedly, to which a relieved Arthur (he had left Hugh's letter unopened for 24 hours) responded amiably. After Hugh's death Arthur recalled how kind Hugh had been to Maggie, except in this instance when he found the new plan for her expensive. "Back to the Priory," he had said. Hugh could be hard.

Long ago Edward White Benson feared that he was to be denied the
happiness of grandchildren. Martin died young, and then Nellie died.
Hugh early on determined he wanted no wife, that he was in every
conceivable way unsuited for marriage, and sealed his word with the
priesthood.[7] Maggie died in an institution. As a young man Arthur
thought he could have fallen in love with Erma Thomas, the sister-in-
law of a friend of Edward, but he was discouraged by her father who
thought the idea of Arthur marrying ridiculous. After a time Arthur
agreed. The truth was with the exception of Mary, Lucy, and one or two
friends, he was not comfortable with women, and grew less patient with
the sex as his correspondence with female readers of his books
increased. Besides, if he married there was always the unhappy
probability of inflicting his prolonged depressions on his wife. At
Eton and now in Cambridge his contacts were almost exclusively with
men. His eye was often attracted to the physical beauty of boys and
young men, and he enjoyed "romantic" male friendships, but these were
platonic friendships, not sexual ones. He was too timid and too
conventional to act upon his urges and remained chaste.[8] Of all the
children Fred with good looks and social connections was the likeliest
to marry and was implored to do it by Arthur who had given up all
thoughts of marrying himself: "We are the only Bensons of our line left
. . . We have struggled into a certain position and it would be pathetic
if we died out just now." It was not to be. Fred was wary of sexual
contact and distrusted it. His affections tended towards male friends, but
not in a sexual way, intimacy being impossible for him.[9] Like Hugh,
he disliked being touched.

It is tempting to draw conclusions about the bachelor lives of the
three brothers, all celibate, all pouring their artistic and sexual energies
into the writing of books in which characters are permitted to speak and
act for them, all three inhibited in one way or another by the ghost of
Edward White Benson, insisting always on propriety and circumspect
conduct. It is equally tempting to speculate how much the Benson sons
were prevented from marrying by the living presence of Mary--their
adored Minnie--who by her wit and kindness and intelligence set up a
standard impossible for other women to meet--all others being dwarfed
by comparison. She provided female companionship and comfort that
otherwise may have been lacking in their lives.

Mary had six children. None of them passed anything on, not a one.

Notes

[1] Philip Caraman, *C.C. Martindale* (London, 1967), p. 123.

[2] "It amused us," Arthur commented, "to draw pictures of the strange interior of Fred's mind, knowing so little of what was going on. We laughed at the kind of pious horror with which Fred explained to MB as if he had discovered it by excavation, the controversy about the Virgin Birth which I had related to him. It was as if she could have no idea what was being thought or said. The truth is that Fred likes to dominate his circle. Funny; he likes to cut jokes and capers and they are often very funny. But the moment it diverges outside what he does not understand he not only thinks it dull, he feels sure it is pokey; it seems to him to cramp the glorious freedom of his own mind. That is why he is so bored at Tremans" (*Diary*, Sept. 13, 1905).

[3] *Our Family Affairs*, p. 215.

[4] *Our Family Affairs*, pp. 99-100. At the time Hugh believed that violent exercise taken to prepare him for heavy steering at Cambridge caused the heart arrest. Later he interpreted the state of unconsciousness as a sign of spiritual paralysis. This incident may have contributed to the elaborate precautions Hugh took against premature burial. *See* Chapter 15, below, for an account of instructions found at the time of his death.

[5] *Diary of Mary Benson*, New Bodleian, Oxford. Maggie's personality and tribulations can be gathered from E.F. Benson's books, and from Arthur's very sympathetic accounts, particularly *The Life and Letters of Maggie Benson* (London, 1917). Fred's analysis of her mental condition was that she had soaked herself so long in her father's papers that before long "they gripped her mind, with the effect that his very personality, dominating and masterful . . . began to take possession of her" with the result that she demanded such flawless rectitude from Mary as Edward might have demanded, and when Mary failed to live up to the ideal, particularly in her relations with Lucy, Maggie began to hate her."

[6] *Final Edition*, pp. 98-100.

[7] Inconceivable physically is a distinct possibility as Hugh even as a young man suffered from what his physician Dr. Leith described as "abnormal physical underdevelopment" (*Letter to Edward White Benson*, 1895).

[8] An account of Arthur's friendships and romantic attachments is found in David Newsome's *On the Edge of Paradise*, pp. 249-66.

9 Brian Masters, *The Life of E.F. Benson* (London, 1991), p. 132. Masters concluded that to Fred the classical ideal of "self-control was all, and disinterested affection the noblest of the instincts." Sexual inclinations and practice were left to his characters to experience. See Masters, pp. 242-52, for a full discussion of the matter of E.F. Benson's friendships.

10
The Hare Street Years

"Oh how I am happy here. Things are far more lovely than I ever dreamed. Meanwhile I tear up to London each Sunday and *bellow* in the pulpit; and then I rush down here again and weed the garden on Monday. I have family prayer in the LIBRARY in the evening; everybody looks through the backs of chairs, and mass every morning . . . " *Letter to a friend, September 1908*

A house had stood on this site in Hare Street for 600 years, so went the village talk, but in fact little remained even from Tudor days beyond a couple of weathered chimney stacks and a single rough plaster wall. All the rest inside and out was 17th century except for the dignified Georgian face.[1] The main garden, closed in on the north by a high brick wall, contained the rose-garden, unfinished, and behind it the brick stable. A terrace and path running from the scrolled gate to the north side of the house Hugh later paved with flagstones from the House of . Commons. He had heard these were to be replaced and rushed to London to claim them, and here they were laid, and remain to this day. Later, he put in a low brick wall capped by stone between the front of the house and the lawn. A row of old lime trees stood between house and the road. There was an orchard and a big walled garden behind, and an old brew-house of wood and plaster with a brick floor, soon to be transformed into a chapel and connected to the main house by a cloister with wooden pillars. The garden was wild and overgrown, and the gardener who lived there a dishonest fellow whom Hugh dismissed. Vegetables went in first, and then flowers. The glory of the garden was to be the rose beds set around a statue of the Virgin rising from her plinth at the center of it all. In the orchard Hugh erected a cross called a Calvary. Hare Street village had known no Catholic until his arrival.

HARE STREET CHAPEL, EXTERIOR

From a drawing by Gabriel J.Pippet

In the guest bedroom hung hand-sewn tapestries of "Death's Progress," depicting every manner of man and woman in the Dance of Death, with Hugh trailing behind, disputing a point hotly with the Grim Reaper. The gruesome subject matter brought squeals of delight-- "Isn't it great fun!" he declared joyfully as the patterns of the dance came together figure by figure. In that room important guests slept in a great four-poster to remind them of their mortality. "Isn't it like an enormous catafalque?" he asked gleefully, rubbing his hands together.

His own bedroom, sparse and brown, sat over the library. He had his manservant Reeman put in a secret panel by his bedstead, and built a priest's hiding hole between the staircase and the entrance hall. On the paneling of the staircase they carved the instruments of the passion, and sundry armorial devices and initials.

Of course, what would Hare Street be without its ghost? Rattlings, footsteps, a groan, and strong impressions were as much as this elusive spirit deigned to reveal of itself. His library he filled with books he never opened, and at the side stood a second-hand Bechstein grand that musician friend Franz Liebich found for him. The dining room was furnished with old oak, and on the wall he hung a portrait of himself painted by his tenant Miss Lyall and also hung the green arras cloth that had caused a sensation at Cambridge Rectory.

In 1911 he put in electricity.

Even at Hare Street it was not in the cards for him to live a recluse's life. Anyway, it would not have suited him; he liked solitude yes, but not the life of a solitary. He liked conversation but insisted on choosing the moment. A guest or two was roaming about somewhere most of the time. "Don't expect too much of me," he warned, but do come, "You fit in." That was taken as high compliment. When he appeared everyone and every thing lit up at once. Also about were the faithful (and invaluable) manservant Reeman, true craftsman, and Margaret the maid, and soon Dr. Sessions came along, a rather mysterious fellow, who gave up a practice to come to stay at Hare Street to think about psychic healing and spent most of his time stitching tapestries. There was the ubiquitous Sophie Lyall, also a convert, tenant of Hare Street cottage from the beginning. (Her father Sir Alfred Lyall paid several hundred pounds to renovate the run-down cottage in "the close" and make it habitable.) She painted Hugh's portrait, helped him deal with his mail, bestowed many gifts, and kept close watch. Gabriel Pippet, the artist-illustrator helped Hugh make a chapel out of the timbered brewery, and together they hammered, and chiseled and stitched until all was tip-top, or nearly so, inside and out. Penitents came, but always Hugh saw them in the chapel (although a few made their way into the house). Dr. Sessions had lived in the early

HARE STREET CHAPEL, INTERIOR
From a drawing by Gabriel J.Pippet

years in the "Doctor's room," and a Captain Anderson occupied the room that thereafter was known as the "Captain's room." E. W. Hornung, creator of *Raffles*, came to visit with his son, and Father Maturin came, and Lord Alfred Douglas (Wilde's "Bosie"), whom Hugh had received into the Church. Of this odd assembly Arthur commented petulantly that what they all failed to recognize was how quickly Hugh would toss them over once he grew bored. That judgment, based on a long-held assumption that Hugh flew rapidly from one interest to the next without a care to what had been left behind, was certainly wrong in the case of his incipient colony at Hare Street. In Arthur's comment there is more than a trace of envy of his brother having found that sweet content that had always managed to elude him.

Hugh had stalls built and carved them with poppy heads and sculpted a bracket of devils and serpents writhing under Our Lady's heel. An old chest with instruments of the Passion painted on the panels served as altar. On the wall hung Sts. Roch, and Anne, and Barbara, and the Blessed Virgin carved out of a pear tree looked out from the sanctuary. The rood-screen, made by himself and Dr. Sessions, was hung with statues of angels Michael and Gabriel wings outspread, and there was St. Sebastian whom Hugh struck arrows into, and St. Thomas Becket with his murderer's sword in his skull; Sts. Hugh and George were there, and the four evangelists, of course, and other saints, all topped by a painted crucifix he had made. "It's just as well that it is so dark that you can't see it," he said of the rood-screen. Getting the right effect was what he was after.

The chapel was very much Hugh, radiant with holy objects, filled with beautiful things, many of them gifts. His admirers delighted in lavishing gifts upon him, and these easily filled the walls until there was scarcely a bare spot--a small American organ which he set in a tiny loft overhanging the sacristy, an expensive pair of candlesticks for his chapel, a set of Stations, a cope-hood elaborately sewn, the jewels in the Virgin's dress, a waxen crucifix that opened at Christ's chest to reveal the entrails. . . .

Morning at Hare Street House began with Holy Mass, then breakfast, downed quickly. If Miss Lyall came by, she helped him with his mail, though by then he might have written off 50 post-cards. Before noon he poked through The Daily Mail, then off he went into the parlor to an old oak refectory table to work. The parlor where he did most of his writing he bordered with a "Grail tapestry" depicting the Grail procession, an idea he had picked up from one of Rolfe's books. All his friends are sewn into it, even to Jack his Irish setter, and his horse Peter trots along with the rest.

And there were neighbors, particularly at Christmas time when he made wonderful parties for the neighborhood children with wonderful games; and a penitents arriving, by appointment or by surprise, expecting to be taken to him directly, and disappointed to find him away. When in the final years Father Reginald Watt came to live there as his assistant, he was protected from callers, most of them women, who liked to show up at the door suddenly. Always there were pets about. Hugh loved dogs, loved cats even more, so much that it was the Church's position on the souls of animals that had delayed his conversion. (In Rome he had been amused at their antics, and when an undergraduate at Trinity had kept an aromatic cat in his rooms.) Roddy the Benson collie had clung to him at Tremans, but one day he wandered off like the tramp he was and never came home. Now there was Kim to take Roddy's place, then Jack the Irish Terrier to take Kim's place, and a cat, and his horse the unpredictable Peter who drew the dog-cart, and Paul the pony--and the pig and the chickens that one dared not get too fond of.

He was the heart of this little world. As long as he was alive, Hare Street House had an almost mystical appeal, every detail radiating his presence. Nothing could hold this world together once the vital link was gone.

Six months later, Mary visited for the first time, taking away these impressions: ". . . A long journey through country of a purgatorial kind to Buntingford--a Tom Thumb Brougham, in which we each took a side and Hare Street! Hugh welcoming us, and taking us in--we were frozen to the bone, and so the house struck us as dismally cold (don't tell him) but it really has a *quality* abt it--nothing common or mean-- quite, even in its bareness, suitable for a priest, and with a stately air about it. I liked it immensely though it *is* bare. Outside the cloister is delightful--absolutely simple. Wooden posts into rough bricks and a red tiled roof which had a queer Italian sort of look. The Chapel is quite good, and looking as if it had gone on being a Chapel for years. No kind of beery suggestion [it had been converted from a brew-house] and though plain I thought quite good. The garden of course this time of year doesn't show the best, but his man seems to have done great things . . . Then we paid a visit to Miss Lyall, who had kindly taken in 2 women in whom Hugh was interested [probably Elizabeth Baker and Miriam Silverstone, see Chapter 11] and we all sat and jabbered. Then after an introduction to the whole household we sat by the fire and talked, and he read some extracts from his new book, nearing its close, till the Pill Box came at 4.30. And Hugh leaves for Ireland and Rome on Tuesday" (*Letter to ACB*, Jan. 29, 1909).

In the afternoons into the garden he went dressed in flannel trousers and a shirt he had worn at Eton. As many seeds and slips as went into the dirt, he had a hard time making anything grow; he had no green thumb, and was reduced (with much lamentation) to buying his vegetables from the green-grocer. Nonetheless gardening was his favorite pastime in the afternoon and he would lay down his novel in progress and hurry out to this joyful labor that bore so little fruit. Everything was precious. Asked to trim the tops of his lime tree, he recoiled: "Never, never, never, so long as the house is mine." When a friend suggested that gardening problems might be solved by getting a new gardener, Hugh was horrified. His servants were friends, not hired hands. It would be a betrayal. As it turned out he was able to secure a position for him in Edinburgh, but there is no evidence the garden profited by it. One day Archbishop Bourne called on him while he was working in the garden. It was quite unexpected. "Bring him into the garden," Hugh said, and so it happened that Hugh dressed like a tramp in old flannel shirt and baggy pants entertained the Archbishop in the garden until four o'clock when they went into the parlor for tea.

Arthur predicted Hugh would find it expensive to maintain this house, and he was right. Money became an issue, but not entirely as Arthur had foreseen. To support this extraordinary life, Hugh took on more and more engagements, gave retreats that took him away from his cherished Hare Street five days out of seven, and launched that relentless schedule, superhuman in demands, that was to wear him out. Yet in 1909 he cried that he was living on the fringe: "I never take cabs; I limit by bills for the entire household--three men, two girls, and a boy-- to £3 weekly (last week it came to £1, 15*s*.). I never go to any entertainment; I never drink wine unless a guest is here; I smoke cigarettes at about 3*s*. 8*d*. a 100." Costs had doubled to £300 per annum, twice what he was now making. He thought of giving up meat and as a last resort, cigarettes--merely a thought. He resolved to spend not a penny on clothes for two or three years, while his family despaired over his frayed buttons and shoes "such as you may pick up on the seashore, sticking out of the jetsam of the waves among seaweed and skates' eggs." And yet Hugh's income had risen to the point that he was able to boast that he made more money than all Catholic novelists put together! As late as 1914, an embarrassed Mary observed to Arthur that "people actually give Hugh money--£5 notes, even sovereigns, which he takes. They think from his clothes that he is poor." He had always been indifferent to what others thought of the way he looked and dressed. His clothes were ill-fitting and worn, his hair uncombed; nor was he entirely clean-shaven always. The sad fact was that, though he gave money to various causes in which he had a personal stake (like the rehabilitation of Miriam Silverstone) and channeled small amounts to favorite charities through friends, watching his money grow had become a habit. He wished someday to own a motor-car like Arthur's, and still dreamed of enlarging Hare Street House into a Catholic colony. And money, lots of it, had to be laid away for that time when he could no longer write novels but still needed to support himself.

As far as Arthur was concerned, his behavior in the Maggie business had been inexcusable, but much fault lay with Mary and Lucy. Neither had any sense of economizing, neither had control of expenses at Tremans. Their laundry bill alone amounted to £120, Arthur groaned. Maggie's money had been used up, and now that she needed it, there was nothing left. The brothers then had to pitch in, with Arthur carrying the lion's share as usual.

Meanwhile, Hugh's nerves were being severely taxed. He caught cold easily, and battled periodic attacks of neuralgia that left him paralyzed with pain whilst they lasted. As early as 1906 after strong pleas by Mary, he promised to slow down: "Yes: I'm trying to turn off steam, and am refusing every single invitation to preach and speak. I'm attempting to dawdle . . . But Lor! There's a lot to do anyhow." Promises were broken. Always the pressure to write more hounded him: "I can't imagine what I'm going to write next. And if I run dry? Where am I?"

Besides reshaping Hare Street in his own image, he was talking everywhere--there were few engagements he turned down--and writing furiously, books, pamphlets, introductions, prefaces, etc. all promoting the Catholic cause. Every minute of the day was filled with plans and schemes, every day bringing a fresh idea that cried out to be acted upon immediately. "I must have incessant work," he wailed. Sleep was not always his to command. He often lay awake at night worrying about tomorrow; or conversely tired to the bone, he fell asleep over a sheaf of papers, and once or twice on his knees at his Office.

At Hare Street he continued his life-long habit of reading his books aloud, this time to his tenants Miss Lyall and Miss Hogge, and other ladies who had settled in the village to be close to him. With papers in hand he would trot beyond the yews under the arches over the stones to the bottom of the garden to Miss Lyall's house. There in the drawing room when the maid had brought out the silver coffee service and they had all taken out their silver cigarette cases, Hugh sipped his coffee as he read last night's work aloud to them inside a cloud of smoke. With cigarette hanging from his lips or fingers, he jabbed his pencil at the manuscript, and fought them tooth and nail over this point or that until they gave in. Seldom did he yield to their criticism. His stammering during these sessions exasperated him. He would clench his fists--"I w-w-won't stammer, it's all a m-m-matter of the will." Promptly at the hour for night prayers he stopped, gave an abrupt Good Night and hurried to the chapel where the servants were already assembled. Soon they were joined by those he had just left, their heads draped with lace mantillas, and all would kneel for compline. That done, one by one they drifted away, leaving him alone, huddled in his place behind the rood screen reading Matins by the glow of the sanctuary lamp.

When home he never ventured out of the tiny village, and seldom even beyond his own road with the result that only a handful of village people knew him or knew he was a Catholic priest.[2] In time, he bought up the adjoining land and the cottage sitting on it, and built a cottage out of bricks in the paddock behind the orchard, letting it all out to Catholic friends. At different times he made plans to establish a home for orphan boys from South London and a temporary shelter for troubled men, where they might recover before going forth to face the world. All of these schemes Hugh mapped out with usual precision, including a horarium of prayer, meditation, solitude and sociability. Nothing ever came of them.[3]

Sometimes he was gone for the week-end, returned on Monday only to leave again on Wednesday. Two or three days out of the week at Hare Street was all he ever managed, but he used every minute to refresh himself upon a thousand activities. If a novel was underway, he worked right through the night, and recuperated by sleeping ten hours in the day. Three times he went to Rome to preach the Lent, and three to America.

There was an occasional holiday in Ireland to fish and hunt (field and stream had always been a passion), and visits to the Lakes or the seashore with Arthur.[4] Sometimes he stayed at manor houses and was given his own room with a chapel set aside for him (Father Benson's suite), and privacy to smoke and write into the morning if he wished, and freedom to do as he liked all day. Word of royal treatment soon got out. irritating other priests and bringing a smile to the lips of those who disliked him. In truth on holiday he liked to be in the company of people of culture and breeding--who doesn't? In social situations he was conscious of social distinctions, but he was not a snob, nor perceived as one by the public; otherwise the fact that his death threw so many of every class into mourning could not be explained. He liked playing squash, and he loved to shoot, and did both whenever he wished thanks to Lady Gifford who had bought an estate nearby and invited him to use her squash courts and hunt in her fields. He would have liked to be a fine horseman, but was not good at it, certainly not on his horse Peter. Nights usually meant a game of cards with friends, or chess.

He was serenely happy in his own house.

Notes

[1] Hugh made a record of the "Early Years of Hare Street House" to accompany a personal chronicle of his years in residence. "It was a saying in the village when I first came to it," he began, "that 'there had been a house where (mine) stands for 600 years," but the oldest work that I can see in it is but Tudor. The foundations however may be much older . . ." He was especially interested in the rumors of a ghost. See "Early Years" and *Hare Street Chronicle* in Appendix (4), below, pp. 210-217.

[2] So quietly did he live that on the day of his funeral, some villagers were unaware Father Benson had just been buried; one or two had never heard of him, but they thought his name musical. "Wrote books, did he?" asked one (*The Universe*, Oct. 30, 1914, p. 5).

[3] Here is the Horarium for himself and for guests.

A Rule of Living for Friends at Hare Street House

7.	Rise: so as to be down by
7.30.	Mental prayer.
7.50.	Prime.
8.	Mass and Angelus.
8.30.	Lauds and mental prayer.
9.	Breakfast.
10-12.	Work alone.
12.	Angelus--letters.
12.45.	Terce, Sext, None (Vespers).
1.	Lunch and recreation or siesta.
2-3.50.	Manual Work preceded by visit to B.S.
4.	Tea and recreation.

[4] Returning from a deer stalk in Killarney in 1912, a touching thing happened. "As I came down from the mountain and was getting into the car," Hugh wrote to Mary, " the keeper's wife ran up to say that a woman was dying in the road, and wanted a priest. So I went up the road and found her lying in the middle of it, stretched out like a crucifix, barefooted. She was able to make her confession; and before she began cried out loud five times 'May the Blood that was shed on Calvary from the wounds of Jesus Christ cleanse my soul from every stain'--very slowly, with the tears streaming down, still flat on her back. And all this in the wilds, with huge hills round, and a sunset, and a group of people who halted with a cart a hundred yards away when they heard what was going on. I don't know whether she is alive to-day or not. The coachman could do nothing all the way back except say how wonderful it was, and what a good woman she must be when there isn't another priest within ten miles!"

11
The Priestly Life

"I don't know what the good of being in union with our Lord is,
unless we try to do what He did--i.e. make *the best of sinners,
and not the worst*--and, above all, never expect gratitude, and
never allow the faintest self-love or bitterness or resentment
to remain in one's heart."

Hugh now embarked on work that would earn him fame. He scarcely
understood how it was he attracted so much attention, but clearly God
was using him to gather souls into the Church, and there were few
opportunities he let pass by.

Hundreds of people consulted him, but he was severe with those who
consulted him to indulge an emotional need. Naive or indifferent as he
was when it came to personal friendships, Hugh's insight into spiritual
motives was shrewd. He was a sensitive observer and critic, capable of
masterly analysis especially when dealing with difficult or desperate
cases. Handling troubled souls, rousing them to a firm commitment
without platitudes or sentimentality while at the same time sifting out
poseurs and cranks who masked their curiosity or infatuation behind a
need to be consoled, was the most difficult part of his work. Letters ate
up three to four hours each day, relentlessly. Away In New York to
preach the Lent, full boxes were forwarded; and when a temperature of
104^0 put him into a sick-bed, a stenographer was brought in to help get
him through the day's mail .

In the uncompromising way religious guides like Mr. Rolls of *The
Sentimentalists* deal with sinners, we see Hugh's methods operating. He
went to great lengths to pull a wayward sheep from the brink and one
can only surmise how many who came to him with serious problems
were saved. An interesting instance of his method applied to a serious

case is that of Miriam Silverstone, a morphine addict being cared for by
a mutual friend, social worker-novelist Elizabeth Anstice Baker.

Hugh of course insisted that she give up her addiction before she enter
the Church. He was more than willing to let her come to stay at Hare
Street, but prudently asked that Miss Baker accompany her: "My
proposal, if you agree, is this. I have a Catholic tenant--a Miss Lyall--
who is taking my cottage next door to this house. She has in it a large
room that would hold two beds without any crushing at all. Would you
be willing to come down with Miss S. for a week, after Christmas, as
early as I can arrange, and stay with Miss Lyall? She is a charming
person though rather nervous: and I would not dare to suggest that
Miss S should be alone with her in the house. My garden and chapel
and library would be entirely at your disposal. . . . During that week I
thought I could see Miss S. for an hour or two for instruction every
day, at least; and, at the end of it I could receive her into the Church.
That week, I imagine, would be her final healing off with the morphia.
. . ." (*Letter*, May 1908).[1] At some point over the next few months,
Miss Silverstone returned to morphine. Hugh was furious at the
betrayal, particularly so as, having been convinced by Hugh's novel *The
Sentimentalists* that to be saved she needed to be dealt with severely,
she had expressly asked him to be a Mr. Rolls to her. He decided that
the best cure was to be "absolutely brutal with her. She is a Poseuse
and Egotist," but she bore up under the brutality, which consisted of
snubbing her until she learned humility, hard penance for one in love
with her priest.

Finally, there is given here a letter to Elizabeth Anstice Baker on the
subject of Miriam Silverstone which Hugh undoubtedly expected her to
read. The letter shows his severe method of dealing with difficult cases.
His bitter disappointment and outrage at the pain her betrayal has
caused, is meliorated finally by an offer to resume the friendship if
certain conditions are met. "I need not say much," he began with great
bitterness, "I am writing in this room which I thought I should always
remember as the scene of a genuine victory: I shall have to remember it
now as the place where the worst treachery I have ever come across was
done. I instructed her here for the last time . . . I am afraid she is
worthless. I don't think I have ever said that of anyone before. The
Love of God came right up to her--as Father Faber says--and looked at
her, and she rejected it. She had better not write to me. I don't want
her to add to her lies and treacheries. I have enough responsibility for
having received her into the Church: I am only more thankful than I can
say that I did not give her our Lord with my own hands. As regards the
future . . . Do you really think it worth while troubling the nuns? They
must of course be told everything: and if they care to take her after that,

it is their own affair. Personally I don't believe she will be straight even there. I don't believe she has ever been sincere, and even wished to be. Please tell her that the £20 I spent on her is cancelled now. I wouldn't take even the payment of a debt from her. I am returning presently a Christmas gift she sent me: fortunately I have not begun to use it; so she can do what she likes with it. I think you must have misunderstood her about wanting my "forgiveness". I am quite sure she values that as little as anything else. It is just one more attempt to wriggle into an interesting pose: and I am not going to form part of the tableau any more. She can go and prance somewhere else."

Now came the turn: "But I suppose, so long as a personal is not actually dead, one is bound to consider that there is a chance left: so one doesn't absolutely finally bang the door, until Almighty God does. *If* therefore she went to the Good Shepherd nuns, and *if* she remained there a long while, and *if* they reported at the end that she was not completely rotten to the bottom of her soul--I suppose I should have to begin to think that a miracle had happened, and that she was converted. But those are a good many "ifs"--and extremely unlikely ones. As to the promised she may make--I wouldn't even allow the possibility of their truth. She has outraged the very last appeal that God can make. She must have received absolution and communion, *knowing that she meant to spit on them.* There is no more to be said of a person who does that. Voltaire recommended the process to any soul unhappily afflicted with a conscience! He said it was final. I wonder whether she went to confession at the Oratory. Did you see her? . . . But at any rate you didn't hear what she said. I suppose it was sacrilegious. This is the worst blow I have ever had. I hope it is the worst you have ever had, or ever will have. But I know--without cynicism--that to be completely knocked over when one is genuinely happy, and to be humiliated to the ground, is extremely good for the soul. I shall take it like that; and try again with other people."

At this point he extended an olive-branch: "I wonder what the situation will be at Easter. I would say some of these things to her, if I thought they would mean anything to her. But I am afraid there is no chance of that. If she goes to the G.S. for a month or two I should be willing to hear from her again."

From the Good Shepherd nuns Miriam Silverstone went to a nursing home, but soon ran away. Persistence did not work, despite Hugh's ultimatums. For months he kept her at arm's length, to ignore and neglect her, thus give her as much pain as possible, to squeeze submission from her. His attitude must be one of "entire alienation, final and complete" until she capitulated. He returned her gifts and a rosary, unblessed. "It is heartbreaking work, but I'm not hopeless yet."

Posing was her problem, not morphine--that ego had to be smashed to pieces. She threatened suicide, she threatened to become a Christian Scientist to spite him, but Hugh dismissed it. Finally just as he was ready to cut her off for good, there were signs of recovery. Whether she was permanent cured is another matter. All this yields insight into Hugh's priestly character, the lack of sentimentality, his firmness and patience in the care of souls--why he was loved and feared. Unfortunately, her addiction was stronger than his medicine, and whatever method he applied failed.

Miriam Silverstone was "a pellucid stream of transparency" compared to the next problem child. From Rome Hugh asked Miss Baker's help in the case of a young girl of considerable sexual appetite. The nuns at three convent schools had been unable to handle her, particularly as she was obsessed by a demon who took the form alternately of a beautiful boy or of an old man, and one time even Hugh's own form! Furthermore she had accused Hugh to a couple of people of being in love with her, complained to Hugh's face that he was "cold" to her and that for that reason she was not able to "get at him." Despite the trouble, Hugh was much taken with her beauty and talent and her personality. "She is, in fact, a very fiery, hot, generous, poetical creature and with all the seamy sides of all those things," apparently unaware of her attractiveness to men, or so good an actress she made others believe it. Lately she was having delusions that she was the daughter of an Italian count.

Friendship came with a price to those he trusted, for Hugh asked Miss Baker to take this difficult girl, on the surface charming and obedient--take her into her home in "endless watchfulness . . . she must not be trusted even for one instant, especially if there is a male anywhere near." Old men, young men, they all went mad about her. Taking charge of her would be like looking after a "charmingly situated powder magazine" and Hugh predicted she would end up either as a fiend or as a contemplative nun, with a passion for suffering.

So many came to him or wrote to him about their plight or the plight of a friend, he had his hands full finding a way to tide them over, or rehabilitate them, often giving money quietly through his collaborator in good works, Miss Baker. Fearless and absolutely determined to get things done despite deafness, her pluck was proved in countless acts of kindness. At his urging, she attended at least one meeting of Rolfe's cultish Order of Sanctissima Sophia. She never failed him, not only in difficult cases like that of Miriam Silverstone, but in routine ones, small acts like finding lodgings for a stranger to the city or work for a lonely friendless woman. Once he asked if she would help him place a "possessed" 12 year-old boy, "frightful in his fits," but in other ways normal. Another time he set her to finding work in London for a widow struggling to keep her sons in school, or if not that, at least a temporary shelter. She died in October 1914, in the same month of his death.

To certain penitents he urged the study of mystical substitution, practiced by such extreme individualists as St. Lydwine of Schiedam. According to this system, the penitent shares in Christ's suffering in expiation of another person's sins. He offers himself to God, asking to bear the temptation and penance instead of another. On a grand scale, this operated in the war, with horrific consequences already being felt in Belgium. To the many who sought absolution he offered this means of sacrifice, urging their suffering be offered up for another. Some wanted to wear hair-shirts, or "take the discipline," beating themselves before God. Usually he discouraged them.   For intellectuals normally he had little hope. "I sometimes think that common sense is a monopoly of the masses, and stupidity of the intellectual class." When people are convinced, they come into the Church; but even when an intellectual is convinced, he draws back, wondering why it is that all intellectuals aren't Catholic. Is he the only one? ". . . And you start off explaining all over again simply because you can't in common decency give the only true reply, which is 'Because they are all as stupid as you are.'" He was stern, even brutal at times, but the brutality was an aspect of the supernatural--"all good religious have it, a kind of ruthlessness towards certain things." Christ Himself showed it when he said it is not meet to take the children's bread and cast it to the dogs. Who else but Christ and His saints could have cut a humble suppliant so deeply?

He took missions everywhere--England, Scotland, Ireland, Rome, New York. There were very few he turned down. An untraditional venture was the Motor Missions, conceived by Father Bernard Vaughan, head of the English Missionary Fathers. With a van equipped as traveling chapel, with altar, harmonium, crucifix, kneelers, the mission took the Faith into Protestant strongholds.   Halls were rented and leaflets announcing the lecture series passed out from house to house. Normally when Hugh lectured, questions were written down by members of the audience and deposited in a box at the door. These Hugh answered before he began, but in the Motor Mission he took questions directly from the floor. Nonconformist groups saw to it that the mission halls were salted with hecklers so that Hugh and Father Vincent McNabb were forced to answer questions of such length as obviously had been prepared in advance. At times Hugh met with tremendous resistance, and as he tried to outshout the catcalls from the rear his rapid-fire delivery and the rise in pitch of his strained voice brought howls of laughter and abuse. The hecklers threatened to become

become violent at times, booing and shoving the priests, but their courtesy and restraint were such that the hecklers were silenced by the crowd and the priests escorted to their van to the sound of cheers.[2] One night Hugh's van was followed from Baldock to Buntingford; another time matters got so out of hand he needed a police escort to the hotel.[3] Apart from these incidents, however, the motor-missions were quite successful, and in some villages like nearby Buntingford (the last place visited in the 1912 tour), parishes grew up where there had been none before. This was a mixed blessing for Hugh personally, because a rival church in Buntingford a mere four miles away would draw worshippers away from Hare Street chapel.

There was not an idle moment in the day that was not quickly filled by somebody's need. Banquets and receptions for charitable causes, particularly Belgian war relief, drew off the bit of time remaining. Ever since the Mirfield days, he had supported St. Hugh's home for destitute boys in South London, and dedicated all proceeds from a book of his poems to it. He often gave talks to Nonconformist groups, but lately these were often on secular topics like the modern novel rather than religious matters, when anti-papist sentiment was liable to erupt--and did so on several occasions leaving Hugh to face an angry crowd. Having first dispelled their fear of scurrilous papists, he might win them another time.

As Spiritual Director Early on Hugh came to understand the value of advertising himself. He liked his work and liked the praise, liked dressing up in his monsignorial robes with the purple sash and red fringes, liked being the center of attention at country homes with his own room (*Father Benson's*--and later *Monsignor Benson's room*) furnished with private chapel, delighted at being seated at the right hand of the Archbishop at banquets, and hearing "Look, it's Father Benson" whispered as he passed on the street, and seeing eyes go up. He was no saint, he loved attention even while moaning about the mountain of meetings, lectures, sermons. . . . From a practical point of view, attention to him meant attention to the Church, and those blazing purple robes left no doubt what he was and what he lived for. His face was famous, his name on everyone's lips--except to the villagers of Hare Street. There his greatest wish was to be left alone.

With men he was usually successful, but with women who made up the majority of penitents he was not always successful. His priesthood, instead of protecting him, draped him in sanctity that women found irresistible. They pursued him genteelly, disguising or subduing or sublimating their secret longings in religion and pious works.

Impulsiveness and passionate outbursts were personal traits that he could never quite master, but at least were curbed when guiding souls. He was convinced that he was the best spiritual director for those who sought him out. The line he walked between total personal detachment from others and extraordinary devotion to their needs was blurred by the intense attention he gave every problem brought to him. "His simple 'Come and see me again next week' did not mean that he only wanted to let events take their course, it meant constant thought and frequent prayer, it meant mementos in Mass, and careful weighing of advice. Spiritual direction was a very serious matter to him; often far more so than it was to those who sought it."[4] He refused to be defeated when faced with an apparently hopeless case, bringing his fist down hard on the table with a roar: "Failure? There is no such thing as failure!"

Women wrote him lengthy letters, expecting lengthy replies. They followed him to Hare Street, were confessed by him, and insisted on receiving Holy Communion from his hands and no other; they arrived long before the appointed time of an interview, and always prolonged their consultation beyond the allotted half-hour. They had no conscience about interrupting his rest when told he was asleep or ill, knowing he would never turn them away. When he went up to London, they flocked to him, ate up hours of his time on days he was to preach, or demanded interviews after Mass when his strength was depleted. They were merciless. Worse, they were proprietary and jealous of each other. He was too patient with them, too generous of the little spare time he had; his nerves were going, but these women were persistent, having convinced themselves of a problem for the purpose of needing to see him. "They are convinced I am good for them," he would say ruefully, "and it that's the way they are going to get to Heaven, I suppose I must let them get there on the end of my cassock." Father Watt called them his worst enemies because they made him extremely irritable and sapped his strength mercilessly, strength he might have called upon in his last illness.

In the case of Mrs. Lindsay, Hugh's innocence when it came to women very nearly caused scandal. Ruth Temple Lindsay was a young widow with a young son who came to live at Hare Street, no doubt to be close to him. Hugh instructed her in the Faith and subsequently received her into the Church, and some time later built a brick house behind the orchard for her as his little Catholic colony multiplied. She belonged to the small circle of friends who met for coffee at Miss Lyall's to hear Hugh read aloud his latest chapter, but she had fallen in love with him. So had they all of course, all fallen in love, but Mrs. Lindsay was bold and unpredictable, and dangerous. Miss Lyall was to call her the wickedest woman she had ever known. Now, Ruth Lindsay was the mother of little Ken Lindsay who became Hugh's ward in 1909 under circumstances that remain unknown. If ever Hugh loved at all, it was children he loved; and nowhere was this tender side more evident than towards his ward Ken Lindsay. In June of 1909 he asked Miss Baker if she knew of a "nice girl, not proud or stuffy, not afraid of loneliness, to come down to rooms here in the village--(two rooms)-- and look after a charming little boy, aged 5 1/2, who is in my house." The child's mother was at that time staying with Miss Lyall, and the child Ken was to be got up in the morning and put to bed at night, and taught reading and writing, and looked after in the afternoon occasionally. "The governess would have quite a nice time of it," he continued, "the use of my garden on decent days, to sit in; and my books to borrow; and we would pay her what was proper. The present one, who is leaving in 3 weeks (a German) has £29 per annum. . . . She would be for the most part left alone. We're not sociable" (*Letter*, June 1909). Arthur's diary for Aug. 6, 1909 gives a picture of a day at Hare Street: "Found Hugh in the garden weeding and in the highest spirits. Female forms flitted about and we found a girl praying in the chapel before the lighted lamp. A charming little boy came up and shook hands. It seems he is to be left in Hugh's charge for sometime, a nephew of Balcarres, with a Catholic mother. We had tea under a yew tree--joined by Mrs. Lindsay, a small pale rather nervous woman--the little boy sat gravely by 'Uncle Hugh' and hardly spoke." Arthur was charmed by the boy, apparently a highly imaginative child who later told him of a great battle in which he had been engaged that morning-- "he had been 3 times wounded and had left 3 men dead in the field"--yet told expressionless with such intensity as if a battle had really happened.

Frequent visits to Hugh's house by Mrs. Lindsay ensued, on the surface perfectly proper under the circumstances. But another diary entry in October described a strange picture of Hugh's troubling contacts with Mrs. Lindsay, an ordeal affecting his health: "Hugh has been here ill and tired. He seems to anticipate a breakdown. He is entirely devoted to little Ken Lindsay but the mother is a dangerous woman. She repeated to Hugh in a garbled version some things about Hugh's lack of prudence which MB had unguardedly said. It must have been a dramatic scene. Hugh is in a queer milieu just now. He has this odd neurotic dangerous woman about--in love with him, I think--the child to whom he is devoted, queer Miss Lyall, a doctor who for some obscure reason has given up a practice." Perhaps Hugh's position as her son's caretaker worked upon her imagination to the extent that in her mind Hugh had entered her family and she was claiming possession. Hugh, oblivious to romantic flights, had no idea what she was up to, but, in fact, gossip was already on neighbors' lips and was drifting into Cambridge and Tremans.

One evening in Cambridge Mgr. Barnes took Arthur aside and told him that Mrs. Lindsay's stay at Hare Street was becoming a scandal. She was known to be very flirtatious, and thought to be in love with Hugh. "Of course no one who knows Hugh will care," Barnes added, "but there are a good many people who know about him and don't know him." When Hugh was told what Barnes had said about Mrs. Lindsay, he became exasperated, but seemed to be aware of the danger. He told Arthur he had always been very careful, "had never gone to her lodgings or had a meal there; and took care that she should always come to see him at reasonable hours--12.30&c. But he said she was a terrible woman, not wholly sane, always making awful scenes, mad to influence people and to be loved by them, but without one single friend. Much as he loved Ken, he would welcome the departure of the two. But he has now built her this house, and I don't see what is to happen. He has evidently suffered much at her hands. He speaks, he says, most plainly to her--he told her the other day that if she left Hare Street, not one single person would miss or regret her. She sate looking at him mutely and stonily. Yet she gave presents to all the servants and twenty presents to Ken. Hugh was bothered, but evidently the plague of her presence, her disingenuousness has been very bad. . ." (*Diary*, Dec. 1909).

At last Hugh decided Mrs. Lindsay must go. By late October, she had left Hare Street, so had Ken--a painful loss to Hugh, the only time Arthur had ever seen him grieve for someone gone away. It was not in his nature to mourn a loss, but he could not have loved a son more than he loved Ken. "We had a quiet dinner and Hugh went off. He seemed to me to be thinking mostly of Ken. Well, I don't grudge it him--and I am glad that a real affection has come into his life," adding wistfully, "but how I envy anyone who can work, and feel, and love!" Hugh never saw Ken again, but talked of him many times.

In 1911, Hugh learned that Ruth Lindsay had written a book and was looking for a publisher, the big houses having refused it. Hugh told his agent James Pinker he had heard "that a book was recently offered to [Longmans] that is either libellous, or very nearly so, by the Hon. Mrs. Lindsay on the subject of ME(!), faintly disguised." He said that he had heard that Longmans had refused the book and asked Pinker to keep his eyes open, and if the book was calculated to injure him to do anything that occurred to him to prevent its publication by warning publishers that he would sue. He went on to say that the story might not be true, and he did not want to be sued back, "but from what I know of the lady, who, to my sorrow, lodged here in the village for a while, I should not think the story entirely unlikely" (*Letter*, March 1911). It was in 1912 that Mrs. Lindsay's book appeared, called *The Guide-book and the Star*, a story in letters of a young widow with a child who moves into a village, takes instruction from the local Catholic priest with whom she falls in love. All in all the book was not malicious, merely embarrassing, for not a soul had the slightest doubt who the priest was.[5]

II

In the Pulpit   He had already made quite a name for himself as a writer, but it was as a great popular preacher that Hugh was most admired. By 1907 he had so big a following that when he preached the Passion on Good Friday at the Carmelite Church in Kensington (his favorite place to preach), the church and sacristy were packed a good hour before the scheduled time. Sliding doors had to be constructed to permit easier exit. Hugh's movements during a typical engagement in Kensington were remembered after his death: "He would arrive here about 1 on Saturday, leave his bag, rush off to a football match, returning about 5, swallow a cup of tea, go to his room, write a report of it for the *Daily Mail* or other paper (sometimes it would be a cricket match or even a sparring competition), then he would take supper with us--always protesting against anything but the community meagre food. Then interviews began, people waiting their turns in the three parlours, and when the female portion had left (oftener at 10.30 than any other hour) he would take some man up to his room, and with a cigarette or two work hard with him at instruction till late. Then he would get a book and devour it, and to my knowledge he often got through a fair-sized volume in a night, telling me he could stand an exam on its contents in the morning. Then up at 7, mass at 8, small breakfast at 9, during which he would read--none of us ever saw him idle. After breakfast he would see people till about 10.30, then to his room to think, and he would come down from the pulpit drenched with perspiration; a hot bath was ready for him and he would soak in it for about twenty minutes--then more interviews--lunch--off to an afternoon sermon or lecture, and oftener than not to an evening sermon too. What struck us most about him was that he could *pigeon-hole* his various subjects so wonderfully and he told us this was the result of very hard work, for he said all his sermons, &c., were the result of real labour to him, and he was *always* nervous. He was most friendly and amiable with us all, and seemed to like being let do just as he pleased here, and felt thoroughly at home in the house. In 1913 he made his yearly retreat here, and would take nothing but our food at all his meals, and you can realise what that must have meant to him, with his brain working so rapidly. Here is the average daily food bill--breakfast, a cup of coffee with some toast; dinner at 11, vegetable soup, piece of fish with potato and greens, piece of cheese, an apple or orange and *sometimes* fruit stewed or other sweet; supper at 7.30, piece of fish or bloater, potato and cheese. Yet he never once complained! When asked what he would like, the invariable answer was "Oh, anything; just what you have," and we had quite a fuss with him to make him eat meat" (*Letter from Father Ambrose*, in M, II, 194-5). It was while on his way back to the Carmelites to preach the Triduum for the Feast of St. Theresa on October 14, 1914, that he took ill and died.

Once in the pulpit Hugh looked small and insignificant, "the bigger the church the smaller he looked. He was in the pulpit and had something to say. Saying it was not enough, he was living it even as the words poured out in a torrent--and he pulled everyone in the church into the torrent with him. "In a child he saw a potential sinner, in the sick and dying he looked on the face of Christ in agony. Everything, everyone had a future more real than the present, everything had romance in it."[6] His voice was harsh and deep, but it obeyed him. The marked stammering which dogged him in every other situation and which friends found so painful ceased completely as soon as he began to speak. His fund of nervous energy simply overwhelmed his audience, body, limbs, head, shoulders, hands--all in motion, throwing himself forward on the table "like a billiard-player taking a difficult stroke: is silent for a moment, and then the words flow in a torrent. Again he draws back as if to get a run at it, and every part of the man follows his effort to get the right word out of the thousand we know are there. Now here, now there, now stretching neck and body over the table to his audience in sheer earnestness, hands in action every moment, drawing, as it were, diagrams of his ideas and arguments. . . . In his hour's talk there is not a flat sentence, a false or uncertain finish. The voice is unsatisfactory. The enunciation is too rapid . . . But the man's personality gets him over these defects. He acts, he lives, he sees every word he speaks. His enthusiasm never flags, his energy is unwearied. You must follow him, must give him your undivided attention. He arouses anger, hope, love, pride, pity, faith at will."[7]

He hated preaching and loved it; it was terrifying and ecstatic. "I need long preparation, much silence, light diet, notes that I can visualise, so that their phantom moves before me. I daren't look at people's faces; I daren't gesticulate unless I find it irresistible--then I do it a lot; at other times not at all." No one hearing him guessed what mental agony he endured in the hours before he preached, huddled in a chair "steeling" himself, frightened, and conscious of slight nausea. No one dared come near him. He prepared meticulously and with infinite care, giving seven or eight hours to each sermon. " . . . he would sit down with his sermon book on his knees, and fidget; he could not keep any part of himself still for a minute, he would cross and re-cross his legs, he would shuffle about in his chair, stroke his chin, scratch himself, and ruffle his hair; he was absurdly uneasy, and very irritable; he would bury his face in his hands, then return to his book, jump up and light another cigarette--of course he smoked all the time--walk about the room, and then sit down again."[8] When he had written down his sermon in points, he would study the page, then put it away.

Finally the moment had arrived, and into the pulpit he went. A little shuffling through the notices, but then pushing them aside, and looking at the congregation for the first time with those round, unblinking eyes, "the trembling under-lip . . . a hissing intake of breath," the body stretching over the pulpit as tension gripped the crowd, everybody alert . . . Then the mad rush forward, a lightning chase for words without an instant's pause. That was essential, because any noise or disturbance of the mental images (the phantoms) moving before him broke his concentration. For that reason he never looked at notes. "They're absolutely fatal. If you get the note habit you never take the trouble to prepare properly . . . don't have anything to do with them. No, no, no! not even in your pocket." And once finished, sweat streaming down his face, a half-hour's soak in a warm bath while smoking three or four cigarettes and he was good as new.

There was little warmth or Mystery in his sermons, just hard doctrine hammered home with stunning physical delivery which made up for defects in eloquence and oratorical skills. Fred, Hugh's sternest critic and no lover of Catholic doctrine, was lost in admiration. "When Hugh preached," he wrote, "the flood of his thoughts carried you off your feet and swept you along with it; you could not stop and criticise, because you were for ever in the rapids, in the grip of his gesture and his eloquence, which were frankly irresistible, and there his genius lay."[9]

The effect he had on crowds was the more striking to those who knew him in social situations where Hugh was a completely different personality, quite shy, "an entirely unaffected and, though so clever and original, a very straightforward and simple man." So Robert Hichens remembered him, reacting to a Lenten sermon preached in San Silvestro to a packed crowd that included fifteen Cardinals. In the pulpit the slight frame, luminous blue eyes, and boyish manner suddenly became transformed into something "startlingly sensational." His voice changed abruptly, alarmingly. His body writhed and started to shake. "Sometimes he would suddenly lower his voice and simultaneously shrink down in the pulpit until only his head and face were visible to the congregation. Then he would raise his voice almost to a shriek and like the figures in a Punch and Judy show dart up diagonally and lean over the pulpit edge until one almost feared that he would tumble out of it and land sprawling among his fascinated, yet apprehensive hearers below." Hichens left the church in such a state of confusion that he failed to recognize his old friend Abbot Gasquet, greeting him instead as Father Maturin! The truth was that he had been so overwhelmed by Father Benson that he scarcely knew where he was.[10]

Being good in the pulpit was not art, Hugh insisted, but a matter of skill and training. From all accounts, it was far more than this, for he was not content only to say what he had to say, he had to live it while he was up there and everyone in the church had to live it with him. His advice to those who asked was never write out your sermon, "I hold most *violently* that even the youngest priest ought never to write out his sermon, even at the beginning of his ministry." The spoken and written word were simply different vehicles. Whether his friend Father Basil Maturin subscribed to this or not, Hugh thought Maturin the best preacher in England.

Among Protestants Correspondence with non-Catholics was quite heavy. Having passed most of his life an Anglican, he understood their point of view, their difficulties with the Roman Church. For Protestants he had nothing but affection, but when it came to religion they were dead wrong and it was important they should be told. Their conversion was his principal work to the end of his life, but for that he had to drive Catholic ideas through Protestant prejudices. To that end, he was provocative, zealous, accusatory (his book *Non-Catholic Denominations* aroused much resentment among the denominations he described), particularly towards Anglicans, for they were children in religious matters and must be treated as such. Conversions were not done in a day, but they could be done. This superior attitude was not overlooked by Anglican critics. His novels were raked by ironic reviewers in the *Church Times*, eager to demolish the weight of Catholic apologetics preached openly by the priest bent on repudiating Anglicanism over and over.[11] Yet of all sects falling under the classification of Protestant--High Church, Low Church, Presbyterian, Nonconformist--Hugh was most critical of Christian Science and took very seriously the inroads Christian Science was making into establishment Christianity. Mincing no words he wrote a scathing review of Mrs. Eddy's book *Science and Health* raking the growing Christian Science cultism. Several difficult "cases" in his care (Miriam Silverstone, for example) used the threat of joining Christian Science to annoy him.

Hugh and the Supernatural   Theosophy and its offshoot
Spiritualism filled a different space. In his Cambridge days, Hugh had
flirted with Swedenborgism and Theosophy, but now accounted these
no more than beguiling cults, whose numbers were swelling with bored
or disaffected Protestants. Particularly alluring to the English were the
claims made by Theosophy to mystical knowledge, connecting it to
Eastern religions and Gnosticism, much the New Ageism of the day.
Dismissing most tenets of Christian belief, Theosophy held that the
One is manifested in all created things, that Man is the highest of these,
that Spirit is supreme, and that all things return to the Creator--a divine
Consciousness--the perfect and eternal One. Our faults lay not in guilt
or anything resembling Original Sin but in our passions and selfish
attachments to the senses, the things of a lower plane.   The
consequences of our deeds, our karma, may be worked out over the
course of several lifetimes and several incarnations. The body is an
equivocal thing; either it is to be despised, or it may be indulged as it is
utterly apart from the soul's development. Meditation is preferred over
prayer, and God is sought in the Self. More challenging to mainline
religion was the Christian Theosophist. For him Christ remains the
Savior, One in substance with the Father; thus, there is no break with
traditional Christian beliefs. Theosophists had no trouble accepting
Transubstantiation or the validity of Sacraments, for these were invested
with special powers, affinities they promoted. Conquering the passions
through an ascetic and contemplative life gives one power over oneself
and others, and in some instances, over matter, as, for example, in the
miracles wrought by Christ and the Saints. Between the two worlds of
pure matter and pure spirit hovers the "astral" plane, a kind of meeting
ground of both worlds, usually inseparable from the body, but
detachable under certain conditions such as death or trance. In the one
instance, Theosophists explain the Resurrection and bi-location events;
in the other, ghosts or phantoms brought back through the heightened
powers of mediums or clairvoyants. Even by Hugh's time Theosophy
had fragmented into several opposing factions, each claiming insight
into esoteric doctrine known only to the adepts of their chapter. In the
early years Anglican ladies particularly, graceful dames in clinging
black "coifed with priceless lace, with one fine string of pearls," passed
with the greatest of ease into Theosophy, a cut above Spiritualism, its
step-sister. Following WW I, Theosophy and occultism attracted many
disillusioned Christians.
    Allied with Theosophy and gaining ground in England was
spiritualism (or *spiritism*, and no longer ridiculed as the province of
cranks as it had been a generation before). With Theosophy,
spiritualism held to a belief in "astral matter," but spiritualism carried

the belief into *séances*, for summoning up disembodied spirits. Hugh hoped to combat the dangers of spiritualism by urging the Church to dispatch a few good priests to séances for the purpose of frustrating evil spirits and saving their victims. "They would have to go disguised; the danger would be extreme; the most violent manifestations would result." He offered to be the first to go, convinced that just now this would be the post of greatest danger in the Church's fight against the powers of evil.[12] When that proposal was rejected, he continued his crusade in interviews and lectures and essays, and ultimately reached a larger audience by exposing spiritualists in the novel *T h e Necromancers*. It would make a great number of people furious, he predicted.

Three theories existed to explain the phenomenon of spirits called up from Stygian realms into the *swami's* London flat. In the Spiritualist theory, disembodied spirits reconstituted themselves out of "astral matter" borrowed from the medium. From "astral matter" the visiting soul was condensed into visible form, materializing in different degrees, sometimes as a mist, sometimes as a transparent body. Another manifestation might be a communication made through the mouth of the medium in a trance, or message transmitted with a planchette [ouija board]. The second, the wholly materialistic Psychological theory held that under certain conditions the human mind tended to produce similar phenomena out of itself, cases in point hypnotism and telepathy, a power within reach of ordinary people. Science had not as yet unlocked the door to explain this phenomenon. The third, the Catholic theory, was not a theory so much as the Catholic position on the subject that held that spiritualism posed a danger to body, mind, and soul to those who persisted in exploring regions obviously closed by God. And exploring to what end? There was nothing to be gained, and much to be lost. Setting aside the ninety-nine percent probability of sheer trickery and fraud, the one per cent remaining were genuine evil intelligences bent on mischief. "Either this or that affair is fraud" and a waste of time, or it is a reality, Hugh warned, "and in that case a sinister and perilous reality."

Hugh outlined specifically how the "inquirer" is subtly roped in, and then indoctrinated into practices destructive to morals, nervous system, and bank balance. The danger was that this new quasi-religion was springing up everywhere these spiritualists went, complete with creeds, hymnals and Sunday schools. Jesus Christ was looked upon as one of the great moral teachers and, more to the point, the greatest of all *mediums*, by which the spiritualists understood His Resurrection was accomplished. For Catholic to whom the spiritual world is an objective reality, evil spirits are real, and the spirits brought up in spiritualist *seances* diabolical. Catholics must beware of dabbling.

Hauntings were another matter entirely. It is fair to say that haunted houses haunted him. Hugh Benson believed in old-fashioned ghosts and old-fashioned hauntings, and was forever seeking them out in upstairs bedrooms, behind panels, under floorboards, along a creaking staircase. At the mere rumor of mysterious thumping or moaning in the night he was off to investigate, armed with his priesthood. Oh, for a sleeve brushing lightly across the face in the deep watches of the night! "I have listened patiently to every ghost-story that has come my way--I have read all the literature I could lay my hands on; I have slept in haunted houses; I once took a suicide's room, with a bloodstain under the bed, and slept in it for a whole year in the hope of seeing a ghost," and the facts were undeniable.[13] That some persons have seen the figures or phantasms of absent friends who are dying or have just died far away he believed totally and offered a reasonable explanation based on the mind's power of projecting a sense image to another sympathetic mind. In point of fact, Hugh was years ahead of his time in examining and describing paranormal events, our extra-sensory perceptions. But in holding with haunted houses, he departed from the psychical research crowd who dismissed them as projections of an overly active imagination. Hugh believed firmly in them and rejected the so-called critical (that is, skeptical) attitude and made his case with rather convincing arguments; for him the weight of popular evidence down through the ages to the present times was overwhelming. The same principle that governed the power of relics and sacramentals to resonate with believers he applied to material objects like rooms and houses. They were impregnated with the aroma of a powerful emotional moment resonating in the mind and senses of the occupant, not visited by tortured souls. That was unworthy of Divine Justice.

Two books stand out as touching intimately his interest in the spirit world, *The Mirror of Shalott*, a collection of ghost stories, and *The Necromancers. The Mirror of Shalott* like *Light Invisible* (which it resembles) gives us tales of diabolic possession and ghostly visitations told by priests sitting around a table in the Canadian College in Rome. But there is nothing run-of-the-mill about these well-told tales. If ever a man craved to be visited by ghosts, apparitions, and related things that go bump in the night, Hugh was that man. Alas, as if perversely they refused to come.

Notes

[1] *Correspondence Between Miss Elizabeth Anstice Baker, TOSD and Mgr. Robert Hugh Benson,* edited by Fr. Simon Tugwell OP, Dominican Historical Centre, Blackfriars, Oxford (1991).

[2] An instance of hostile protests raised against religious themes as commercial entertainment occurred in London about this time. This was a protest mounted against Max Reinhardt's spectacular production of Maeterlinck's version of the medieval miracle play about a runaway nun whose place is taken by the Virgin. Hundreds of clergy of every religious sect were invited to attend a special matinee performance only to be met by a Nonconformist procession outside carrying signs that read "Four Thousand Romanisers Support Rome's Latest Miracle" and "Down With Popery." Protesters demanded a meeting of Protestants to protest the revival of nunneries, convent schools and Popery in general.

[3] These were not the only dangers he faced. After publication of an essay by Hugh on the subject of celibacy and sexual purity in an odd little book *Give Us White Men,* militant Suffragettes took to the warpath, interrupting High Mass at the Carmelite Church and threatening violence often enough that police needed to watch his house. He kept a whistle under his pillow. On another occasion the Reverend R.J. Campbell of the City Temple quieted a noisy gathering of hostile Protestants dead set against Hugh's lecture on Catholic doctrine. Campbell an ex-Presbyterian, ex-Anglo-Catholic, now a Nonconformist of the most liberal pantheist breed, remained a friend.

[4] Reginald Watt, *Robert Hugh Benson, Captain in God's Army* (London, 1918), p. 168.

[5] The book was noticed in the *Times Literary Supplement* for Thursday 15 July, 1911 (299c): "THE GUIDE-BOOK AND THE STAR, by Ruth Temple Lindsay. 7 1/2x5 165pp. Evelyn Benmar. These are letters to a friend by a young widow with a child, who is in a remote country place in close touch with a Roman Catholic priest. They are written in a very intimate gushing style which always looks to unreal in print; but they make rather a clever apologia for a convert to Romanism."

[6] Watt, p. 149.

[7] Flyer quoting Father Collier in the *Catholic Fireside* (n.d.). Hugh was scheduled to give the annual sermons for schools at St. Thomas of Canterbury Church, Waterloo. Admission to morning and evening sermons was 2*s*. Hugh sent Mary Benson a copy on which he had drawn a hand over a face, with the comment "I blush."

[8] Watt, p. 147.

[9] *A Mother,* p. 203. A sermon Hugh often preached answered the objection that the Church lavished too much money on beautiful interiors. He liked to cite the contrast of the use of precious stones for the adornment

of women, "concluding with a flash of withering invective that if they would not crown the Saviour with gold and jewels He could still wear the Crown of Thorns." Joseph McMahon in *American Catholic Historical Records Society*, 26 (1916), p. 61.

10 *Yesterday* (London, 1947), pp. 164-5. "He seemed an entirely different man from the charming and unaffected visitor with whom I had conversed a few days before." Hichens was not the first to be taken by the disparity between the man they knew socially and the public Father Benson. Mgr. Ronald Knox who had been deeply influenced by Hugh's books and sermons was disappointed upon first meeting him in person. With friends Hugh had no poses, with strangers he was shy and unprepossessing. Nevertheless, his sermons in San Silvestro brought out every English-speaking priest and seminarian. Twice on Good Friday he preached continually for three hours.

11 In a caustic review of *The Conventionalists* the anonymous *Church Times* reviewer accused him of attacking "the faith and practice of English Churchmen by innuendo, by taunt, by caricature, by misrepresentation," continuing into a personal attack on his overall abilities: "Four of five years ago Mr. Benson might have dealt interestingly with this theme of a Carthusian vocation . . . Today it is a task beyond his failing powers" (Nov. 13, 1908), p. 652. Hugh was incensed and at a subsequent attack in the November 20th number and again on November 27th in which he was accused of "knowingly misrepresenting facts" in advancing the Catholic cause. Hugh had by then fired off a reply, which the *Church Times* failed to publish or even acknowledge save for the insertion of his initials among "letters received." In desperation he sent his letter to *The Tablet*, aware that he had been peremptorily disconnected from the audience he needed to reach. "To Anglican readers, therefore, of The Church Times I am made to appear as a discredited controversialist who vanishes in silence at the first hint of opposition. And rather over four columns are devoted, in three consecutive numbers, to my discomfiture--which is, of course, complete--by showing up my mental deterioration, my gross ignorance, and my wilful disingenuousness, without permitting a word in self-defence." Hugh noted that the period of mental decay evidenced in his writings was "the last five years, curiously enough, the years of [his] Catholic life" (December 12, 1908) p. 934.

12 H.S. Dean in The *Month*, 124 (1914), p. 503.

13 This was the Cambridge undergraduate who had shot himself. When no one wished to move into the suicide's rooms, Hugh jumped at the chance rather callously, to the consternation of the dean man's friends. Psychic investigation was no novelty to the Bensons. Mary Benson was a member of the Psychical Research Society, which had been jointly founded by Edward and her brother Henry Sidgwick, and was currently presided over by Mrs. Sidgwick.

12
The Artist in Him

"When he was writing a book, he was like a man galloping
across country in a fresh sunny world, and shouting aloud
with joy." *Hugh*

When Hugh was at work on a novel, "he wrote with such ferocious
energy that it would not have surprised you to see the paper scorch
beneath his pen, and the whole bent of his brain was occupied with the
teeming thought that seemed to leap and bubble from the ink from the
ink pot on his paper"--so a correspondent remembered him, and it was
Arthur's recollection as well.[1] He never needed to search his brain for
an idea--it came when summoned; nor was there much agonizing over
images or stylistic effects. He went at writing headlong without
introspection, relying on his remarkable ability to forge the precise
detail that carried the whole impression. His skill as a novelist lay
mainly in the ability to establish immediate intimacy between readers
and characters. His characters were vivid and exciting, and what became
of them mattered from the moment they entered the page. In the
modern novels, readers were taken into country homes and shared in
country pleasures like trout-fishing or rabbit shoots, while our hero
moved inexorably towards a spiritual crisis, helped into and out of it by
a Catholic advisor, usually a resident priest in ill-fitting clothes. (There
was no special pleading for priests, who are often presented as
ineffectual or humorless taskmasters.) You went to Father Benson's
psychological novels prepared to see a soul raked to pieces before being
reconstituted. There was a moral lesson to be learned, delivered in a
realistic setting. Divine truths could not be grasped by the modern anti-
Christian mind as a set of propositions; they must be presented
indirectly in scenes and attitudes that would not cause them to be
rejected out of hand--in concrete images that stick in the imagination,
not in abstract ideas that do not.

Even his critics who considered his novels shameless Catholic tracts came back for more, not to sneer, but to see what Benson was up to now, and in many instances to read his books in secret. To critics who deplored his propagandist methods, he pointed out that all novelists worth the price of a book preach; they have an opinion and try to influence public opinion, whether preaching Marxism, Capitalism, Patriotism or Nihilism. He preached Catholicism. Fiction conveying a religious idea was tantamount to a sacramental and as such was conveying truth as nothing else could. It is the writer's business to see that the inner and invisible mystery is adequately portrayed and presented outwardly through the right visible sign. A case in point is the incomparably described Mass in *By What Authority?* where the poetry and beauty of Catholic liturgy is presented without loss of dogmatic truth. The images sink into the imagination and the doctrine is absorbed.

He had exceptional talent for describing nature. With a keen eye for detail he brought a grandeur to familiar things: birds and trees and clear streams, fragrant gardens, the sun rising, landscapes. They rolled effortlessly off his pen. Yet he was never known to react passionately to nature, or to give more than a passing nod to some spectacular moment of natural beauty. Impressions that struck the senses in an unusual way sank into his head rapidly and could be recreated on paper, but things beautiful in nature never really detained him or sent him into raptures. He looked at them with a photographic eye, and passed on.

Sweeping vistas came alive in his books--great swaying crowds and colorful pageants and frantic chases to set the heart racing, all of these panoramas executed smoothly as if a mere change of expression or an arm thrown out casually were being described. History especially presented opportunities for his "set pieces," long descriptive passages reconstructing with gem-like brilliance a particular moment that happened precisely as he was describing it, or should have. Another strength was his handling of convincing motivation. In the modern novels where great life-and-death struggles must be scaled down, the hero is usually "one of us," that is, someone so ordinary he is scarcely noticed even by his family. Into his life comes a crisis of decision, the choice is made, ending in the Soul's victory over world, flesh, and devil. It has been an initiation truly, spiritual and actual, in which the protagonist ends up quite apart from the world, enlightened and unique. The rejection is mutual. The novels are filled with mannerisms, repeated phrasing, digressions, curious facts, music and sensation, and a fascination with odd physical and psychological states, going hoarse, going blind, dying. A plot-line is frequently sacrificed to long descriptive passages, beautifully crafted, but distracting. There is a love interest, there is even passion, although today's readers would have to hunt for it. Women and social conventions pull the hero in one direction while God pulls in another. The victory almost always falls to God.

Hugh liked to show off his talent for recreating the mystery of physical death, as in the stunning interiorizing of the final moments of Mary Tudor's life or of Nevill Fanning's in *Initiation* as the body lets go of the soul. One striking habit that delighted readers and irritated critics was that of revealing characters from the inside, slipping into the skins of ecstatics, worldly types, callow youths, footmen, lovers, Wagnerian sopranos, boys, cats, dying baronets. That talent for interior monologues from multiple points of view might have amounted to something had he bothered to refine technique instead of merely testing his powers--other writers like Woolf and Joyce were experimenting along similar lines. But this was Hugh Benson; once he had made his point, all the rest was mere literature.

His novels were flawed. He wrote too much, he wrote too fast. Eventually writing became too easy, formulaic; and towards the end, driven by timetable, he became careless and over-confident. The story conveying the moral imperative was of first importance, the characters no more than a means of elaborating it, so while there might be faults of characterization, the tale itself seldom faltered. There were too many digressions; careless phrasing and unsystematic punctuation abounded. With his reputation secure, as time went on he often resorted to the ellipsis to save himself the trouble of completing a thought. Perhaps thoughts rushed from his pen as they rushed from his lips in the pulpit, so his hand was not able to keep up So much weight was given to the dash, the reader felt suspended in space. And the overused parenthesis (for every nuance) suggested a disdain for matters of form.[2]

He made quick work of a book without bothering about revisions, boasting "publish every word I write, you bet." That was certainly true once he had established a reputation. In 1908 *The Conventionalists* was delayed for weeks by revisions, however. The "Charles II" book hatched long ago in Rome he revised many times, and finally after throwing the fifth attempt into the fire, gave the project two weeks of solid uninterrupted work. *Oddsfish!* was the result, but he was not satisfied with it even in its sixth and final version.

In the Elizabethan novels (*By What Authority? The Queen's Tragedy, The King's Achievement*) the myth of Tudor saintliness was smashed, a healthy but short-lived correction of Protestant English Reformation history promoted by historians like George G. Coulton.[3] It was Hugh

Benson who created unforgettable portraits of tyrants and martyrs, who lifted the prejudices passed down of monasteries as great treasure houses and monks as greedy sensualists. His books insist that here is what really happened, if only the schoolmasters and Protestant propagandists let it be known. Writing historical novels really suited his talents best, but modern novels without the need for months of research were far easier to write, and addressing as they did the problems of his day, were more useful in bringing Catholicism to England immediately.

In the historical novels but less so in the modern novels, Hugh was completely dominated by his characters. In the modern "psychological" novels, the upper classes ossified by conventionalism were frequently his subject. Yet his novels take such pleasure in the world of the country home where everybody dresses up for dinner and men retire to the study for the obligatory port, that a reader may be forgiven for missing the allegorical purpose at least in the first four or five chapters. "Hugh Benson can never describe a house where there is not a second footman, a critic wailed" (M, II, 181), yet it was the spiritual emptiness of these people of breeding that he sought to expose. In one novel after another, shallow or disappointed parents, feckless children, incompetent or inefficient clergy, wasted days, wasted lives in a crumbling fortress petrified by low Church religion--these fill his pages. From his novels one learned how the genteel life was lived and squandered just before the death blow dealt by World War I. His heroes were ordinary men without noticeable gifts, weak or sometimes disagreeable, who are suddenly put to the test spiritually. Readers followed them through the several stages of discovery from discontent, to suffering and atonement, to illumination. Hugh had a favorite woman as well. She was the forthright, high-spirited outdoors type who knew how to ride a horse smartly, and who spoke her mind at critical moments, often sending our hero into a spiritual tailspin. Instead of finding fault with these frozen well-scrubbed, well-mannered, well-born English maidens, women readers found them attractive and modern, and never insisted they possess any more depth or dimension than Hugh had given them. In his fiction they were strung along the allegorical thread, incidental stages in the spiritual ascent or decline of the hero.

With few exceptions, the most interesting female characters inhabit his historical novels, as if the opulence and grandeur of Olde England were the complement of their genius. Not a character in the modern novels can match the vitality and wit of Mary Corbet or Isabel Norris of *By What Authority?* or the intellectual precocity of Beatrice Atherton, Thomas More's young friend in *The King's Achievement.* Dynamic Elizabeth I sweeps in and out of his chapters, gloriously imperious and tyrannical. Women of the modern "psychological" novels fall into several categories; there are the strong, sensible, capable, and fickle; or strong, but temperamental and spoiled; or strong, competent, smart, and brave. Wherever one finds her, she is usually an accessory, urging or obstructing the hero's spiritual progress. There are a few exceptions. In *The Winnowing* the focus is Mary Weston, wiser than her husband; and in *Loneliness* , Hugh's final book, a woman takes center stage again literally, for Marion is a soprano who having wrecked her voice and lost her fiancé, chooses the Lover who will never fail her.

He was accused of lacking any real human sympathy for his subjects, that the suffering of his characters (particularly in the late novels) expressed a thesis rather than a living emotion, yet the critics' view did not reflect the attitude of the public, who found his entire work resonating with personal confession. That may be the key to his power over the reader. Aspects of his personality were to be found in his fictional characters, it was widely believed, and while it may be true that Hugh fed this predisposition by continually re-inventing himself for purposes of his novel, the conflicts were sufficiently real in his experience to be convincingly portrayed. The public saw him mirrored in their favorite characters--Anthony, Chris, Algy, Robin--so they came to know him intimately, or thought they did, and believed that in examining the personal and religious conflicts of his heroes he was letting them into his life. Whatever the facts, there is no other way to explain why so many people who hardly knew him or knew him only through his books felt at his death they had lost a personal friend.

Long ago he decided that *The Light Invisible* he liked least of all his books because he had expressed his own Anglican yearnings for Rome in a veiled way, substituting subjectivism for doctrine. *The Dawn of All*, chronicling the final triumph of Rome, he called a deplorable book that should not have been written. *Richard Raynal* was his favorite; so much of his ideal self living the ideal life had been poured into it. Written in the style of a recently discovered manuscript, it was assumed by readers to be a real history of a real Richard Raynal. Hugh was perplexed how readers could understand it as anything other than fiction. "Poor Richard Raynal," he wrote to Wilfred Ward, "Really I don't know what more I could have done to make the facts plain, unless I had printed in capitols--I MADE THIS UP--on the title page." And when after *Lord of the World* he left the field of prophecy and Apocalypse to return to an historical setting in *Come Rack! Come Rope* everyone was relieved. It is an unforgettable novel that did more than any other work of fiction of the time or since to change Anglican attitudes about the cruelties of the English Reformation. Dry periods struck the craftsman,

but infrequently. When *None Other Gods* appeared in bookstalls in
1910, he was two months into another novel which had lain idle on his
writing desk for six weeks.

While he wrote, his mind and body were fully engaged, but once
finished, he absorbed himself in the next project, with no interest in
what he had done yesterday. Talking about his books bored him, except
for the novel being created at the end of his pen. All interest lay in the
present and future, in what he was doing at the moment, or would be
doing next week or next month.

By all accounts he became quite the astute businessman, a far cry
from his irresponsible younger days at Cambridge when all he managed
was to rack up debts. Figures eluded him, he liked to say, but not
when it came to sales of his books and his talent. He had contracted
with Methuen for novels in series of three (not three novels a year in
perpetuity as rumored--though in one year he managed to produce three
novels, and articles besides). *The King's Achievement* had sold about
10,000 books. Sales of *The Queen's Tragedy* had been extremely good,
but others of that year 1907 (*Richard Raynal, Lord of the World, The
Sentimentalists*) faltered somewhat by comparison. On that basis, his
publisher offered an advance of £350, 400, 450 for three novels of at
least 75,000 words, but Hugh resisted, insisting that he needed to make
more money. These books turned out to be *The Conventionalists*
(already nearing completion), *Oddsfish!*, continually in progress, and the
Thomas Becket book, to be written jointly by him and his collaborator
Frederick Rolfe, in the manner of a contemporary memoir like *Richard
Raynal*. By April 1908, however, he had had straight talk about Rolfe
from Arthur and Mgr. Barnes and as a result of it advised Pinker that
Rolfe would be acknowledged only in the preface. In March 1908 he
asked for an advance on *The Necromancers* of £200. By April 1908 *The
Conventionalists* was finished and he sent the hand-written manuscript
to Pinker, but he proposed delaying publication until Autumn, unless
he had a historical novel done by then, in which case that ought to go
first, in expectation of better sales for both. He was uncertain how the
novel would sell, offering to change parts of it if needed, and in May of
1908 he worried about losing largely should a cheap edition of his
novels be published prematurely. He was even then at work on a life of
Thomas Becket different from the projected Rolfe collaboration.
Meanwhile, foreign rights for *Lord of the World* in Spanish and Italian
translations were being negotiated, and though Hugh insisted he knew
nothing about these matters, he scrutinized every article of the
agreement. His *Nativity* play, illustrated by Gabriel Pippet, went to
the printer in late summer 1908. By December 1908 Huchinson asked
for another novel, and incredibly by March 1909, a mere three months

later, *The Necromancers*, his demonic book, was all but finished. In 1910 he assembled a number of successful sermons, demanding specially good terms from Benziger in America where he had enjoyed great success during his trip. By June of 1910 he was at work on yet another novel. He badgered his agent James Pinker to get the best terms and widest circulation, which meant American and foreign rights and printing cheap editions spaced decently apart after the more expensive first edition had run its course. When offering an article to a journal, he was direct: how long? what type? how much per thousand words? He preferred the larger houses to Catholic publishers who offered lower terms. Faced with a repair bill or sudden expenditure, he grumbled to Pinker that Arthur's books made more money than his, yet in reality he had little to complain about. *Lord of the World* made a lot of money, so did *A Queen's Tragedy*. *The King's Achievement* not so much, which naturally affected his advances.[4] His works were translated into French, German, Spanish, Portuguese, Italian, Hungarian, Dutch, Polish, Swedish, and Braille, all at the going rate.

Among literary people he was the foremost writer of religious novels, a friend of co-religionist Hilaire Belloc and G.K. Chesterton. To his good friend Hornung, whose novel about the society burglar Raffles was making such a smash, he dedicated the manuscript of *The Coward*. He was frequently consulted on ecclesiastical matters by other writers. For Ford Madox Hueffer (Ford), he compiled extensive notes on ecclesiastical protocol, which Ford used in *The Fifth Queen: and How She Came to Court*, a book about the short reign of Queen Catherine Howard.

Hugh was not selfish about publication and went to great lengths to encourage young writers just starting out, writing them letters generous with praise and recommending their books to publishers. He never criticized a new writer for errors, remarking about a first novel, "I think if I wrote that book now it would be hailed as 'another masterpiece by Mgr. Benson,' and if I'd written it twelve years ago I'd have got the sort of reviews he'll get; I do hope it won't stop him writing though." As for reviews, it was always unsatisfactory work, painful to write because "you are so liable to pick up a book with the one object of finding out its faults, and, having found them, you write about them, and having damned the book completely you shove in a few remarks like 'showing promise,' 'a strong scene,' 'vivid imagination' . . ." It was too difficult to be both conscientious and charitable when a writer's career was in the balance.

He needed to express himself in all sorts of art forms, but it was the expression more than the finished product that he delighted in. Carving, gardening, medievalism, hiding holes--his passions seemed boundless. He loved especially old things that link us to the past, from old books to old houses. Nothing is to tamper with history. So he might admire a decrepit set of posts barely holding up a roof because they had been gnawed by cattle for centuries. Inspired by Miss Lyall, he took up painting. Two pictures, one not very good one of Hugh, hung in the library. "You know Miss Lyall is jolly good, but she never knows when she's finished; she will go finicking on--that's how she spoiled that picture of me; and in the end I had to do the hand myself." Once having developed a passion for painting he painted everything in sight, the neighboring duck pond, his own chapel, the two windmills on the hill behind the house; he painted Miss Lyall's balcony from his garden, he painted his garden from Miss Lyall's balcony. "Just look at them!" he said, pointing to a whole row of his little canvases, "Averaging more than one a day! No R[oyal]. A[cademician]. could do that."[5] He took one or two lessons from eminent landscape painter Sir John Lavery, whom he met in Ireland, and Austin Spare, artist and ex-prizefighter, was a frequent guest at Hare Street, though Spare's art leaned heavily to the bizarre and fantastic. It was not that Hugh was spreading himself too thin, he was all over the place, as if there were nothing beyond his talents, no skill he could not master.

Love of the theater was an old story for him, beginning with childhood fantastics in the family who played seriously at everything, and continuing solidly into Eton and Cambridge days. For the children of Hackney Wick and Kemsing he had created elaborate productions.[6] He believed in drama as a teaching tool for the Faith if only Catholics produced plays equal artistically with those the world produced, and urged using the new motion picture "cinematograph" to evangelize England. He wrote *Maid of Orleans* and *The Cost of a Crown*, a play about the English Martyrs. That one had all but reached the West End stage when the backers alarmed at the cost suddenly withdrew. It was a bitter disappointment. His *Play in Honour of the Nativity of Our Lord* successfully imitated a medieval Mystery play, and *The Upper Room* was being performed as late as the 1960's, and it may well be that a Catholic audience is seeing it even today. Towards the end of his life when he was convinced nothing was beyond his abilities, he dreamed of becoming a successful playwright although theater-going was forbidden him. He dramatized the demonic novel *The Necromancers* and wrote several plays: The *Mother* (and a shorter version *His Mother's Game*), *Within Limits*, and *The Brothers* about a young man's sexual indiscretion. All but *Within Limits* are signed "James Percival Head," his pen-name. Not even the Benson reputation could have carried off these limp melodramas, however..

Physical things are of utmost importance in the spiritual journeys of his characters because the senses are instruments for receiving spiritual truth. So, to say that hell smells of brimstone is a sort of sacramental way of understanding a mysterious quality of hell, just as to look at a rose is to see the Beauty of God. He pointed out that it is precisely that method by which the Evangelist was instructed in Revelations. Here lay his interest--in the bizarre and abnormal, in the Lydwines and the Durtals of a world slightly off its axis.[7] His peculiar ability to work himself into his character--that ability of writing from the inside--operated for pain as well, so efficiently that after writing the passages on the torture of the martyrs in *Come Rack! Come Rope* he claimed that his fingers and wrists actually had begun to tingle. Ironically, his tolerance for pain was low (the prospect of pain terrified him), yet he firmly believed pain to be the first step to sanctification. It is certainly so for the martyrs of his novels. From martyrologies, particularly Huysmans' version of the life of St. Lydwine of Schiedam, he learned how suffering could be put to good use. "Love and death and pain are the bones on which life is modelled," he said in *The Necromancers*.

One amusement of his was to catalogue his books, most of them unopened and unread, but important possessions if one was to have a well-stocked library. He was not a connoisseur of the Classics by any means. The great crowds he spoke to on the subject of "The Modern Novel" were undoubtedly many times better read in great books than he, but he spoke with authority and his reputation as a novelist gave weight to his opinions. He preferred contemporary novels to historical ones and often dismissed important writers with a flippancy that suggested commanding knowledge. He had no taste for Sir Walter Scott of G.B. Shaw. Newman, Stevenson, Thackeray and Meredith he liked very much. The Brontës produced for him the impression of "being in a nightmare with too many clothes on the bed." H.G. Wells, whom he referred to as "that amazing genius," was his favorite writer; there was nothing about Wells's art to dislike except his politics. At least Wells had a point of view and went straight towards it, wrong as it might be. Kingsley's *Westward Ho!* which he had loved as a boy was exciting romance mired in gross distortions of fact and anti-Catholic polemic. Among essayists, Chesterton had genius, but Hilaire Belloc (Hugh's good friend) was more enduring. The Celtic Renascence very much on the ascendant he brushed aside as pagan and Protestant, not in the least expressive of the Irish soul. Shakespeare, Milton--any writer before the 19th century, in fact--were of little interest apparently, but the 19th century inspired him, from Flaubert to Pater to Huysmans.

In Eton at the tender age of thirteen he became enamored of Joseph Shorthouse's *John Inglesant.*, and while at Cambridge he discovered J.K. Huysmans, the French convert and former occultist, a fanatical lover of all things medieval, and inspiration of aesthetes and Decadents. With unbridled enthusiasm Hugh buried himself in Huysmans, as he would do for Frederick Rolfe later. When a correspondent called the favorite *St. Lydwine of Schiedam* a hideous book, he pounced on her mercilessly for the sacrilege. Yet, what besides atmosphere was it in Huysmans that attracted him? There is no plot to speak of. Characterization? Unlikely--too many characters walking through Huysmans' novels are at best disagreeable, at worst repulsive. But in the setting, there is no lack of luxurious medievalism with its intoxicating appeal to aesthetic or neurotic sensibilities. Hugh sensed disease in Huysmans' creations, specifically his hero Durtal the aesthete, connoisseur of the odd and eccentric. Durtal's world uniting aesthetic and symbolic was fantastic, disturbing, swarming with moonstones and gargoyles and thrusting spires. Hungering but incapable of being satisfied, Durtal is physical and spiritual flotsam until he finds the Roman Church, refuge of sinners. Huysmans' character has been wicked, indulging his perversions in back alleys for the greater glory of experience and salons for the greater glory of Art. Finally he is driven to the magnificent ritual of the Catholic Church, the last glimmer of hope before facing the barrel of a gun. What draws him to the Church but hooded saints and chants in darkened chapels? For Huysmans votive lights, faded roses, clasped hands raised in adoration mean redemption; without them Hell yawns. This is Rolfe's world too. In these shadowy reaches of the imagination where the nervous sensibility has its home, Hugh and Rolfe and Huysmans were kindred spirits.[8]

Notes

[1] From "Mgr. Benson in Private Life" in *The Universe* (London, Oct. 30, 1914), p. 6.

[2] The view held by those not disposed to his overlook faults was that he wrote fast to make money fast. "You show symptoms of being infected with the common deplorable form of Modernism which is called Hysteria," wrote his friend Maria Storer, the wife of Bellamy Storer the American Ambassador at Vienna under President Taft and Roosevelt. ". . . Now this may be a way of making money rapidly. Whether it is a justifiable way, you know best, or ought to. But I think you have now come to the point when you ought to decide whether your career is creditable. You are a great popular preacher, a capacity simply sown with innumerable fatal pitfalls. You are also a great popular writer . . ." On she went without apology--"Preach or write, she insisted, "and give yourself to one career or another, all without advertising the fact in the papers." She preferred the preacher to the writer.

[3] Today, that correction of the earlier view is being carried on by historians Scarisbricke, McGrath, Duffy, and others. In developing characterizations, plot, and setting Hugh strove to be a careful historian; he kept a record of books consulted for *The Queen's Tragedy*, among them Camden Society publications, Holinshed, Stowe, Wrothesley, and various collections of state papers. But he was writing fiction with a point of view and obviously selected his material accordingly.

[4] *Correspondence between Robert Hugh Benson and James Pinker 1907-14*, in the Berg Collection, New York Public Library. He realized £36 over his advance on *Lord of the World*, a small sum today, but in those years books sold for a few shillings. James Pinker also represented Arthur Benson, Joseph Conrad, James Joyce, Henry James, John Galsworthy, and H. G. Wells.

[5] Watt, p. 26.

[6] He wrote many plays and published three rhymed books for children, *A Child's Rule of Life, Old Testament Rhymes* (written on the back of a paper book during railway journeys), and *An Alphabet of Saints* (a collaborative work). Gabriel Pippet illustrated them.

[7] From childhood days macabre tales were his contributions to family story-telling adventures. As a child writing for the family Saturday Magazine, a joint literary effort of the Benson children, Hugh "produced adventures so bloody, that out of sheer reaction his audience rocked with unquenchable laughter" (*Our Family Affairs*, p. 93). Drawings of gallows and axes and victims being dragged off to dungeons may still be seen among his papers, presages of the hero's tribulations in the novels of adult life.

[8] Dorothy Brennell in "Mgr. Benson and Huysmans," *The Month* (Dec. 1917), pp. 512-19, concluded that Hugh was less saturated by medievalism,

cleaner and more substantive in his mysticism than Huysmans. The article is of interest chiefly as indicating that the affinity was not overlooked by Benson's contemporaries. A more penetrating essay (though evasive in drawing exact parallels) is Canon William Barry's "Mgr. Benson--A Literary Note." Pointing out keen sensitivity to symbols, Barry, an astute critic of 19th century literature, held that Benson learned something of his craft from Huysmans, intimating deeper connections in these "melancholy places" than admitted: "Dark threads run from his first volume to his last; again, like Huysmans, he lived not in the sunshine. To my feeling he [Huysmans] is never merry, acute, brilliant, with points of satire; he deserves the epithet of severe. . . . They belong, as far as I know them, to the Bible of Repentance; they dwell constantly on the mind diseased which cannot be its own physician. Now and again they lapse into pathology, as records of the sick-room" *The Universe* (October 23, 1914), p. 7.

13
Benson Abroad

America always had a warm spot in her heart for Hugh's books and welcomed him to her shores three times: in 1910 in Boston (then a city sixty per-cent Catholic), in New York in 1912, and again in 1914. Each time he enjoyed a greater success than before. An invitation was first made by Maria Storer, wife of Bellamy Storer, the American ambassador in Austria. Before moving to Hare Street in June of 1908 he had traveled with the Storers to Lourdes, pausing at Versailles for a month to absorb its "thousand apparitions" and at Chartres, locale of Huysmans' *La Cathédrale*. In Lourdes, he was overwhelmed at the sight of pilgrims, thousands of them, many crippled and diseased, and was moved especially by the intensity of faith that engulfed them like a great mystical cloud. He knew Zola's brilliant but misleading book on the phenomenon. With Maria Storer acting as translator, he consulted the official records of miraculous cures for the purpose of setting right Zola's glaring distortions in his own book on the subject. Hugh had arrived somewhat of a skeptic, but returned absolutely convinced of the propinquity of the Blessed Virgin at Lourdes.

His friends the Storers kept an apartment on the Fenway, very close to the palatial residence of the grandest of Boston Brahmins Mrs. Isabella Stewart Gardner, an ardent Bensonian. Under Mrs. Gardner's patronage Hugh gave ten lectures at Fenway Court over a two week period to a great crowd of friends and admirers.[1] Apart from this dazzling event, his sermons at Holy Cross Cathedral created surprisingly little stir outside of Catholic circles. With typical Benson zeal, he did much sightseeing, racing here and there, and in Chinatown took copious notes on the mysteries of the opium den.

In 1912 he sailed for New York for a full menu of lectures and Masses from South Brooklyn to South Bend. He was already enough of a celebrity to bring out reporters for a dockside interview and the next day his picture and appeared in the New York Herald with a full report of his remarks upon arrival.

No American church gave him quite the welcome of Our Lady of Lourdes. It was resounding. For the first time a complete Lent was to be preached as a "connected series of sermons" in the diocese of New York, and no less a personality than Mgr. Benson would preach it. McMahon was immensely flattered by his guest's visits--after all Father Benson was quite the celebrity--and Our Lady of Lourdes enjoyed unparalleled publicity the entire time, and unparalleled profits. No newcomer to good business methods in parish administration, Father McMahon accompanied him to functions in the city and nearby New Jersey and on his travels westward.

Notices went out announcing that Father Benson was an earnest thinker who had found the truth in the Catholic Church and curiosity-seekers were cautioned they would find nothing sensational in the event. Thirty thousand tickets were printed. When the advance demand for seats turned out to be even greater than expected, Hugh offered to add the Three Hours' Agony on Good Friday. At first curiosity did indeed bring out New Yorkers. Here was no less than the Catholic son of an Anglican Archbishop of Canterbury, a renowned novelist and apologist who had taken the world by storm, about to preach in a New York City church. On Ash Wednesday, 1250 jammed into the church which seated 850, so many of them Protestants that local parishioners found themselves listening from the steps through the open doors. On a return visit in 1914, numbers were even greater and additional lectures needed to be scheduled in the auditorium.

Strangers who happened to be passing and managed to make their way in were captivated by this slight figure of a man in a black soutane girdled with a monsignorial sash, with nervous hands and expressive face. So wrote President Finlay of the City College who on the way home from Palm Sunday service in his own church dropped into Our Lady of Lourdes. "I found the main floor so crowded that I could not get in, so I made my way to the gallery which was also very much crowded, but I found standing room there. An English priest was preaching, and his remarks impressed me so much," Finlay said, that he wished he could have brought him along to say the same to his meeting. There were perhaps 5000 people in the audience, and also 100 or more priests.

Vibrant, living Catholicism untrammeled by skepticism was what attracted him in America. "Here is the smallest parish in New York-- with eight Masses each Sunday, and all packed," Hugh marveled. "They bang about and get red and hot on the side of the Church." Asked when

England would return to the Church, he spoke of the confusion in Anglican circles and the compromises in dogmatic religion that were shaking Protestantism free of all sacred principles.

"Things going tearingly here," he wrote to Dr. Sessions in March of his prima-donna treatment, "if only I could sleep a little more. It's really not good enough to sleep uneasily through nightmare after nightmare--all about dead people and their corpses--for five hours; and then to lunch out, and tea out, and to lecture or preach six times a week. I fainted wholly and entirely on my way over here, and have no idea even how long I was unconscious--and all without any premonitory symptoms. I just found myself emerging from eternity on the floor of my cabin. I wonder if death's like that. I hope so. . . . I'm lecturing in the ball-room of the Astor Hotel twice; tickets from one dollar to three and about 2000-2500 people in the audience!! And I dine with millionaires and ladies with $2000 worth of jewellery on. . . . So you must pray for me that I may not come back bloated and arrogant. I have also grasped the hand of the President and the Chief Justice, and am to dine with a railroad king next week. So you must pray, or I shall be wearing a fur coat!"

He continued his heavy schedule speaking in churches and cathedrals, fashionable salons and clubs, and at the podium in important universities and convents. In Brooklyn he talked on modern psychical research and again the next day at the Hudson Theater (in later years a notorious burlesque house!); then it was off by train to Detroit and points west. On the way he made sure to try out all means of modern locomotion, the subway, trolley car, and limousine. At Grand Central Station he hopped a train and rode with the engineer all the way to Albany, emerging with his face covered with black soot. It was a thrilling ride of hair-pin turns he would not soon forget. At Sing-Sing prison, he asked to be strapped into the electric chair, and was. Hugh liked America, liked the bustle and the noise and the slang, the kindness, the independence of its people and their vigor. He was not uncritical, however, about the high crime rate, the noise, and the American habit of demanding instant gratification. Perhaps because it was a country without a long history, he reasoned, America lacked ability to reflect on the past.[2]

Even in America, he was pursued by unrelenting correspondents. "Open everything," he had instructed Father Watt as he was mounting the dog-cart at Hare Street, "and tear up all the rubbish. Deal with everything you can, and tell me what you've done; send on anything that looks private . . ." Of course, so many of these letters wanted his personal handling that there was little rubbish to dispose of. Hugh sent his replies to Father Watt (or whoever happened to be acting as his secretary at the time), who posted them in England. Americans too were pitiless when it came to letter writing. Among the stacks of letters arriving daily were invitations to dinner, invitations to lecture, or join in a panel discussion on some controversial point, questions about points of doctrine, questions about what course of action ought to be followed by the obedient correspondent.

When it came time to depart for home, gifts rained down upon him: jewelry, gold boxes, gold cases, gorgeous red vestments, gorgeous green vestments.[3] On the *Olympia* for the return voyage he found his cabin crammed with them. He wrote his thanks to Father McMahon, moving at once to the momentous event that had just taken place on the high seas, the sinking of the *Titanic*, the *Olympia*'s sister-ship. "The shock of the Titanic tragedy has been awful here," he wrote. "A good many people have had friends on board, and the stewards, some of whom nearly joined her, and others of whom had relatives on board, have suffered most of all. And then this is the sister-ship: and we were close to the scene and actually passed ice, ourselves, the following night. I said Mass for the souls of all that were lost, next morning; I had quite a congregation. I am writing this letter, and shall leave it open till the last moment in case I think of anything else. Will you please give all messages of gratitude and affection to the other priests? I feel I haven't thanked anybody sufficiently for all their kindness and patience." £1000 was collected "for Titanic sufferers on board here," he wrote the following day, and to his surprise he had been made treasurer. "Needless to say, the accounts are hopelessly muddled."

In 1914 he left for New York again aboard the *Olympia*. Twenty-four sermons were scheduled for Our Lady of Lourdes. Additionally, he had five "conferences" ready to go (one of them, "Why I am a Catholic," based on chapters in his *Confessions*), all of them given before, all to be given again repeatedly. He paused in Boston to talk on "Philanthropy" and "Modern Dangers of Religion," and went on to Princeton, then to Philadelphia. At the University 200 students waited outside the auditorium unable to get in. Three times he spoke to audiences in Chicago--at the Mediaevalist Club in the University, and at St. Anne's Church; and was inducted into the Knights of Columbus; then traveled on to the University of Notre Dame and convent-schools in and around South Bend where he had talked in 1912, returning finally to New York for a round of lectures at Our Lady of Lourdes and farewell feasts at the elegant Delmonico's. He enjoyed many pleasures denied him back home--a Turkish bath, visits to theaters and music-halls, and mounting his own play *Maid of Orleans* for the dramatic Guild of Our

Lady of Lourdes (he had done the same during his visit in 1912 for the *Nativity* play). John McCormick, the famous tenor, sang for him at a drawing-room concert assembled expressly in his honor. This was the best preaching engagement he had ever had, combining a "magnificent congregation, and very satisfactory remuneration." In the two visits of 1912 and 1914, over 100,000 people heard him preach or lecture.

By now the pattern was fixed to preach in Rome and New York in alternate years; thus, he would be returning to New York in the spring of 1916.[4] 1915 was to be a relatively quiet year, with a shooting holiday in Newfoundland the only transatlantic journey.

Between New York and the final months at Hare Street, Hugh joined the Bellamy Storers again at Zermatt, with high hopes of climbing the Riffel Alp, the same peak down which years ago he had been carried half-dead and Fred poured brandy down his throat until he came to, good and drunk but alive. In August then, an inspection of the Swiss Alps; and in September off to Cannes for a solid retreat "full of graces."

He returned home rested and vigorous, itching to get on with planting a rose garden, with the statue of the Blessed Virgin at the center of it. His creative powers had already peaked, yet the public showed no signs of abandoning him; they wanted more, and more they would get. *Oddsfish!* was about to hit the stalls, and next year they would have *Loneliness?* Already another novel was brewing in his head, this one about the War, now in progress and raging in Belgium.

Living life so abundantly, Hugh never suspected that for him a mere month of life remained.

Notes

[1] In a May 1910 letter Mrs. Gardner told Bernard Berenson in Rome of Father Hugh Benson's lectures, enjoyed by all apparently. She refers to him in letters familiarly as "Hugh," a liberty even the great lady would scarcely have taken to his face. These courses in Boston were made up of sermons he gave at San Silvestro in 1909, and again at the Carmelite Church, London. Having been talked to saturation level on two continents, they were sent to the publisher and appeared in print as *Christ in the Church*.

[2] Father McMahon recounted the amazing schedule for 1912 in Our Lady of Lourdes' parish news: "Monsignor Benson was exactly 56 days in this country. During that time he preached 26 sermons, in our church in course, besides giving the Three Hours' Agony, and the Servite Service of Maria Addolorata. He gave the five Conferences in the AUDITORIUM; two lectures

at the Hotel Astor; two lectures at the Bellevue Stratford in Philadelphia, Pa., and one to the Catholic Girls' High School; two lectures at Cathedral Hall, Boston. He lectured at the University of Pennsylvania and at Princeton. He preached at St. Peter's, Poughkeepsie; at St. Mary's, Chicago; at Corpus Christi Monastery, Hunts Point; at the Convent of the Sacred Heart; and at Marymount. He lectured at Notre Dame University, and at St. Mary's Convent, South Bend, Ind., at D'Youville College, Buffalo; and at Notre Dame Convent, Longwood, Chicago. He addressed four Lenten sewing classes in New York City; spoke to a very large audience in the Amphion Theatre, Brooklyn, made an impressive appeal at the Conference of Catholic Charities, and closed this strenuous work with a splendid lecture before a magnificent audience composed of the Catholic Library Association and their friends, on the eve of his sailing. Altogether, by actual count, he spoke to 50,000 people in his 57 appearances."

3 "Words fail, speech is inadequate, for any just or complete appreciation of your labors here," said the spokesman for the parish, overcome with emotion. ". . . It has been duty, duty, duty with you all the time-- unrelemittingly, with zest of spirit, with vigor--such vigor of mind and body, such deep abiding fervor of heart and soul--showing us vividly, in yourself, the effects of the cultivation of the interior life--helping us to battle through 'those times in between'--why my dear Monsignor, you have given our lives an epoch! We have been at your hands re-baptised, confirmed again and again, in our faith; while you have sent us to the Holy Table, with renewed and more vibrant comprehension; it has been wondrous!" Hugh's 1912 essay on impressions of America is printed in the Appendix (3), below, pp. 205-209.

4 In the summer McMahon was to be Hugh's guest briefly at Hare Street House. It was through Hugh that Basil Maturin, at that time chaplain to the Catholic undergraduates of Oxford, became known to Father McMahon. In May 1915 after preaching the Lent at Our Lady of Lourdes, Maturin sailed for home aboard the *Lusitania* and perished when the ship went down. He was 69. A paycheck from Our Lady of Lourdes was found in his pocket and returned to Father McMahon.

14
Among Priests

"With the clergy as a whole--I mean the Catholic clergy--Robert Hugh Benson was not really popular. Of course there were a certain number who really knew him, and if you knew him well you were bound to like him; but with the large body of clergy, who knew of him, and perhaps had met him at public functions, or in some case had got him to come and preach on some great occasion in their churches, the large body who declared loudly that he was a poor novelist, and nevertheless made a point of reading all he wrote, with that great body he was not popular, though he was undoubtedly useful to them." *Father Reginald Watt*

The considerable discomfort felt by other Catholic priests when it came to Hugh Benson had several causes, in part distrust of Anglican converts generally who became Catholic priests, in part envy of the independent life he led. They remembered how he had wasted time in 1903 in Rome and how strings had been pulled on his behalf. That at 33 he was older than most seminarians; had been an ordained priest in the Church of England, had offered Mass and heard confessions and clearly did not need the classroom routine required of beginners meant little to them. Except for one or two fellow Englishmen like Father Vincent McNabb whom he had met at Woodchester Priory, and a few Americans, he did little fraternizing with other priests and so they did not get to know him.[1] Shy with strangers, Hugh wished not to call attention to himself, but he did precisely that day after day walking alone to the 8 o'clock lecture rather than *in camarata*, looking a little disheveled, his arms laden with books; so deficient in Latin that his responses brought laughter from the class. With the help of a private tutor, he got through Moral Theology, but just barely, so that a year's further study was made a condition of being granted faculties to preach or hear confessions.

Socially, as the son of an Anglican Archbishop he was courted by well-to-do English and American converts. At the same time, his upbringing, his tastes, the Eton and Cambridge education and everything that went with it isolated him from other English-speaking priests in Rome, most of them Irish.

It was Father Martindale, Hugh Benson's biographer, who re-ignited resentment smoldering since the Rome days when he printed Hugh's letters to Mary--letters obviously never meant to be made public-- disparaging Catholic priests generally and Irish priests particularly. A formal dinner for a few priests, in every way a dignified affair, was exaggerated as a Bacchanalian feast: "We have had a huge dinner party as usual again today--12.45-3 p.m.!--more wearisome than once could believed possible, with about eight courses and a great deal too much to drink, and a quantity of tiresome people. I beguiled it by doing conjuring tricks to Scotch and Irish respectively, and asking a lot of riddles about two trains, and 'that man's father is my father's son.' And I had positively to write out the whole thing and draw a portrait in a gilt frame before the Irishman could see it" (*Letter*, Feb. 1904). This vignette and others like it, related when he was fresh out of an Anglican household, irritated many priests, already distrustful of converts. What Martindale's motive was in printing the offending letter at all, particularly as it (and others) was addressed to his mother at a moment in his life when he had just crossed over from Anglicanism to Catholicism, and why he introduced them with a little preface about Hugh's "displeasing portraitures of priests, his relentless ridicule of ecclesiastical art and jargon and mannerisms . . ." (M, I, 287) are open to question, but the upshot was that Hugh's comments were remembered against him by other priests for years after his death.

Too much was made of Irishness. A single passage in *By What Authority?* in which drowned bodies are despoiled by "Irish savages" was seized upon and broadcast as insulting to the Irish while very many remarks praising Irish faith and Irish hospitality were ignored. Now, Hugh was English through and through, with an English soul and definite ideas about governing Ireland, which did not include Home Rule, and for this too he was reproached. Politics aside, he liked the Irish and they liked him. Later when his name could summon 4,000 together in a church in Dublin or Cork on a single day, Ireland was unquestionably his favorite place to preach and to visit--the air throbbed with grace and faith. In *The Dawn of All*, Ireland is the center of European contemplative life.

Priests were divided in their opinion. Many a teacher, priest and catechist dipped into his books repeatedly although the circles Hugh's characters perambulated were seldom those visited by Catholics. On the surface priests lauded his success in advancing the Faith, but many did not like him. They remembered against him how Catholic clergy in *Lord of the World* had saved their skins by deserting the Church, and how Protestants had gloated that the internal machinery disclosed by Benson in that novel had brought discredit to the Roman Church.[2] They were weary of the adulation piled upon this priest who had lived very comfortably and independently outside of a parish. He seemed always to be on his own, doing what he liked, making lots of money, and not in the least interested in them or their tribulations. His early Rome letters printed by Martindale rekindled the bitterness felt by other priests who had not come to their vocation so romantically.

At first he criticized the seminary system for producing stupid priests- "they are hopeless"--but certainly held a different view later on when he wrote *Papers of a Pariah*: "Yes, yes; the Catholic Church is amazingly adroit; she has managed to produce grapes from thorns and figs from thistles, and men of the world from seminaries. I have not an idea how she does it, unless her own explanation of it is true--which is that the knowledge of God is the short cut to knowledge of man, that time spent in prayer is the most economical investment of a working hour, and that meditation on supernatural mysteries and familiarity with supernatural thing confer an insight into ordinary affairs of common life that can be obtained in no other way."[3]

Tactlessness plunged him into indiscretions. On the larger scale were the two futuristic novels. In Rome in 1913 he let slip that while in New York he was never once asked to dinner by the Archbishop. Eyebrows went up at the impudence of a young priest expecting to be handed such an invitation. The fact was, Father McMahon had written to Archbishop Farley informing him that the eminent priest who had done such remarkable work to advance the Catholic cause had arrived from England, fully expecting that a meeting could be arranged. It was not, and Hugh went unnoticed officially.[4] The snub embarrassed McMahon, and Hugh obviously had not forgotten it. Mentioning it to other priests irritated them all the more.

But the worst wound to his *confrères* was in the way Hugh presented the Catholic priest in his novels. "Almost invariably he is a man devoid of culture, lacking any spiritual insight, incapable of understanding or guiding any spiritual development in the souls he meets."[5] In *The Conventionalists* he is powerless to help Algy solve his problem. Wise Chris Dell (who has graduated from Mr. Rolls's course of spiritual cleansing) is the one consulted by troubled souls while the priest stands around mumbling into his breviary. At least he is doing no harm. In *The Winnowing*, it is the Mother Superior of a nunnery who imparts the wisdom, not the well-meaning but amateurish

priest. Who could be more unappealing than the Benedictine chaplain
of *The Sentimentalists*, "a little prim brown old man like a clerical
monkey"? or Father Mahon of *The Necromancers*--sympathetic and
helpful but not very intelligent--dismissing the palpable threat from
the malevolent force though he as priest has the power to defeat it.
Attractive priests are to be found here and there, but they are either
monks like Father Hilary in *An Average Man*, or Jesuits who are better
educated. Above them all rises the sublime hermit-mystic Richard
Raynal, hardly your typical priest. Of secular priests, only Father
Maple of *The Coward* comes off as a wise and patient counselor
restoring Val Medd's character in the eyes of his family after he has
died in a fire. Father Denny in *Loneliness*, a man resembling Hugh in
physical appearance, is presented as timid and tactless. The worst of the
lot is the entrenched Father Richardson of *Initiation*, tactless and smug,
wholly missing the point of our hero's suffering. And if an Anglican
clergyman is anywhere in the vicinity, the contrast is unmistakable.
Education, tact, breeding, charm--all these qualities mark the Anglican
clergyman, and all the clumsiness is in the Catholic priest. Lost was
Hugh's subtle point that while Anglicans certainly have the corner on
the rules of etiquette, they are helpless in a spiritual crisis.
    Now these are social differences the reader might overlook, but a
priest would not be likely to overlook them. They gave offense. Hugh
argued in his defense that every priest or nun need not be painted as a
model of perfection; the strength of Catholicism is its doctrine, not
personalities. It is the Church herself that is infallible because divine,
however imperfect her children may seem on occasion. The Faith is
greater than the individual priest.
    Why didn't he treat the priest in his books with common decency?
asked Father Conry in an article that appeared after his death. "To him
the priest was always an unshaven creature who could not appear in
polite society without making a fool of himself," while Anglican
clergy were presented invariably as well-bred, well-educated gentlemen.
Yet had he not always been treated with kindness and hospitality by all?
    Here was the son of an Archbishop of Canterbury hurried through
theological training, hurried into Holy Orders and permitted to live an
independent life writing books that portrayed other priests as ineffective
clods, doctrinally correct but often clumsy and smelling of tobacco and
wine. Furthermore, it had got around that many who had suffered a
slight from another priest came to him for relief, and then, properly
comforted, went off to do what duties were expected of them, soothed
and reconciled. This situation created a wall between Hugh and other
priests that was bound to become unbreachable without a genuine effort

on his part. Hugh was shy by nature, not mean or indifferent, and it would have taken a supreme effort for him to deal personally with those who disliked or distrusted him, assuming, that is, he saw the need and had the means. At all events, nothing was done. Life as he was living it was richly satisfying; he was sought after and by so many that the resentment felt by other priests went unnoticed, until the matter of promotion became an issue. It was only after intense lobbying in Rome of his good friend Father Dolan that he was named papal chamberlain in 1911. That, though people in high places were bitterly opposed to him, particularly Archbishop (now Cardinal) Bourne, who had never liked him.[6]

Priests who had spent a lifetime laboring in the Lord's vineyard resented public adulation that amounted to cultism, and they resented the hollow elitism depicted in his books in which he seemed to take such pleasure and was living out to some extent at Hare Street House. It was no secret that however good he was a spiritual director of men and women of all classes, socially he preferred the company of people of breeding and culture. He traveled with them on holiday, or was a guest in their country manors. Many priests held that Hugh ought not waste his time on modern novels when his duty lay with lifting the prejudice of the English towards Catholics, best done by revealing the brutal methods of Protestant reformers. And besides, in the historical novels priests were courageous and self-sacrificing, while the modern novels generally depicted priests in an unflattering light. The reason he left off writing historical novels, they concluded, was that modern novels, thrown together faster, made more money. There was some truth in that.

How much money was rolling into Hare Street coffers was often a topic of conversation at home and abroad. Arthur's frustration with Hugh's apparent love of money was echoed by others. They saw it in his ragged attire and felt it in his penny-pinching. It was no secret Hugh liked money, and other priests were scandalized by his stinginess, and complained how hard it was to get money out of him for any cause.[7] Yet his new religion provided him with a river of money that showed no sign of drying up. He possessed a positive genius for profitable self-promotion, it was claimed. In New York in 1914, he wore himself out running to engagements (on one occasion five in a day, with long distances to be covered between each engagement); for his Lenten course at Our Lady of Lourdes Church, a leaflet with a list of booksellers carrying his books was given out with advice that all parishioners should familiarize themselves with his printed sermons beforehand. It was all quite business-like, and he made money. Of course those disposed against him had no way of knowing about gifts made quietly through Elizabeth Baker or his support of homes for destitute boys in Southeast London or other projects like endowing the livings of Anglican clergy wishing to convert but fearful of losing their livings. A disturbing story he had heard in Rome was of such a man who was unable to find work. Such a fate befalling Mr. Main, the suffering servant in *An Average Man*, shows that problems of Catholic converts from Anglicanism whom nobody wanted was much on his mind. Still, the ugly suspicion that the Church was being used for profit continued to simmer, rooted as it was in genuine consternation or genuine envy. Either way, Hugh had got under their skin.

Notes

[1] They collaborated in the Motor Missions in 1912. Father McNabb wrote an honest, unsentimental tribute upon his death for Chesterton's Distributive journal *The New Witness*.

[2] In a review of Martindale's biography in *The British Weekly* (May 25, 1916), p. 151, "Claudius Clear" reminded readers that [Fabian] Sir Oliver Lodge thought *Lord of the World* was written "with great ability and singular internal knowledge, to bring discredit upon the general outlook of the Roman Church." The reviewer was at pains to point out that Hugh was of the stuff of which Romans are made. He had supported Loisy until the abbot was condemned, after which Hugh ceased to think of him.

[3] *Papers of a Pariah* (London, 1907), p. 51.

[4] Father McMahon asked that Hugh be granted faculties to preach, adding that in Rome the previous year crowds had to be turned away. Besides the spiritual advantage of his coming, McMahon cited the financial profitability, which alone was good reason for having him back. "I need not point out the distinction achieved by Mgr. Benson in his own diocese. At his recent lecture on Modern Religious Problems, His Grace the Duke of Norfolk, England's leading layman presided." In his reply, Cardinal Farley explained rather testily the reason the diocese reserved the right to grant faculties to visiting preachers was not to discourage the practice, but to prevent incursions of Modernism.

[5] Father James P. Conry's "Benson in Rome," *Ecclesiastical Review*, 58 (March 1918), pp. 274-89. For a spirited rebuttal see Father Reginald Watt, *ER*, 59 (Sept. 1918), pp. 265-74.

[6] The office of papal chamberlain was an honorific that brought along the title of monsignor. He and Father Watt joked once in a while about his becoming a bishop some day, but when Hugh returned to the subject days later, it had become a real possibility in his mind.

[7] "I recognise in myself one grave vice--avarice; and I have been giving it several shrewd slaps this morning by signing large cheques" (M, II, 123-4). One of these checks went to Arthur for Maggie's hospitalization.

15
The Final Chapter

"Not often did he give his heart away; he admired greatly, he
sympathised freely; but I never saw him desolated or stricken by any
bereavement or loss. I used to think sometimes that he never needed
anyone. I never saw him exhibit the smallest trace of jealousy, nor did
he ever try to possess anyone's entire affection. He recognised any
sign of affection generously and eagerly; but he never claimed to keep
it exclusively as his own." *Hugh*

By 1913 Hare Street House was firmly stamped, Hugh Benson all
over. He had been living there since June of 1908, and in those five
years made good use of every moment. His engagement book was
filled for months and months to come, and he was making money, but
at the cost to himself of days and weeks spent away from home and
immeasurable strain on his nerves. More than once in these last years,
in moments of deep fatigue Hugh admitted that he wished to be out of
it all. He was tired--not on top, but deep down inside. Even on top,
signs of decay were showing. Until 1912 he had enjoyed good health.
He was strong, vigorous, with a sound heart and indefatigable body.
There had been painful bouts with neuralgia, the usual flattening colds,
but beyond that nothing serious. He was operated on after a bad attack
(probably hernia) during Midnight Mass at Christmas, and spent a
month in a nursing home recovering. It all seemed routine, with Hugh
in very good spirits. Yet something indefinable was happening--middle
age that seemed before to have passed him by was now rushing in upon
him: perceptible changes in the face, bowing of the shoulders, a slower
step. The operation had been a complete success, and the month's
convalescence in the nursing home provided him with material for his

next novel *Initiation*), but he was never quite the same after it--so everyone said after his death. It was the beginning of the end.

By June of 1912 Father Reginald Watt had come to Hare Street to assist him and to look for a site for the new Buntingford church, which thanks to Hugh's Motor Mission work, was now becoming a reality.[1] Hare Street House was running smoothly, to his delight. There were always major expenses to be met, but his continued popularity as a preacher and a writer was proof against financial worries for a long time to come. Visiting Hare Street in August, two months before Hugh's collapse, Arthur lunched contentedly in the shade of the yew trees in the garden walk, near the chapel, drinking golden wine made from Hugh's own vines, thinking the whole place "now beautifully laid out and kept, full of flowers and paved walks. . . The house enormously improved-- fine panelling up everywhere and the whole thing much more dignified and interesting. Curious books everywhere, much of my old furniture recognisable. . . . It was nice to see the whole place so well kept and beautiful and to feel Hugh's enjoyment of it" (*Diary*, Aug. 13, 1914).

But for the last two years or so of Hugh's life dangerous signs were mounting. Eccentric habits became more pronounced. There was not a moment when a cigarette was not between his fingers and his head not afloat in a cloud of smoke. He tried several times to give them up, and gave them up at last but too late to do any good. He prescribed a water-cure for himself consisting of drinking gallons of water daily, and not only water, but hard liquor as well to calm the nerves--with the result that he sometimes fell asleep, drunk or nearly so. Always, nerves and a nervous system demanding more work lured him on. Friend Maria Storer cautioned that he suffered hideously from "nerves, sleeplessness, and the other signs of masculine hysteria." Preach or write, she insisted, one or the other, before his "headlong prancings" brought on total collapse.[2] There was talk of Hugh's tireless driving of the engine, but he insisted that he must be allowed to live his life in his own way. It was better to burn out than rust out.

Change was not physical alone, but mental as well. He became convinced there was no creative act beyond his capacities. Just as he had set his heart on becoming a playwright, so he suddenly set his mind on mastering the piano. All his life Hugh had played piano and organ by ear; now he wished to make a systematic study of musicianship. He learned enough from a friend Franz Liebich to rescore church music for his choir and composed a litany for Sunday which he banged out from the little organ loft of his chapel. A newly bought but-not-new Beckstein grand drove him on to the heights. "Now, listen to this, then tell me if you don't think I really am getting on," he said eagerly to a visitor, settling him into the armchair. On he would go at the piano until he hit an intricate passage, then he would "attack again and again--each attack more rapid and furious than the last; until his patience becoming exhausted he would roar out, "Oh! oh! oh!" and bring both fists crashing down on the unoffending piano, pummelling the keyboard, crying out he was hopeless and would never be able to do it."[3] A few days later after hours of practice, the passage was conquered.

His artistic powers were becoming an obsession--as if there were nothing he could not write, no idea he could not build an edifice upon. Galloping through his head came pieces of plot, ideas, phrases that kept invading his work, his thoughts, interfering even with his Mass. A kind of artistic hysteria had taken hold of him, with inevitable danger to the nerves and heart. Outbursts of temper already severe became more frequent. Lately he was forgetting appointments, joking to a reporter in Chicago that after having been invited to meet H. G. Wells at Cambridge, "I entered the wrong house at the wrong hour!" Unhappily, it was a harbinger of things to come, but such signs had been building for at least a year. Very tired and looking ill, he went off to Rome to preach the Lent following his surgery, and spent his spare time in his room in front of a heater wrapped in blankets, and when he preached spoke for the first time in his life from a chair in the pulpit--twenty-two sermons in ten days that left him drained and exhausted.

Signs that his nerves were under attack were becoming all too apparent. In Rome he complained at table about stingy breakfasts when in fact his plate was full. And there was the excruciating incident of the honey. A jar of honey had been given him to use at breakfast, and one morning when Hugh went into the refectory to get it, he found the jar empty. What had become of the honey! Who had eaten the honey! He became furious, inconsolable, while other priests looked on and wondered. Inquiries were made, but the culprits (probably two servant boys who had helped themselves) escaped. Causing a scene about ten cents worth of honey was dismissed at the time as a childish tantrum (Hugh's notorious temper was no secret), but it was another signal, a rather sad one, of coming collapse.[4]

Perhaps the strangest of Hugh's acts this last year of his life, the one underscoring the broken state of his nerves, were the precautions he took against premature burial. His reading of macabre tales, specifically (in Fred's opinion) Rolfe's tale "How I Was Buried Alive," convinced him of the need to take steps to prevent it should he die suddenly. In 1912 he wrote out elaborate instructions for the handling of his body after death, asking that his grave should be "a little brick chamber, accessible from outside, with steps leading down to it, closed by an iron door, which can be opened from the inside; that the coffin

AT TREMANS, 1913

A.C. Benson   Hugh   E.F. Benson

ROBERT HUGH BENSON, SEPTEMBER 1914

should be placed in a loculus in a shelf on one side, which could be forced from within; that the coffin should be lightly made, so that in the event of my being buried alive, I could escape, and that a key should be placed in the coffin. After one month, I should wish all this to be sealed and closed." If this arrangement was impossible, then an artery in his arm was to be opened "in such a way that death would not be caused if I were alive (since that would be suicide), but that if life were still in me, the fact would be unmistakable." "I *entreat* this," he wrote.[5] In the end death came so swiftly and unexpectedly there was no time to carry out his wishes for such a vault, which would have taken a month to build, but at least Arthur as executor could see to the opening of the artery, done the evening of the day following his death, as Hugh requested.

From 1912 Mary's letters had sounded the panic and he promised to put on less fuel. It was an empty promise, however.[6] In Lent in New York he gave 60 talks in 50 days, preaching hard as many as five times in a day, traveling great distances between sermons. A fever of 104° and a grippe slowed but never stopped him. To those annoying friends at home worried about the dangerous pace, he said firmly, "It is better so: I know myself: it is better to let me lead my life as I know it." Sustained by an odd theory that sounds like medicine from St. Lydwine's pharmacopoeia, he believed best work was done in a state of unhealth.

This was 1914, a fatal year. He had spoken out forcefully on the subject of the imminent war, and in August, when the conflagration began Hugh, although terrified that he would be sent to the Front, nevertheless offered to serve as military chaplain to the Forces, fully expecting to be called up. Father John Ayscough, another popular contemporary Catholic novelist, was already in Belgium. Word of German atrocities, photographs of ruined cathedrals, ruined cities, villages pillaged and wiped out, Belgium in flames, horrified and bewildered him--all the evils coming swiftly, apocalyptically, upon the death of Pope Pius X that summer. Every day the newspapers carried long lists of the English dead. Five out of eight friends of his had been wounded. Before England entered he fretted that she would disgrace herself by standing pat, and now that England was in, he expected to hear any day that Germany was done for, and lived in terror of being called up until that day came. Turned down--with thanks--on health grounds, his feelings were of mixed relief and guilt. It was unthinkable to do nothing while sending other young men off to die. If he was unfit to serve one way, he would serve in another. From that moment he threw himself into the war effort, writing articles and writing letters of encouragement, sponsoring benefits on behalf of Belgian refugees, and composing a patriotic playlet for Belgian war relief that he never lived to see produced. For armed forces use he put together *Vexilla Regis*, a book of devotions for each day of the week, but died before seeing the proofs. An outline of a war novel, its hero a priest, was found among his effects. Then came a brainstorm to use his name and influence to make the British case known to isolationist Americans. Who can say that this most admired of English priests might not have changed American opinion?[7]

Breathlessness and pains in the arms and chest continued to plague him. His physician Todd diagnosed the condition as false angina, a form of neuralgia, and insisted that Hugh cancel his engagements to Christmas, which he agreed to do. At the same time he took up Arthur's invitation to come to Cambridge for a couple of months to rest and do whatever he pleased, or do nothing. "There, that's what I call a real invitation--that is what I shall do," he told Reeman. But first, he asked Todd if he might meet engagements scheduled over the next few weeks. One engagement especially, in Salford where he had preached many times before, was a favorite of his and he wished not to disappoint the bishop. Hugh was a poor patient, with a low threshold of pain and an excitable nature; to avoid alarming him, his doctor agreed reluctantly.

In September he left Hare Street to spend a week with the monks of Caldey Island, commenting sadly to Reeman as he climbed into the dog-cart that the leaves would all have fallen from the trees before he returned. Remarkably, in the crisp Caldey air he recovered his vigor, ate with the monks, bathed in the sea, and, inspired by the setting, pondered his Catholic colony of artists and contemplatives, and whether the nearby island of St. Margaret reachable from Caldey at low tide was just the ideal place for his own idyllic Little Gidding.[8] He was on the surface his old charming self, entertaining the monks with ghost stories, but extreme restlessness of chronic neurasthenia was evident-- eyes darting here and there, a lot of trembling, little bursts of laughter. His brain was too busy, too easily stimulated into turbulence. "He could not for a moment cease from constructing plots, and working out new novels; even at Mass their ingenious developments would harass him. His anxiety raced onwards, at times into panic. He believed himself the victim of obsession. . . . It is enough to say that the spectre of acute neurasthenia began to haunt him, and to recall, more threatening than ever, the conviction that his collapse would be soon, sudden, and complete" (M, II, 426).

From Caldey he went to Westmoreland, where Arthur was staying with Archie Marshall and his family. The final days at Caldey had left him refreshed and happy, and except for breathlessness still plaguing him, he seemed fit again. He painted, and stomped about in woods and streams until forced to turn back because of chest pain.[9] Hugh informed Canon Sharrock at one point that he was unwell, but in a second letter announced that, having been declared fit to undertake the mission, he was coming after all. "Here I am," he wrote a worried friend from Ulverstone. "But I'm not up to much, and with 'False Angina,' and no smoking allowed, and exercise impossible because of instant pain" and a series of lectures still facing him. "I feel terribly ill," he confided, "but I'm told that's all part of the 'falseness' of the Angina," and it all seemed terribly plausible to him and the "falseness" of it mildly comforting (M, II, p. 429).

Now, after the few years of country houses and country pleasures, it was fitting that Hugh's last work on earth should be in a parish made up mostly of poor Irish.

At Ulverstone a public hall had been booked for Monday's lecture, and from Tuesday to Friday evening Hugh spoke from the pulpit as usual, showing no signs of ill health. All of Wednesday night, however, he had been kept awake with pains so acute he cried aloud several times; but by Thursday evening he was himself again, a lively dinner guest, entertaining everybody with his good humor and stories. With another priest he visited the nearby shipyard to see a battleship ready for launching, although he needed to stop to rest several times. Feeling better on Friday, he saw a few callers, and made ready to depart for Salford the next morning after spending a quiet night. As he waited for the cab, he was asked by a young maid-servant for his autograph, and wrote in her album, "*Jhesu, Jhesu, esto michi Jhesu!*"--Campion's last words on the scaffold--and as it turned out the last inscription Hugh Benson wrote on earth.

Back at Salford on Saturday he was met at the station by Canon Sharrock who was struck at once by his changed condition.[10] Moving very slowly and stopping every few seconds to inhale deep breaths--the stairs were a terrible challenge for him--Hugh repeatedly assured him that his doctor had diagnosed the pain as "false angina," very painful indeed, but had pronounced his heart sound. Sharrock pleaded with him to give up his work for the month of October. It was futile. On Sunday evening, October 11th, he preached quietly in a low voice and without the familiar gestures, and went to bed early hoping to make up for a week's lost sleep. "After an awful night of pain and great restlessness," Canon Sharrock recalled, "he decided to leave for London on Monday, October 12th, by the early morning train. We had not gone many yards towards the station when he bade me stop the taxi, and drive to the nearest doctor, as he could bear the pain no longer. With great difficulty I got him back to the house, and sent for the nearest doctor, who came immediately." That very day Hugh informed the rector at Bury, Lancashire (where his next engagement was scheduled) that his condition had been diagnosed as an abnormal state of heart nerves brought on by overwork and that the doctor had absolutely forbidden him to preach: "I don't know how to express my regrets. But--there it is! I can't even walk upstairs now--more than three steps at a time! So please try to forgive me."

On the Monday afternoon he felt well enough to go to a "picture-palace" and enjoyed himself. On Tuesday he went to the picture-palace again but this time felt exhausted after it. That night excruciating pain returned and continued all Tuesday without stop and into Tuesday night and Wednesday morning. On Wednesday night he had a very bad attack of pain. Father Gorman found Hugh in pajamas in anguish, his chest and arms shot through with pain. "He tried to make him go to bed, but he would not, nor would he put anything on, though he was streaming with sweat. He roamed about the room and corridors, Gorman with him--he even went out into the court. He leaned for nearly two hours on the mantelpiece. Gorman could do nothing with him at all. At last it subsided and he went to bed." Too late, for Hugh already weak and sinking had caught a chill that brought on pneumonia. Not until Wednesday noon did the pain relent. Hugh hoped to recover his strength with sleep, but even this was denied him, as sleep was broken by acute restlessness. By this time two physicians, the local physician and a specialist, were in continual attendance. On Thursday congestion of the right lung began to show itself, and by Thursday night both lungs were involved--bronchial pneumonia had set in, painful and exhausting, but not necessarily life-threatening. In fact, everyone expected Hugh's "splendid vitality" to see him through--so they said to keep up his spirits, and theirs. Where was the strength to put up a good fight to come from?

Real danger became evident on Friday; and on Saturday as a precaution, he received Last Rites and calmly made his profession of Faith. Sunday morning saw a change after a restless night which had tried the endurance of both doctor and nurse. He was a difficult patient, very excitable, very impatient of pain, very restless, had hardly slept at all, wanted to smoke, always insisting the doctors try different medicines. During the night he got up and paced back and forth on bare feet, unable to lie down, unable to stand without support. Sweating profusely he went out into the Court to escape the heat. He would not listen to pleas to come in out of the night air. They got his coat on but he was so hot he could not bear it. In this weakened condition, the pneumonia worsened. On Sunday morning, when it was clear he was fading, Hugh received Viaticum, making all the responses, even correcting Canon Sharrock when at the *Misereatur* the good man was overcome with emotion. Hugh informed Sharrock that he would be quite well by Tuesday, "though this hard breathing is a terrible bore." Yet had he not lived his life in a state of breathlessness as if preparing for this death?

On Saturday evening Arthur found a wire from Canon Sharrock to say Hugh was dangerously ill of pneumonia. He wired Sharrock for news and asked if he should come, but Sharrock in a return wire said that Hugh was better. He determined to go anyway. "I got to town very late, took a train that crawled, but there was time enough, and . . . I had however a feeling which was very strong that Hugh would get through." Arthur stayed the night at a hotel, and reached Hugh's bed early Sunday morning to find him exhausted, but somewhat improved from the previous night. His mental faculties were as keen as ever, his strength appeared good, but the terrible strain on the heart from the pneumonia was severe.

Arthur's moving account of Hugh's last hours speak not only to his tenderness and strength but confirm the deep affection binding the two brothers: "I went in to see him--his voice was strong when he said 'come in'. He was in the bishop's study, a big room full of books . . . He was propped up in bed with back to the light. He looked very much himself. I simply said I felt anxious and wanted to see how he was." (Many people gathering about his bed would certainly alarm him.) "He seemed pleased, said he was much better and added that I should be able to return tomorrow. His throat was painful and he had a constant hard little cough and they told him not to talk." Hugh asked about Maggie and if she had consented to the operation, then raised the question of his will which he did not think was legally drawn. Arthur assured him that at all events his wishes were known and would be carried out. "He smiled and said 'Oh, it's only a precaution. I don't feel like dying at all. I feel every so much stronger today. I am not going to die.'" The legality of the will came up again, and Arthur assured him again that he knew that Hugh wished to leave Hare Street as a house for the Abbot of Westminister and that he entirely approved. That satisfied him. They talked on a little and Hugh laughed at Arthur's stories about his friend Percy Lubbock and with characteristic generosity brushed off a vicious remark made about him by the Bishop of Calcutta. As Hugh needed to rest, Arthur left, took breakfast, and returned at one o'clock to find Hugh cheerful. "You'll be able to go back tomorrow," he said, but Arthur saw that he was uncomfortable and seemed anxious. "I told him some stories and he said 'Delightful!' once or twice as in his old way. He was polite as he always was, and said he was sorry I had the trouble of coming. . ." Then Canon Sharrock came in "a strong sanguine man, a very fine fellow full of kindness and tenderness. 'Now, monsignor' he said, 'You must not talk--be content to listen.' Hugh ate a baked apple, but with much difficulty. I went out with Sharrock and had a talk in the front room. There was an oxygen cylinder on the table." Sharrock explained everything, how he had preached on Sunday last, nearly fell when leaving the pulpit, and had much pain and breathlessness; how he had been forced to come back after starting out for the station.

A little later Arthur returned to Hugh's room and found him "very faint and collapsed. I gave him a little whiskey which was on the table and he revived a little. The doctor came and I could see he was anxious. He gave him some drug, and then oxygen--it was some time before it would work. I was there for nearly two hours. Hugh hardly spoke except to ask them to try something, and he could not get a breath. It was very dreadful to be so helpless. At last the breathlessness went off and he settled down, saying to me 'What bliss!' The doctor took me away, and said I had better move my things down to the house. 'I don't like the look of things at all,' he said, 'and your place is here. Don't disturb him. He is sleeping now.' The old man spoke very feelingly and affectedly about him and said that he himself was quite ill with the anxiety. 'It's touch-and-go," he said, 'he has much vitality, but he is worn out.' 'By what?' I said. 'By pain,' he said, 'and by his incessant work.'

At dinner Father Gorman and Canon Sharrock tried to keep his spirits up, but Arthur had already abandoned hope. "The doctor came at 10 and I just looked in to see Hugh. He was dozing, but woke, smiled and gave me a little nod. Sharrock said I should be called at once if he was worse. I went to bed [in the adjoining room] but did not sleep, tired as I was. At last when the house was quiet I heard the priests going to their rooms." At one o'clock Canon Sharrock was summoned by the nurse at Hugh's request and knew as he entered the room that the end was near. Hugh told him so himself with the words, 'God's will be done.' He asked, 'Is my brother near?' 'Yes, he is in the house.' 'Thank God' said Hugh. 'Tell him to come at once!' . . . Sharrock came along the passage, looked in, and said 'Mr. Benson, you must come down at once--don't delay--he is sinking.' I put on some things in a strange dream-like way. I found a nurse. We went straight through the dark throne-room. I went in. Hugh was sitting up in bed--a chair had been placed beside him on the bed, with a cushion, so that he could lean upon it. He was pale, and breathing very fast--he did not seem in pain. He hardly coughed at all. When I came in he fixed his eyes on me, and said 'This is the end!' Sharrock was there with a red stole over his coat and a book . . . the nurse was wiping Hugh's brow and cheek." Arthur knelt down near the bed as Sharrock began to read prayers for the dying. Once when the canon paused Hugh urged him in God's name to go on. Hugh gave the responses, crossed himself once or twice very faintly. "'One moment!' he said to the canon "and to me--'My love to them all!' The big room was brightly lit, and something boiled over on the hearth. The nurse went to the fireplace and returned. Once Hugh said 'Make certain I am dead.' Then he said to the nurse 'Is it any good resisting . . . making an effort?' She said quietly, 'No, monsignor, it is no good.' He closed his eyes after this, and his breath came quicker. Then he opened his eyes and seeing I was looking at him he said softly 'Don't look at me Arthur' and to the nurse 'Stand between me and him.' The nurse moved and I saw his face no longer." At one point he commended his soul to God. "Jesus, Mary and Joseph, I give you my heart and my soul." Sharrock went on with his prayers. "Twice Hugh drew up his hands to his chest--but there was no struggle. I heard him moan a little very faintly, but more like one who was tired out than in pain--and the nurse kept feeling his pulse. I heard his breath no longer, and she said 'It is over.' Then I saw his face, fallen forward, the underlip dropped, very pale and helpless, but looking very young. The nurse laid his head back on the pillow. I kissed his hand which was warm and firm, shook the nurse's hand and went out with Sharrock. He said, 'Mr. Benson, it was wonderful. I have seen many people die, and never anyone so easily and quietly.'"

At 1:30 A.M. on Monday morning Hugh Benson died, his eyes fixed on the priest. It was just as if he had gone to sleep.

So Hugh was gone. If ever Arthur was touched by Hugh's kindness and chivalry, it was at this moment when his last thought had been to spare his brother the pain of seeing him die. At the end Hugh had been "so brave, so thoughtful, it was if he had but turned a corner, had opened a door and was going in." It was not so much a death as a departure, for there was no humiliation, "and so little suffering that I thought that if it had not been the end, how he would have discussed it with pleasure afterward, not as a thing too hard to be spoken of, but as an adventure. 'My word, it was awful!' he would have said with a laugh. It seemed to me a simple and natural thing to die. I did not feel I had lost him--or at any rate that he was *there*. I slept calmly and with no horror or misery at awakening" (*Diary*, Oct. 19, 1914).

When Mary and Lucy arrived at Salford the next morning they were brought into the bishop's study where Hugh had died. He had been dressed by then in cassock and biretta, and had his rosary in his fingers. He looked very young and very like himself--no trace of suffering, and a little smile, as if asleep. To avoid throngs of mourners it was decided that the body should depart by the midnight train, but first the doctor was asked to open an artery to make sure he was dead, in accordance with Hugh's own directions. "I *entreat* this" Hugh had begged, and so it was done.

On Thursday Arthur motored to Hare Street. A lot of people were there--Father Morgan, "a nice Trinity man" who would be rector of the new Buntingford Church, Father Reginald Watt, now a chaplain in the army, Mrs. Hogge, Hugh's tenant who had been present when he wrote out his will, along with many others. The coffin had been put in the chapel, and candles around it. Arthur was overwhelmed: "It was pathetic to see the house and garden, all so carefully designed and just finished. He had never seen the new rose garden--and all so full of little signs of his ingenuity. Fred came down full of good nature. He had found the will with its seal broken and an unfinished letter in it in an open portfolio in the table. I looked at a few papers. They had begun to dig the grave in the tangled grass of the orchard and golden leaves were falling everywhere. Reeman, Hugh's man, and Margaret, the pretty girl housekeeper . . . The intense attachment to Hugh among all these people is wonderful. He was somehow very lonely with it all. He charmed people, but he did not need them--I don't think he needed anyone--and he kept all his friends separate."

Arthur claimed correctly to know him better than any other living soul. "But one must not be sentimental--he would have hated that. In fact, at his deathbed, I felt how he would have loathed it if I had been emotional or tearful or kissed his hand or done anything of the sort--he didn't like to be touched. And about this house, I am sorry he did not enjoy it longer, but it all meant an immense happiness to him of a very vivid kind."

On the night Hugh died the Bishop of Menevia, sleeping on the bed Hugh had recently occupied in the monastery of Caldey, dreamed of his death.[11]

The zeal of thy house has eaten me up.

Notes

[1] At his death the new church (for a long time informally called the Benson Memorial Church) was under construction and about to be hurried along thanks to donations made in Hugh's memory. On the day the first stones were laid, a procession of priests and laity headed by the Bishop marched the two miles from Hare Street to the construction site. There Hugh preached from a wooden platform. Hugh felt an ambivalence towards the new church. As much as he wished for there to be a place of public worship in Buntingford, the church would draw some of its flock from his own Hare Street Chapel. In the early years Buntingford boasted the smallest parish in Hertfordshire, but the Father Benson connection attracted many Catholics to settle there. Within a few years a convent was established.

[2] In 1914 two intellectual problems particularly absorbed him, Spiritism and Lourdes. Put on the trail of French scientist Dr. Alexis Carrel, who diagnosed the miraculous cures as a transference of vitalizing force, Hugh related the Lourdes phenomena to Gospel miracles where faith is the integral element in the cure. While in New York in 1914 he wrote an introduction for a reissue of *Lourdes*, and in June lectured on the subject of "Modern Miracles" at Caxton Hall, G. K. Chesterton presiding.

[3] "Mgr. Benson in Private Life," *The Universe*, October 30 1914, p. 6.

[4] Conry, "Benson in Rome," p. 287.

[5] Martindale, II, pp. 429-21. These instructions were found among Hugh's papers at Hare Street. Fred thought this began with obsession began with Hugh's reading of Rolfe's short story (a tale of pure fiction laid in Renaissance Italy), but Rolfe's tale is pallid fare compared to Poe's tales of premature burial. "Mr. Bosanquet's Tale," one of Hugh's best short stories included in *Mirror of Shalott*, deals with dying and return, or near-death experience. It is an exquisite tale of the strange passage into the Other World at the total expense of the Self. At all events, whatever the influence, it is a sizable leap from reading about being buried alive to taking steps to prevent it at one's own death.

[6] In March of 1911 she had spoken anxiously of her fears that he was running for a fall "NOT of death, but of the enforced rest . . . when things won't work." When the usual warnings went unheeded, appeals became more passionate, calling upon his obligations as a son, as in the letter of March 8, 1912, when, after Dr. Sessions thought he heard an irregular heart beat, she begged him to see a specialist in New York--"what happens to you touches my inmost core Hugh dear, don't break my heart." Again, in a letter of June 22, 1912: "DO modify your work or there will only be about an inch

left in the middle of the candle, and poor stuff at that" and on November 10, 1913: "Dearest, I have had a letter from Arthur and he thinks you're rather <u>overdoing</u> it. O Hugh, please don't (I SAID O Please). Think of your mother, think of your sister, your brothers and your Country, and think of your books which will suffer, and your sermons. I know you won't think about yourself because you have a ridiculous theory that work is better done by in a rather unhealthy condition. Ye gads! O HUGH! Couldn't you please your mother. Try to modify or you'll vanish into blue flame." And on June 3, 1914, she wrote cautiously lest her worry not be construed as meddling: "Dearest: I lay my hand upon my mouth--I wish I could as firmly (and I pray for always) quiet the heartbeats of anxiety at the life you are leading. . . . you need about 48 hours in each day to do half of the program in which you are immersed." Finally, she wrote on August 24: "I hope with all my soul that you are feeling less depressed and my mortal mind desires that if there IS physical over-tiredness, that might be met by physical remedies. Hush! I've done."

7 Apparently American isolationists misunderstood his position. A few days before his death an item appeared in *The Pilot*, diocesan newspaper of Boston, repeating a "special cable" from London giving what it reported were the war views of Archbishop Benson in the archiepiscopal palace of Westminster. American opposition to the war is all over it. "In the purported interview Mgr. Benson, who will smile at being called the Archbishop of Westminster, said it is impossible to imagine any Catholic in the world taking any other side than that of the Allies." To which the writer added that the entire story was about as accurate as the title of "archbishop." The writer was no doubt unaware that a lengthy letter in defense of the English cause in the war had appeared in the latest issue of *America*.

8 Originally Anglican communities, the monks of Caldey and the Benedictine nuns of St. Bride of Malling Abbey (for whom Hugh had a special fondness) had gone over to Rome en masse in 1912. They were part of the wave of conversions that appeared to signal the imminent conversion of England.

9 Arthur noted in his diary for Friday, Oct. 11 that "poor dear Maggie is to be operated upon tomorrow, Saturday, at 10 o'clock--and Hugh is ill and nervous."

10 Events of Hugh's final days are drawn from Arthur C. Benson's *Diary* entries of 17-19 October 1914, and Canon Sharrock's narrative first published in *The Tablet* and reprinted in the posthumous *Poems by Robert Hugh Benson* (London, 1915).

11 "On the Tuesday following, Dr. Mostyn, the Bishop of Menevia, who was travelling at sea from Caldey, said to a fellow-guest, 'I had a dream on Sunday night which told me that Mgr. Benson was dead . . . I remember thinking, in my dream, how happy it was that Mgr. Benson had only just previously made a retreat.'" The other guest was startled: he had heard the

news that Benson was ill, and asked the Bishop if he had known of this. He had not. When they reached the mainland, they walked together to the railway-station bookstall for a newspaper. "On the front page it was announced that Mgr. Benson was dead," the bishop reported. From "In a Dream," subtitled "Distinguished Catholic Learns whilst Asleep of Mgr. Benson's Death," by a Staff Correspondent, The *Universe* (Oct. 23, 1914), p. 5. Martindale repeated the story in the biography, adding that Hugh would have been delighted to make a note of these strange details. Among the mourners at Hare Street was Hugh's good friend Father Edmund Walsh of Liverpool, where Hugh had gone many times to preach. To all who saw him that day Father Walsh appeared overwhelmed with grief. Returning to London from Hare Street, he died that night at the hotel in which he was staying.

16
Reputation

"I take the lowest plane . . . put myself last . . . I embrace all others
with charity . . . I renounce all perishable things . . . all that is not
Thyself . . . all vanity . . . impurity . . . self-seeking . . . I resign
myself to Thy will . . . from lowest depths of my being . . . I pour out
my will into Thine . . . May Thy Will be done in me . . . with me . . .
by me . . . in time and eternity . . . I offer myself . . . ready to
embrace with my will whatever I know to please Thee . . ."

From *Aspirations*

When a man becomes so much a part of a national consciousness that
it refuses to accept that he has died, then inevitably it comes to terms
with the fact of his death by soaking in endless recollections,
memories, dedications. From the instant Hugh's death became known
his name was on everybody's lips; every fact, every gesture and nuance
of a gesture, the complete memorabilia of his identity--started to
collect. Though there were horrific events happening abroad, a World
War in progress and lists of war dead making the papers every morning,
his passing seemed the only thing worth talking about. Over the
coming days and months tears and tributes poured in. So, after being
remembered in countless ways, in newspaper and magazines, in
conversations, in tributes from the pulpit by friends and foes alike, the
public let him go at last.

From Salford his body was taken to Hare Street and there buried in
the orchard on October 23rd, a sad moment stamped into the memory of
the invited guests present that day, family, friends, villagers who knew
him simply as a man who led a holy life and loved children--a crowd of
various people in obvious grief who had been helped by Hugh in
different ways, Arthur noted, remarking on the intense attachment to
him among all these people. The sole invited newspaper correspondent

painted a vignette of the day's events for readers of *The Universe*, describing first the little screen of ancient woodwork separating the sanctuary from the rest of the chapel, where was placed the simple altar at which Hugh had so often celebrated Mass--"Before this altar his coffin lay all Wednesday and Thursday, with chalice, biretta and stole resting upon it. No sign of mourning was there except the black pall that covered him and the unbleached candles that burnt around. The altar, with its fittings of soft dull blue and dim silver, remained as it had been during his life, and the violet curtain before the low tabernacle was the only funeral sign. In the chapel some thirty people gathered for the Requiem. Dr. Driscoll celebrated the Mass in the presence of Cardinal Bourne, who afterwards gave the absolution." Six Westminster Cathedral choirboys rendered the Gregorian plain chant [from the organ loft]. . . . There was no funeral oration. "Slowly, to the sound of *In Paradisum*, Mgr. Benson was carried out from his beautiful chapel, through the garden he loved so well, to the orchard. There the Cardinal blessed the grave, and to the tones of the *Benedictus* the coffin was laid therein. The brief last rites of the Church--so simple and sincere in their noble directness--followed by a few short prayers in English, were then read, loving hands cast flowers upon the coffin, and the Cardinal withdrew, reciting the *De Profundis* with his clergy as he returned to the house."[1] On that day in London a low Requiem Mass was celebrated at Westminster Cathedral, and at St. John's Cathedral, Salford, on the following Monday Bishop Vaughan spoke of him from the pulpit at the solemn Requiem Mass.

What was it Hugh possessed that his death should have wounded so many who never knew him apart from his books and sermons, and what did he leave behind? First, he was a man of amazing versatility, proven in his power to draw great crowds and hold them--none better--so talented an amateur in so many arts, that it is difficult to know where to begin to sum him up satisfactorily. Certainly he was an individualist with many endearing idiosyncrasies and some not at all endearing. Cravings for activity of mind or hands needed to be instantly gratified, and every change of pace, from bird-shooting to piano playing to laying bricks, served as an antidote to restlessness. He giggled, he often played a game of talking through his nose while he worked, mispronouncing words and mimicking the bishop's speech--such silliness that sent him into hysterics. He made his own wine. He was positively gleeful playing at cards and chess with friends. On the other hand, his fierce rages over trifles often hurt those who loved him--his eyes would widen and flash and he would stomp about the room saying cruel things meant to wound. "There! I told you I was a scorpion," he roared, and after a moment's regret offered the most abject apologies.

Unlike his favorite literary mentors, his aestheticism or, more precisely, the fascination for beautiful things and consuming curiosity never became pathological, never crossed the line into obsession. He was a pagan in art only. Even to those friends and family closest to him "he was extremely undemonstrative, and to the end there were only five or six people whom he addressed by their Christian names. Of course he was claimed by crowds as their especial friend and confidant; confidant he never was to anybody, friend, to very many" (M, II, 151). He was unsentimental, dominant, and hard. "Get down beneath all the vices and virtues, to the very heart of things--to that little hard lump called self, and *smash it"* he told one penitent; and to another suffering from drug addiction, "Perhaps you will think you are going to die. Well, then die. I would a thousand times sooner you died of exhaustion and misery, than that you went back to the world uncured" (M, II, 243). God is Love was not to be mistaken as God is Good Nature, he insisted. "Love is terrible and stern."

Opinions about him differed wildly. He was a child, most lovable when least disciplined whether anyone approved or disapproved; he was subtle, he was sincere, he was always dressing up; he would go to the wire for you, but the moment he was uninterested he let you slide; he was gentle, he was rough. . . . He was all of these, he was none of these. What does this prove but that intensely interesting men like Hugh are paradoxes not easily catalogued. Certainly he was trustful in the extreme, and in personal friendships frequently lacked insight--it was part of the boyish innocence--but he wasted no time in extricating himself from difficult situations once he had made up his mind to do it.

When his family described him, with one voice they declared he was a boy at heart, transparently honest, with childlike love of play, a delightful raconteur and companion, chivalrous and absolutely fearless. Father Martindale accepted this characterization, and drawing upon other sources, notably Hugh's voluminous correspondence as well as his own powers of analysis, built a multi-dimensional picture of a priest equipped with ample gifts to serve if not lead the flock.

One indisputable Benson fact emerges, and that is it was impossible to unseat Edward White Benson from the consciousness of his children; in Hugh's case the inheritance from his father was two-fold: an independent spirit determined to assert itself and strong artistic sensibilities. For both father and son the keen artistic temperament found a heaven in ritual and pageantry, in church music and church windows; but while Edward's method of approach, no less ardent, was deliberate and intellectual, Hugh was intoxicated by beauty and beautiful things, especially by Church ornaments, a passion shared by a parade of aesthetes, symbolists, pre-Raphaelites, Decadents, and even one or two bourgeois conventionalists. His sensibility was a romantic sensibility that fed on the strange and exotic, leading him to writers whose artistic tastes resembled his own: Pater, Flaubert, Huysmans. It was in him from the beginning, in the strong, unhealthy imagination that sought out those dark corners where the timid dared not tread, an imagination saturated with colors and textures and sensations.

His mother was and would remain the woman of his life in perfect understanding cemented at the time of his conversion: "Between my mother and myself there is simply not a shadow; in many ways we are nearer to one another than we were before" (M, II, 256). He needed no other woman. There was no need to hide behind the priest's collar to avoid marriage as that issue had been put to rest before he entered Mirfield when he declared himself unfit for marriage from every conceivable point of view. His celibacy was real, not forced upon him by timidity although physical impairment may have decided the matter. He was not romantically inclined towards women (or men) even though women were drawn to him as to a lodestone. Like Arthur, he preferred the company of men. The closest he came to romantic infatuation was Frederick Rolfe, a disappointed man, who, after their bitter falling out, came to hate him and mocked his asceticism. A fog of naiveté blinded Hugh to Rolfe's egoism and intentions, and so it was whenever in his boyish ebullience he relaxed his natural reserve and "put on too much fuel." Hugh was incapable of dishonesty, was open in his motives and emotions, confessed himself too fond of money, too impulsive, and too quick to anger. Every whim needed to be satisfied at once rather than at last; he was the first to concede this was a fault. Father Martindale did not like him but nevertheless accepted this commission at the request of Cardinal Bourne. One suspects Hugh's amazing popularity and success as a writer annoyed his biographer who was by any measure the superior scholar, learned in classical languages and the arts, and much sought after in his own right. No doubt Martindale represented that segment of Catholics who envied Hugh because he had made such a great success without having paid a great price.

Some admirers were quick to call him a mystic. Perhaps in powers of concentration and detachment he glanced at it; certainly he had tasted such mysteries as are revealed to a soul in prayer. But the true mystic's life was beyond his reach. One can only marvel at his implausible dream of one day becoming a Carthusian, for he had no vocation for the contemplative life except in his imagination. It asked more interiorly than he possessed. Solitude in the abstract appealed to him and certainly privacy appealed to him, but the reality was he lived life externally, fiercely and noisily, with a need to express himself in a thousand ways.

There was nothing hidebound, nothing prudish about him. That he loved old, familiar things dearly never interfered with common sense in facing the realities of changing times. He enjoyed writing historical novels, but chose to write modern novels because in addressing the problems of his day they were more useful in bringing Catholicism to England. He recognized early on how the power of the press and the stage to influence behavior was potentially greater than that of the pulpit as he pointed out to a friend: "No doubt it is more picturesque to ignore modern methods; but a society that is only picturesque and mediaeval certainly is not Catholic in the widest sense. Further it must be remembered that the printing press is here anyhow; and is being steadily used against Revealed Religion in a hundred ways" (M, II, 223).

At the age of 32 he had burst upon the literary scene with *The Light Invisible*. From then on he wrote steadily, one book after another for a total of nineteen novels, and had already mapped out the twentieth when Death took him. Had he lived longer he might have become a great novelist, some mused, and tilted with the likes of Joseph Conrad and H. G. Wells, and so the early death was doubly deplored for the loss of talent. That was a pretty fable. No art for art's sake for him; at the very least every novel he wrote was conceived with the idea of getting a moral lesson across, every novel promoted Catholic doctrine. Hugh knew his strength and knew whence it came, nor did he fancy he wrote for all ages. He was a man of his time, writing for men and women of his time about themselves and their spiritual dryness and the one prodigal among thousands who finds his way home. It was not meant for him to throw his gifts away on trifles. He lived and wrote at the edge of apocalyptic change. In the aftermath of World War I, England and America were to be swallowed up by hedonistic materialism (the visionary *Lord of the World* realized), but even in Hugh's day--the twilight of grace and courtesy but like all twilights the herald of night-- decay was rapidly setting in. Realism was slowly giving way to nominalism; and Christian spirituality succumbing to the lure of occultism. No matter how many warnings were sounded in private correspondence, in the press, and from the pulpit, the slide could not be stopped.

There was something of triumphant materialism even in the disappearance of Hugh Benson's name from the lists of best-selling writers of the day. While his reputation certainly declined with the crumbling of the pre-War age to which he belonged--only the strongest or luckiest are able to survive earthquakes--there were moments when he might have been restored to public favor, when a Hugh Benson revival seemed possible. Articles continued to appear into the Twenties. In the

Forties there was a minor revival spurred by the re-issue of a number of
novels by Burns and Oates, and in the early Sixties, inspired possibly
by the election of a Roman Catholic President, *By What Authority?*
Oddsfish! and *Come Rack! Come Rope!* were reissued by an American
publishing house. Nothing came of it. Today there remains a glimmer
of interest from reprint houses, mostly Catholic. Where did it all go,
the fame and adulation? Perhaps we must look to his personality and
presence for the answer. Personality was the secret of Hugh Benson.
While he lived, a physical presence to be talked about, with a book or
two always to be found in the book-stalls--with still another surely on
the way to outrage and delight Protestants and Catholics alike, he
commanded the stage. Lectures, sermons, Masses--these were public
events, and that public needed the actual, the provoking, prolific Hugh
Benson in the flesh--now in Edinburgh, now Leeds, now Dublin, now
Boston. Through his exciting personality he claimed them and held
them. But his literary remains without the vivid personality--body and
soul--standing on the sidelines were not strong enough to survive by
themselves.

Different critics had at him for different reasons, those who disliked
his mystical books, those who thought he wrote bad history, or
deplored the drenching propaganda, or sniped at his modern
psychological novels as being inferior to those of George Eliot.
Ironically, any single group while disapproving of one kind of novel,
were often shameless readers of another. They no less than the humble
masses were smitten with Bensonitis or Bensonmania, that affliction
causing the sufferer to wallow unapologetically in Hugh Benson's
novels and pine for more of the same.

There had long been talk about Hugh's morbid streak, mutterings
about a sadistic side based on the considerable volume of blood
splattered about in his books. No one disputed his power in describing
suffering and death; the process of dying whether from natural causes or
under torture had long fascinated him, deepened by his own terror of
pain and mutilation. He spoke often of the uses of pain and suffering,
and in a few cases practiced or attempted to practice "mystical
substitution," offering to suffer for the sins of others, a considerable
sacrifice for one with low tolerance for pain. Of the sufferings of others,
particularly the English martyrs, he had much to say, and said it in
books and plays frequently and in detail. He brought the horror of
Tudor racks and Tudor prisons directly to readers--not in the manner of
Foxe's martyrology that for all its lurid excess leaves the reader fatigued
rather than stimulated--but recreating the mental states of men under
torture to the fullest extent that language could manage it. Here he is
not, as usual, the external observer, but has slipped into the skin of the

sufferer to speak from the inside. Does that imply a sadistic streak running below the surface of respectable history? If so, his audience who continued to buy his books must have shared his predilection. Hugh's aesthetic sensibility was certainly stimulated by tales of danger and brutality, but morbid curiosity whether rooted in bad nerves or bad dreams worked itself out in his books, and one can surely argue that he turned his neurosis to the greatest good, bringing English audiences face to face with terrible cruelties practiced upon Roman Catholics in the reign of Gloriana. However, the impression of his unhealthy preoccupation with the subject held, an impression reinforced by gossip about The Dance of Death tapestry at Hare Street and the special instructions on how he was to be buried. Undeniably a morbid streak ran along the surface of his nervous temperament.[2] It is another facet of his personality.

He wished to be buried in particular vestments, and asked that his monsignorial robes be buried with him also. A little copper chalice kept on the shelf near the parlor was also to be put in the coffin; Hugh had it made up expressly. It was standing atop his coffin during the funeral and went into the grave with him. Why this chalice? Symbol of his priesthood, certainly, but more besides, for it raises the question of the power of prescience or revelation--how should the phenomenon be explained? A strange dream dreamt one night in Egypt in 1897 had became reality in 1914. It is worth repeating again. "I was on a seashore, and a figure rose from the sand holding two chalices," he wrote in his diary the next morning. "The figure was mostly in shadow, but lighted in redlight from the one chalice. The figure lifted a dark chalice and poured what looked like red liquid fire from it into the other, and the other glowed red as the liquid fell in; a voice kept on saying 'The blood of God.' The chalice was held out to me; and I dipped the tip of my finger in and tasted it: and it tasted like sweet fire: and again the voice kept on saying 'seventeen years.' I know too that I connected that in my mind with my own lifetime--that I should live seventeen years more." In that curious dream his term was set, and seventeen years more was given him exactly.

Even in death he was embroiled in controversy. Hugh had drawn up a will leaving the bulk of his estate (about £12,000) and the house to the Diocese of Westminster to serve as the Archbishop's country retreat. An additional £4000 was to go to Arthur and the family, but two problems arose. First, the will was not properly signed, so from a legal position Hugh had died intestate. As a formality, the family filed suit against the Archdiocese and won, at which point they turned everything over to Westminster Cathedral, including all copyrights to Hugh's books. All was all done just as Hugh had wanted.[3] Second, the family could not be sure the Archdiocese would accept the house without an adequate endowment to keep it up. It was a reasonable caution, though Arthur was a little annoyed that all should go to the Catholic Church--with their strings of proper financial endowment attached![4]

Hugh's individualism was not cold; he had passions and enthusiasms, and a boyish vivacity that charmed everyone in sight. But he had no great emotional depths that sealed him to another human being, man or woman. That is not to say he had no compassion. He hated cruelty above all things and would not tolerate injustice or rudeness or discourtesy, but the deeper currents of emotional life eluded him. He loathed the thrusting and parrying of controversy--"it seems to ruin everything"--but found himself somehow embroiled and frequently embroiled. He had passionate convictions, but no passions--he never lost himself in an intense friendship, except for his brother Arthur, whom he dearly loved, but even there religious and temperamental differences interfered with a perfect understanding. Like a child whose affections fly to the pleasure at hand whether others approve or disapprove, he threw himself heart and soul into every activity. Of this childlikeness, when it was simplicity itself, he approved as the key to the spiritual life: "It seems to me that 'childlikeness' is the secret of everything--of faith and life: and the key to all holiness . . . there are innumerable virtues springing out of it--realisation of the supernatural--absorption , in the right sense, in one's affairs--or intensity of purpose--a terror of Sin: and an absolute taking for granted the means of grace" (M, II, 238-39). He was charmingly selfish, and most charming when least disciplined. He loved being talked of and lionized, but on his own terms. Arthur marveled how many admirers thought Hugh's life to be an utter complete subjugation of will, when it was just the opposite--a complete expression of his many selves.

In religion he was a fighter standing up for principles, sublimely fearless in firing up tepid Protestants and lazy Catholics alike. "Let 'em have it!" he thundered mercilessly. There was nothing anemic about his Catholicism. Once in the pulpit the little untidy man ceased to exist; he became the inspired prophet filled with holy fire--"I live, now not I, but Christ lives in me"--talking in a language understood by intellectual and laborer alike. It was the same whether he was talking to ten or to thousands--the slight body quivering with nervous energy pent-up within--swaying to one side then the other, first up then down, balancing itself on toes, always at the point of toppling, but never quite toppling. His sermons were muscular, metaphor-crammed, picturesque, with little warmth or mystery in them, but plenty of hard doctrine of Christ. Unflinching moral hair-shirt was what he offered, and everybody listened and hung on every word. That it lay in every priest's power to become a good preacher he firmly believed, citing his own example: "If ever there was a man who had everything against him as a preacher, I am that man," he said. "I've got this beastly impediment in my speech, and I'm as nervous as a chicken."

Benson the convert, the priest, the missionary, the preacher, the *enfant terrible* capable of probing the interior life and the surface world of Nature with equal vividness--his admirers ranged round him devotedly. His imagination was white-hot. Count up what he created in his dozen years of Catholic life--twenty novels and books on religion, dozens of prefaces and introductions and pamphlets and commentaries and reviews and a river of correspondence while penitents clamored at the gate. All this in addition to interviews, receptions, lectures, and courses and retreats in churches, in monasteries and convents until every minute of the day was eaten up. It is true he enjoyed writing and that his life was as bound to it as it was to breathing, and true he profited greatly from his novels enabling him to live as he wished, but his apologetics recognized that Divine truths needed to be presented in a manner that would not cause them to be rejected out of hand, and novel-writing was that manner exactly. Novels gave him the wider audience he needed to reach. There were thousands reached from the pulpit, but hundreds of thousands reached through the printed word. To those who claimed he was a better preacher than writer, he protested "Oh no! no! no! My novels are far better than my sermons, they reach a far bigger public, they have a much better chance of sinking in, they do far more good."

He wrote five books of popular apologetics, *Christ in the Church*, and *Friendship of Christ*, based on sermons preached in New York and in Rome; *Religion of A Plain Man*, intended to liberate Catholics and Anglicans from the tyranny of Higher Criticism, *Paradoxes of Christianity*, and *Papers of a Pariah*. It was the very fact that his apologetics did not get bogged down in theological language that made them so attractive, so readable to a public that would not have sat still for five minutes had these truths been presented as theological tract.

Even before becoming a Catholic, he was recognized everywhere as the best preacher in the Church of England. His conversion and subsequent success as a Roman Catholic sat not at all well with Anglican clergy by whom he was disliked privately and criticized in print. The *Church Times* that had applauded the display of talent by Anglican Hugh Benson became indignant at the success of Hugh Benson the Roman Catholic. After reading Hugh's *Confessions* that had minced the Church of England into polite bits (inevitable a religious *apologia*), the hysterical reviewer slashed away at his positions, going as far as to question the reliability of Matthew's "You are Peter . . ." in

order to refute Hugh's claims for Apostolic succession. Sighs heard
following his death from that quarter were of mingled regret and relief.
Anglicans of the establishment bade him glad farewell.[5]

Not only Anglicans scoffed that Hugh Benson's life was a piece of
self-advertisement. In this they were joined by a few Catholic priests
who while he lived had smiled and said nothing. His growing fame, his
legions of readers, his unrivaled popularity as a preacher--all these were
unsettling not only to Protestants but also to other Catholic priests,
life-long Catholics, who also labored in the Lord's vineyard. It is only
human. While it is true that he never entered fully into English
Catholic life--the circumstances of his birth, who his father was, his
Anglican attitudes worked against it--and while it is also true there was
lingering resentment that he had come to Holy Orders too soon and
lived a far too independent life, the Church in her wisdom recognized
that he must be allowed a longer tether, that a wealth of souls waited to
be harvested by this charismatic young priest. Who can know how
many thousands entered the Church as a direct result of his work, and
the tens of thousands brought in indirectly?

On the other hand, he remained indifferent to ecclesiastical politics
and as a consequence stumbled into "blazing indiscretions" like
disclosures about ritualism in the House of the Resurrection, Mirfield,
made quite innocently as part of his *Confessions*[6] He never resented
being corrected, and made amends if it lay in his power. Because he
held the ear of the non-Catholic world to an unprecedented degree,
because thousands hung upon his words, special obligations fell to
him. Like it or not he had become a spokesman for the Church, and
Catholic positions were often adduced from his books. Was he aware of
the tremendous responsibility that had fallen upon him as a result of it?
The lack of systematic training dogged him his entire Catholic life and
showed up in his dogmatic works. His occasional ventures into
theological writing contained errors that were edited before seeing print;
and as for the accuracy of the historical novels, he eagerly consulted
learned men like Dom Bede Camm and Abbot Gasquet, leading
authorities of the time. Only through the persistence of friends in
Rome was he made Papal Chamberlain to Pius X, an honorific that
carried the title of monsignor, granted despite strong opposition from
Cardinal Bourne.

Even in death, Hugh refused to be silenced. *Oddsfish!* with its new
tenderness and "passion of romance" (inducement for female admirers,
surely), appeared in November, followed by publication of the final
novel *Loneliness?* and a Mystery play *The Upper Room*, in 1915. The
public fell in love with him because they fell in love with his
characters. They thought his heroes were projections of himself: the

tenderness, innocence, toughness--everything his heroes endured he had endured. He was letting them into his life. Why else did people who had never met him feel they had lost a personal friend? Then after the flood of tears and panegyrics, the memoirs and memories, and the pleas to have done with this Bensonmania, when all appeared to be subsiding, three more books appeared--Arthur's *Hugh*, Olive Parr's treacly *Robert Hugh Benson: an Appreciation.*, "a simply idiotic presentment of Hugh,"[7] and Mrs. Warre Cornish's sympathetic sketches in *Memorials of Robert Hugh Benson.* Her fantastic memorial for the *Dublin Review* had painted Hugh as a great mystic. "He was nothing of the kind," shot back Arthur, furious that Hugh had been "impounded by the R.Cs."

Whatever dismay Father Martindale felt as Arthur's book *Hugh* appeared in advance of his own, he never said publicly. Did he think Arthur's rushing the very personal memoir into print a bit of treachery, like having one's pockets picked by a friend? In 1916, more than a year after Hugh's death, Martindale's authorized *Life* was in the shops-- 300,000 words filling two thick volumes--for a man who had died before his 44th birthday? And so the floodgates opened up once more and the articles poured forth, all the while Europe was being pulverized by German artillery. How does one explain it?

The women in his life   For the stream of penitents who came to his door or flooded him with letters as if he were their exclusive property he had infinite patience. Women were a terrible trial. They adored him politely, but made incessant demands upon his time; they became dependent upon him, dedicated books to him, and dreamt of being buried by his side. In the last years he had been hounded by starry-eyed spinsters and widows in search of--what? Poor Hugh! He liked to be noticed, to be needed, to be at the center of things, but quietly, without displays and without strings. Women who had made Hugh's life miserable with their demands pursued him into the afterlife. There is Olive Parr (whom Father Martindale thought unbalanced) pouring out spiritual intimacies about her soul-mate Father Benson for the world to read, and Sophie Maude dedicating her novel in "deathless gratitude" to him, and Agnes Lewis who begged to be buried by his side. Agnes Lewis was a pianist who had come on several occasions to Hare Street to play Mozart for Hugh and after his death posted sections of her passionate diary to Arthur--"odd passionate things, very devotional, impassioned, which show how she fell deeper and deeper in love with him." She was not embarrassed to tell the slightly disgusted Arthur that in Paradise Hugh's spirit turns to her in love: her own soul she has put in the wound of Christ's left hand, and Hugh's soul into the wound in Christ's right hand. She demanded to be buried beside him "on the grounds of a spiritual union--like Joseph and Mary, and. This she knows exists by intuition. She says he has put off his priest in death and their souls flow together, and that it is Hugh's wish that they should be buried together. If so, then it is very odd that he does not give me an intuition, when I could arrange it, but only to her, who cannot" (*Diary*, Sept. 3, 1915). Such sentimentality would have convulsed Hugh; and as for their two souls flowing together, it was a dream--Arthur did not believe for a second that Hugh had the slightest touch of sexual passion--"he liked friends, and he loved children, but he shrank from women."

But when these female votaries found themselves unsatisfied, they shifted their attention to Arthur. Gentleman that he was, he allowed himself to be pushed--or pummeled--to the limit. One of Hugh's "wild" women fights with Arthur via the post. A running debate begins between him and a woman from Torquay to whom Hugh had written hundreds of letters: "She's one of the females who sucked Hugh's lifeblood and is now trying to suck mine. She writes endless letters, and now she becomes controversial. . . . But I don't intend to write daily to an ignorant woman." And again a month later he complains after she has gone on and on about her idiotic reminiscences, writing every day those arch, sentimental letters. "The wretched Miss Martin again on the warpath. These women!" Still more--"Very unpleasant letter from Miss Martin. . . ." To which he threw up his hands in despair: "These women lodged themselves like parasites in Hugh's mind, and now that he is gone, they try to find a home in mine" (*Diary*, March 7, 1915). There were exceptions to the rule like the devout Miss Kyle whose letters from Hugh had appeared (with his consent) in the American *Ave Maria*, and were subsequently published as a book *Spiritual Letters to a Convert*. But in most cases after Hugh's death they hovered like harpies laying claim to his possessions, his fountain pen, his rosary beads, a breviary--personal things he has handled, written with, prayed over, even the earth he lay buried in.

Of course there was Miss Lyall, ubiquitous, devoted Miss Lyall, comfortably settled in Hare Street cottage with a maid who served after-dinner coffee in a silver pot. At news of Hugh's death she had rushed to Salford, hysterical with grief. Faithful to his memory, she stayed on at Hare Street to look after things until the house was firmly settled upon the Archdiocese. It was Miss Lyall who arranged for the building of the beautiful chapel of "St. Hugh of Lincoln" that today soars over Hugh's undisturbed grave. On the flat stone slab near the altar is an inscription ringing with echoes of *John Inglesant*--

Robertus Hugo Benson,
sacerdos Catholicae et Romanae Ecclesiae, Peccator Expectans ad
Revelationem Filiorum Dei.

In contrast to the gentle Miss Lyall was the greedy Miss Hogge, Hugh's troublesome tenant in the cottage he had built for Mrs. Lindsay. She had witnessed Hugh's will (which turned out not to be legally drawn) and now demanded that Arthur give her Hugh's most personal things: "I woke and worried about having given Hugh's pen to the leader of the Harpies Mrs. Hogge. I could see Hugh pull it out of his pocket and uncap it! Yet she had asked him for it--that's amazing enough--and he had laughed and said that she might ask me about it. And further she chose as the moment to ask him for that and his Breviary and his Rosary the evening when she witnessed his Will, which he made because he was going to Switzerland and thought he might be running some risk! She handed me these requests in a note on the day of the funeral . . . She is a gaunt, hungry-looking woman with long teeth and a peering eye" (*Diary*, April 6, 1915). Her demands and when she made them--on the eve of his going abroad while making out a will and then staking her claim on the day of his funeral--filled Arthur with disgust. In March of 1915, Reeman, Hugh's manservant, was still drawing up lists of mementos. Arthur took away one or two trifles, like a little crystal ball dug up in the garden. But the place was looking desolate; it was a house meant to be lived in, though no human presence could fill it as vividly as Hugh had filled it. Then he went to the grave "beautifully kept with turf and flowers. But I had a sense that Hugh was somehow near me, glad to have got away and that he felt like a caged bird released. It was a pretty and well-ordered cage. But he is free, he has flown to the shadow of the pines. I discover gradually how many serious and anxious episodes there were in his life--relations with rather evil people, out of which he had to extricate himself as best he could. I don't think these got much on his mind--he had a wonderful power of detachment. . . . I write all this with a little fountain pen which I have Hugh, but he seems not to have used it" (*Diary*, March 30, 1915).

While it is true Hugh made a lot of money, he made it only in three years out of the ten, and he worked hard for every penny. It was true he became tightfisted with money--and that must be counted against him-- and there were few appeals able to force that fist open. There was much muttering about it by fellow priests; yet thrice he took up Father Dolan's invitation to preach at Rome for pay that scarcely met his expenses when preaching in America brought in 100 times that. It was scandalous that he cared little about how he looked in public--his buttons were frayed and his cassock a little ragged and greenish. Asked just before ordination what kind of priest he planned to be, "an untidy one," he replied, and he lived it up to the hilt.[8] As Frederick Rolfe had pointed out, Hugh paid scant attention to this temple of the Holy Ghost.

Listing Hugh's lectures and sermons would tire the enginer, range as they did from delights of mountain climbing to preparing Catholics in the universities to the dangers of groping about for spirits in séances. He was a man traveling up and down England, talking everywhere, talking to girls, talking to boys, giving interviews, attending benefits, accepting every invitation until his engagement book was solidly and dangerously packed. Father Benson had become a national event. As often as he wished out loud to be left alone, he courted publicity and advertisement and in his public persona rather enjoyed basking in the limelight. In Rome during three Lents--1909, 1911, 1913--priests of every rank, from seminarian to Cardinal attended his bi-weekly lectures, giving up their free afternoons to crowd into a packed church to hear him speak. In 1907 he first preached the Lent at the Carmelite Church in Kensington. It became his favorite place in London and he was, in fact, on his way back to London to preach the Triduum for the Feast of St. Theresa there on October 14, 1914, when he took ill and died.

His lectures and sermons were fierce emotional performances that left audience breathless, from sophisticated intellectual to your ordinary man in the street. Stalking ghosts in haunted rooms often kept him busy-- he was determined to coax them into an appearance. And if these disembodied wraiths from the spirit-world refused to oblige, what of it? It was the quest that mattered. Everything that struck the senses, that smacked of romance or of the abnormal fascinated him. A friend who knew him well remembered warmly how everything in God's world was too interesting to him to be passed by; it must be proved, dissected on the spot, then talked over into the small hours of the night: "He was all flame. That is the key to his character; that is 'the secret of Benson.'"[9]

Arthur often wondered why Hugh who insisted on having his own way in all things could not find a home in Anglicanism with its greater allowances for personal liberty and individualism, its refinement, moderation, and courtesy. The answer, of course, was "Authority." Because he was a priest he was expected to be as gentle as a lamb, as deep as a well, but he was neither of these. His faith was too fiery and busy and unreflective, but he reached the absolute height of his capabilities, without the assistance or sanction of official Catholicism, but by the force of his own personality. Someone said of him once that his Roman Catholicism sat but lightly upon him: to the end he was

Hugh. So he was, if being Hugh meant fearlessness and zeal in working towards one goal, the conversion of England. That it sat lightly upon him is refuted by certainty that "as to the Catholic Church there is simply no question at all, *It is it*, and that is an end of the matter."

Before the dawn of Catholic life Hugh showed no particular promise. He was then as laterexceptionally sensitive to impressions, quite impulsive, mischievous, humorous, self-absorbed, undisciplined, theatrical; at Cambridge he spent his energies chasing after disembodied spirits, rowing, writing satires, and got on "by the skin of his teeth." He became a priest of the Church of England as the path of least resistance, but only when he became a Catholic did his life catch fire. He became a priest and remained a priest, and accomplished three works as preacher, spiritual director, novelist. In his life he maintained a detachment from others that left many who loved him unsatisfied, keeping watch over the human heart without giving his own away. To do what God wished of him was his purpose even to the last breath.

"Is it any good resisting?" he asked before the end came and the wonders of this world were closed to him, and when told it was no good, he went out of this world and into the next eyes open, unafraid, with arms outstretched, greeting his Lord in that husky voice so well remembered and dearly missed--*Oh, my dear, isn't it all tremendous? Isn't it all great fun?*

Notes

[1] By a correspondent, *The Universe* (October 30, 1914), p. 5. It was possible still to find a spot of humor in the general lamentation. The "Miscellany" page of *The Universe* reported that "a correspondent suggests that Mgr. Benson has done more in the direction of the occult than is generally imagined. The assumption is based upon an extraordinary statement which appeared in, among other papers, the *Daily Telegraph* and the *Cambridge Daily News*, to the effect that Cardinal Manning officiated at the Requiem which preceded the interment at Buntingford last Friday of the mortal remains of Mr. Benson. This record of the post-mortem activity of the great Cardinal is certainly remarkable. Cardinal Vaughan has been "raised" many times (we ourselves once broke the spell of his repose); but the phonetic values of "Vaughan" and "Bourne" are so nearly equivalent that telephonic carelessness might result in confusion. Now that Cardinal Manning has been thus recalled, there seems a chance that Cardinal Pole or Cardinal Wolsey may yet be dragged into contemporary history." This was not the only mistake. Hugh's coffin went into the grave with his birth-date

incorrectly inscribed as November 17th (the feast day of St. Hugh) instead of November 18th. The 18th was put on the plate originally and then blacked out.

2 Martindale offered an analysis of this preoccupation with pain dismissing its "morbid" character though not denying that it might have been so "had he not, owing to temperament, 'passed on' too quickly to the next thing to become really a brooder over pain or in love with it or tempted to inflict it. Moreover, his singularly practical tendency always forced him at once to register and *use* it for some outside end, nor suffered him to hug it and live with it interiorly. " Hugh was too pre-occupied with his duties and obligations to practice any "dangerous tendencies of religious asceticism" (M, II, 356). His hatred of all cruelty has already been noted.

3 In February 1915 the case came to court. The legatees under the will drawn in 1912 were duly represented, but the will was thrown out as invalid. Gabriel Pippet, who had witnessed the will drawn up by Hugh just before he left for Switzerland, testified that Hugh had taken it with him, and that the second witness Mrs. Hogge had not been present when he signed, nor was he present when Mrs. Hogge signed it at a later date. The will was judged not properly executed (ACB *Diary*, Feb. 1915).

4 When Arthur came by in August (with Fr. Martindale) "vague females appeared wandering about looking into the windows. The Cardinal complained that it was all rather infested by people who marched in to see chapel and grave. . . The orchard is full of long grass, just as Hugh liked it, and the grave with its flowers looked strangely embowered" (*Diary*, Aug. 2, 1915). He was pleased that Bourne intended to keep things as Hugh liked them, and was touched when the Cardinal, bare-headed, said a little prayer over Hugh's grave (as recently as March Hugh had mentioned that the Cardinal did not trust him one bit). One of Hugh's lady admirers had arranged for the planting of rose beds exactly as Hugh had designed them. Nevertheless, without the vital presence of the man who made Hare Street his little Paradise, nothing was the same, nor could be. When Father Martindale visited again in the course of writing the biography, he noted the house was like a stage set for RHB; and not only was the actor, who alone justified the scenery, not there, but the incongruous Cardinal and his secretary were, both quite out of place--as he himself was, sitting there "like a fool" with the intention to observe and write (Caraman, p. 142). The Buntingford Catholic Church was for a time informally referred to as the Benson Memorial Church. On the second anniversary of Hugh's death Cardinal Bourne paid three visits, saying Mass at 8 in the new Lady's Chapel, which had been donated by an American friend. He stayed on to hear a sung mass later, and in the afternoon gave the solemn Pontifical Blessing.

5 A remarkable tribute came from the Rev. Robert Campbell, a leading Nonconformist minister who often had invited him to speak at City Temple- "Robert Hugh Benson belonged to Heaven," Campbell wrote, "Heaven has claimed him, that is all. I never knew a man less worldly. He was out of place in a utilitarian world like ours. His was the substance of which saints

are made, with not an atom of self-seeking in his nature." (Hugh used to relate with pleasure how Campbell suppressed a hostile demonstration at a meeting where he was explaining the position of the Catholic Church. It was decided Hugh that thereafter he should lecture on less inflammatory topics). On the other side, while ill at Salford Hugh heard that Welldon, the Bishop of Calcutta, had very recently called him a "hell-hound." He mentioned it in passing to Arthur the day before he died. The *Church Times* obituary notice was at best polite. Their view of his literary remains was that of all his books only *The Light Invisible* written while he was an Anglican was worthy to endure. In the following issue appeared a warm appreciation by a curate friend of long-ago who assisted him at the Eton Mission and much admired how remarkably he had applied the parables to the lives of the poor and unschooled--a polite reminder that it was among the poorest and most ignorant that Hugh Benson found an audience for his spiritual fiction, a ludicrous assertion. Martindale's biography was a further irritation to those who had had enough of hero worship, as the publishing arm of Nonconformism *The British Weekly* proved in its front-page declaration of TOO MUCH HUGH BENSON, jabbing at his memory, astonished that (as reported in Martindale's biography) Mgr. Benson had not read his father's biography until ten years after publication! Dead or alive, it seemed, there was no escaping Father Benson! That Hugh's success had annoyed Anglicans and some Catholic priests was no news either, but how was one to deal with the rumor floating around Cambridge that Jesuits had hastened Hugh's death by poisoning him? "What century are we living in?" Arthur asked angrily.

6 Among these indiscretions was a comment about the local squire, a very low Churchman, "who, though himself a most charming and courteous old man, was something very like a fanatic on the side of ultra-Protestantism" (*Confessions*, pp. 50-51). A number of incidents in his novels caused consternation to authorities, among them the description of romantically inclined cats in *The Necromancers, a*nd the execution of the heretical monk who refuses to recant in *The Dawn of All.* See H. S. Dean, "Robert Hugh Benson," in *The Month* (1914), pp. 501-508; also Fr. John Keating, "De Civitate Dei," *The Month* (October 1911), pp. 390-402.

7 "Miss Parr prays to him and he sends her messages. She lives in the hope of having his company all to herself in heaven. That is the difficulty of Heaven. Is Hugh to have no say? Is he to be claimed by Miss Parr? I can imagine his horror at the prospect." There were lighter touches as well. Of a friend's comment to Mary Benson that Hugh was now an angel in paradise, hovering over her as she prayed, Arthur smiled, "I can imagine with what helpless convulsions of laughter Hugh would have gone on hearing this."

8 In Rome in 1903 an old man, unshaven, in a filthy cassock and hat but with one of the most ethereal faces he had ever seen was pointed out to Hugh. Father Vaughan whispered to him that he was going to be a saint some day. "It is one of the things in Rome to see him say Mass! and he, of course, is frankly impervious of it all. It's interesting to see a saint in the making!" (*Letter* to MB, Nov. 1903). Could that have been behind Hugh's carelessness? Probably not.

9 H. S. Dean, p. 503.

Appendix

1

*A Sermon on Sacramental Communion Preached in the House of
Retreat November 2, 1901*

[*Hugh Benson's best sermons were meticulously prepared and supplied with
elaborate points in outline, not written out as essays as was this exception
that follows, composed and delivered at Mirfield.*]

Sacramental Communion notes the double condescension of Our
Blessed Lord. Not only in His Incarnate life does He condescend to
terms of space, but also to terms of *time* in the Blessed Sacrament. At
His Incarnation He came down from heaven to earth and took human
nature to himself and then lifted it up to a Heavenly Life. But there He
is, separated from us by centuries of time. Therefore, now in the
Blessed Sacrament, he makes another act of condescension to our
weakness. He comes down to us day by day, in the Blessed Sacrament,
so that we may kneel before him, morning by morning, and say "My
Lord and My God." (St John xx. 28) The presence of Our Lord in the
Blessed Sacrament is His Heavenly and Eternal life translated into terms
of earthly and temporal existence. There is no need for us to throw our
imagination centuries back, and picture ourselves kneeling at His Feet,
gazing at His Pierced Side; we can kneel here, as we do this morning;
and, without types or images, worship Him really present in His
Divine and Human nature, expressed in these terms of time and space.

The method, then, of our Saviour in the Blessed Sacrament is the
method of the Incarnation. At His Incarnation the Pérson of the eternal
Word, the Creator of Heaven and Earth, stooped down and took particles
of that human nature he had created, and made Himself a Body from the
flesh of the Blessed Virgin Mary. In the Blessed Sacrament He stoops
to earth again, takes the material particles of bread and wine, and "lo!" a
Body prepared for Him again in the Blessed Sacrament.

(ii) It has been thought that, at the Last Supper, our Lord, as He took
the bread and broke it, took part of it, and ate it, and it became His
Body by a natural process, while the other half became His Body by a
supernatural process. As we consider this great Mystery thus, how
extraordinarily simple it becomes! Apply to the Blessed Sacrament the
same laws by which He worked in His Incarnation, and many of its
mysteries become, I will not say clear, but at east luminous.

(iii) We may think thoughts of this kind out for ourselves; but, after
all, though they may possibly be helps to us towards realising the truth
about the Blessed Sacrament; yet since it is not all people that can share
or understand them, they cannot be necessary to the unity of the Faith.

All we need believe is that it *is* His Body and Blood, and that He gives us Himself. In fact, if we think too elaborately about this Great Mystery, we shall be apt to lose something of its grandeur or of its simplicity. For example, God shows us the glories of the Blessed Sacrament by the wealth of types by which He illustrates It in the Scriptures. Our Lord Himself makes use of the type of Heavenly Manna given to the people in the wilderness, as we read in St John vi. 41. Or we may think of It as under the type of Heavenly Meat brought to Elizah (1 Kings xix). Yet it is quite possible, that if we dwell too much on this and other glorious aspects of the Mystery, we may become so dazzled as to lose the sense of the wonderful simplicity with which our Lord comes to us. This may be illustrated by the visit of the Queen of Sheba to Solomon (1 Kings xiii.). We read that after she had witnessed the splendour of his court, "there was no more spirit left in her." Solomon was grateful for her awe and admiration and loaded her with gifts; yet that queen was not so dear to King Solomon as his own children who came running in and out of his presence, and who could climb on his knee and lay their head on his breast; for to them he was not the wise or glorious king, but the tender father to whom they could come for a caress.

So the simple soul that cannot put three words together theologically, and understands nothing whatever about the types and symbols of the Blessed Sacrament, can be far nearer to our Lord as she nestles up to Him in the Sacrament of His Love than all the theologians in the world who have not her childlike faith or her simple love. For the way that leads to God is so very simple. As Isaiah said: "The wayfaring men, though fools, shall not err therein." (Ch xxxv. 8). It does not require learning or cleverness to be near to our Blessed Lord.

(iv) But now let us look at this great mystery in another and a different aspect. Let us shift our position so as to catch another light that we have not meditated on before, perhaps; and this, not because it is, of necessity, a better or an inner light, but because variety is good for human limitations.

We have thought of Holy Communion as a coming to our Lord, as our coming to Him and seeking Him. Let us think of it now as our Blessed Lord coming to us and seeking us. In prayer, we desire Christ; in Holy Communion Christ desires us. Now as ever Mass ought to be, as it were, a great love-story consummated in the union of the Soul and her Beloved. You all know the story of King Cophetua coming down in his royal robes and making the beggar-maid his queen. So should it be in the spiritual history of each soul; for thus does our Lord humble Himself and lift up the beggar-maid, which is human nature, to inherit

His Princely Throne. It is more true to say that at the Eucharist Christ comes down to us, than that we lift up our hearts to Him, for He acts continually along the lines of the Incarnation, when He "for us men and for our salvation came down from heaven." It is quite as true, if not more true, because *our* desire is weak and faint, and *His* desire is always white-hot; for He Who says: "If any man thirst, let him come unto me and drink," (St John vii. 37) says also from the Cross: "I thirst." (St John xix. 28) He thirsts for *us*--desires *us*. And He Who said: "Ask, and it shall be given you, seek, and ye shall find, knock and it shall be opened unto you," (St Matt. viii. 7) said also: "Behold, I stand at the door and knock." (Rev. iii. 20). So, when we feel our communion cold, our desires languid, our appetites feeble, it is good to cast ourselves into the thought of *His* desire; all that He asks is that we put no obstacle between our self and His Love; our best preparation is to lie still, passive and content, when the great Lover of souls comes to court us and to unite us to Himself in the wedlock of that Sacrament.

There are some souls that are scrupulously anxious as to whether they have made sufficient preparation for their communion, whether they have hungered and thirsted *enough* after the Lord through Righteousness. But let us lay aside all undue anxiety, remembering that His desire for us is never satisfied; He cannot rest until every part of our being is consecrated to Him. If, then, we cannot trust the perseverance or intensity of our own desires, we can, at least, trust the perseverance and intensity of His.

It is a beautiful suggestion of Coventry Patmore's that, not only is God the food of man, but that man is also the food of God. The original idea of sacrifice was that the beast slain was offered in man's place as food to God. Thus in Holy Communion not only do we feed on Him, but He feeds on us. So that, as we look around on nature, we see everywhere an upward movement towards God. The mineral creation is taken up into the vegetable as the grass absorbs the chemic of the earth into itself; the vegetable creation into the animal, as the sheep feeds on the grass; the animal creation is taken up into man, as he feeds upon animal life. And in the Blessed Sacrament, man becomes the food of God. Thus there is an upward movement of all creation towards God. Each "order" of life rises by death into a higher order, and the last step reaches God. "Behold a ladder set up on earth, and the top of it reaches to heaven." (Gen. xxviii. 12). The idea may seem at first a little fantastic, and yet it conveys a deep truth.

When St Ignatius of Antioch was on his way to martyrdom, his prayer was, "that he might be so ground by the teeth of the wild beasts that he might become the pure bread of God."

We want to think of Our Lord as *Our* Bread, and of *our* hunger being satisfied through partaking of Him; let us take sometimes the opposite idea and think of His desire for *us*; and that longing of His may be satisfied as we come to Him. He, the great Husbandsman of the world, the Sower Who sows the seed, sees all the travail of His soul and is satisfied in the human soul that gives itself back to Him to be the Sustenance of His love. And, after all, the glory and satisfaction of God are greater things than ourselves.

Spiritual Communion

Here let us pray, first, that Spiritual Communion is not a fantasy, but a *fact;* that, really and truly, by every longing aspiration, every lifting up of the heart to Our Lord, we receive Him into ourselves. Spiritual Communion is such an important devotion that a great spiritual writer tells us that, when the desire for it comes, we should stop whatever we are doing, and make the active Spiritual Communion. There are so many things that may provoke this desire on the part of those who are seeking to find God in their soul. For instance, we may be reading the Gospel, and a sudden flush of joy will come over us; it is a sign that the Bridegroom is at hand; we should close the book and go out to meet Him.

Conclusion of Talk and Retreat

Once more. Evening is the best time for meeting old friends. Perhaps there was a time when we thought that Religion must be brought "to square with modern thought" and we talked a great deal of nonsense about "the stereotyped ways of Christianity," and indulged in absurd dreams of the "religion of humanity," and loved high-sounding theories and philosophical terms. But at the hour of death we shall crave for simpler things than those; we shall want to fall back on the old plain and solid doctrine of God, and wholeness; and sin, and forgiveness, and Heaven and hell. We like to think that, when we come to die, we shall have beside us, not sin and forgiveness, and Heaven and hell. We like to think that, when we come to die, we shall have beside us, not an elaborate religious system, nor high sounding theories, or philosophical speculation, but Jesus Christ to receive us on our death-day, and out Mother Mary to pray for us, and our Guardian Angel to help us.

2

Two Letters to Mary Benson Written at the House of the Resurrection, Mirfield

[*These letters laid out the difficulties Benson faced in the Church of England even as he explained the reasonsbehind his imminent conversion. They are presented here as synopsis in his own words of his intellectual position.*]

May 1903

My dear Mamma,

Very many thanks for your letter. It wants a lot of answering. (1) I will first say that if, after writing this, you will feel you would like me to see the Archbishop[*] or anyone else you care to name *as a representative of the moderate school* I will very gladly see him. (2) I will now try to say what I feel about the moderate school *as a school.* But please absolutely dissociate that from what I think of the persons who form it. Subjectively I have the greatest love for them. I mean all my associates and so on are wrapped up in them and theirs. For example, people "staying" for Communion, always give me a thrill, because it's all mysterious and solemn: and I feel real joy in that, because I know that they are in good faith, and I love to "stay" too to watch it, and to pray; but objectively it appears to me quite *terrible*, for many reasons that you can guess. I only state all this to show that there is a very deep difference between them and their tenets.

It is the duty of religion to instruct the intellect, kindle the heart and influence the will (this is not a Brampton lecture!). I can quite frankly and without bitterness, say that my early religion scarcely did any of these things. Almighty God did; and you and Papa did--but NOT my religion. I could not have given in the *least*, a connected account of my religion, so as, e.g., to have taught it intelligently. I didn't love God, really, at all, and I lived an unconverted life. I remember, for example, frankly stating in writing, that the sonship of JESUS CHRIST was only different in degree from our own. Then I began to learn what I now believe to be the "Catholic" Religion, in fragments. Each fragment was like a revelation. To understand that "THIS IS MY BODY" was just a simple fact: and that it was *true*: and that "He *hath* given power and commandment. . ." meant what it said--these were amazing things to me--to think that I could go to a priest as to JESUS CHRIST and hear him say "Go and sin no more" &c! These things were not taught me by the "moderate" position. I'm not denying for a

---

[*] Archbishop Randall Davidson who succeeded Temple in 1902.

moment that they were not believed by many in the "moderate" position, but they weren't brought home to me at all. Then gradually I became aware that Our Lord was a loveable person, who was as much here and now, as there and then in Palestine and that the Sacramental System made that into a fact instead of a fancy--so I owe absolutely all that I have to these revelations that came to me through the *"extreme"* party,** no doubt built on a solid foundation of the "moderate party." But to seriously go back now, would mean real treachery to light. *The "extreme" theory has answered.* It appears to me that God has been slowly bringing me up a ladder, each step being a new revelation and now it *seems* as if the last step were beginning to appear in the fog. To turn and go down again!

If I do go to a "Moderate" what can happen. (1) I may be persuaded that it is the true representative of the church of England. Then I should feel that the church of England was just a desperate apostasy--and I fear I should be bitter against her. At present I am not bitter against her, because I believe that her true position is on the whole on the side of Catholic truth. (2) I may be persuaded that the "moderate" party is not the only possible platform for Christianity at all. Then I should have to condemn centuries full of millions who have died for another faith. I myself should lose any little zeal or intellect or love for God that I may have. It's simply inconceivable to me. It appears to me that I can see the elements of which the moderate religion has been formed. But I won't state them. Really I'm sorry for all this: but I can't lose all control of myself when I'm asked to take the "moderate" position seriously. It is just work of amateurs, and it hasn't answered.

(3) That is *an aspect* of Christianity. But I know that already and that it contains many Christians far nearer to God than I am, or every will be in this world. Yet for all that, it is not an aspect for me. It fails to satisfy my intellect, *or* to kindle my heart, *or* to touch my will, although I know it does all these for others.

After all, surely what one has been brought up in, one does know best! If anything, I think you haven't considered enough the claims of the *extremist* possible parts in the church of England but have passed through it too quickly. Remember too that I hold, positively, *all* that I was taught as a child--you are wanting me to take a negative step, to deny my later spiritual experiences--for that is what it would come to if your plan were to come off. But I can hardly even contemplate future existence from the moderate standpoint. I think I may truthfully say that the practices I have learned from the extreme party--Confession,

---

** By extreme is here meant the High Church or Anglo-Catholic party holding to sacramental Confession and Communion.

Communion coupled with objective faith &c, Meditation: these things give me keener joy than anything in the world. To go back to a colourless, inchoate scheme, seems like a sort of nightmare, like turning back from the Gates of Heaven, to consider, after all whether life in a Provincial Suburb is not preferable.

Now, I've given myself away entirely in this letter, and made a large number of statements that I can neither defend nor justify, but have deliberately not restrained myself, in order to shew the kind of fundamental feelings I have about the "moderate" religion. I have *deliberately* allowed them to boil over. So please don't make this letter a test of controversy: because I'm quite aware that it is full of holes and loose statements. But do you think it much good my seriously considering the moderate position? If you do, I WILL DO SO, and will seek advice from any true representative of that school. But indeed I don't want to be bitter and fierce at the very thought of the church of England, because she contains so many loveable people. And, once more--if anything I've said, hurts--please distinguish once again between the system which I HATE, and the people, such as Papa and yourself, whom I LOVE. Ever your loving son.

May 11, 1903

My dear Mamma,

Thank you immensely for your letter. I had been rather regretting my last letter in some ways ever since I sent it, but now I don't any longer. May I try to answer as frankly as possible? 1. I think you used the word "understand" in two senses: and in order to get one's position clear one must discriminate.

(a) Understand--intellectual grasp. This I think I do already. I see that the "moderate" party appeals to the Scriptures as interpreted by the Primitive Church, and as being slightly modified by modern constructions. At least this (apart from modern constructions) was the [definite] *Tractarian* standpoint: and the continuations of this in the system I learnt at home and school seem to me to be fairly represented by my second clause ("as . . . constructions"). I *reject the position as a whole*. It appears to me, for all kinds of reasons that I will gladly go into in conversation to be entirely untenable--or if tenable at least untenable *by me*. (I should have thought from what we've talked about together that this was unsatisfactory to you too, and that the "modifications" in your case as well as in mine, were very much more than "slight," and that you allowed very largely [indeed] for development. But perhaps I have misunderstood you.) [He goes on to argue the Protestant position that the church evolved from the seed planted by Christ.]

Now these are, roughly, the facts. And it seems to me that one must just say "I'll have that"--well (1) Anglican position (2) (I fear) RC position (is it not simply that Evolution and Development of Doctrine emerged so simultaneously?) Now I don't honestly think that any amount of talking *could* convince me that (1) was true. It seems to me contrary to Scripture, History, Science, Common-sense &c. It isn't this or that disputed point that makes the difference or a question of texts: your reminder that Pope Alexander VI was a beast: or that "the educated class in Italy" are opposed to religion: or that the *commercial* (!!) prosperity of England has steadily grown since the Blessed Reformation: or any little transitory thing like that--but we are on deeper and wider ground altogether. These things are fundamental, and concern one's view of God and Man and the Nature of things--and *above all* the hidden spring of one's own soul and the movements of one's inner life. (2) Understanding--Sympathise with--See the *point of view &c . . . in the emotional plane.* This I frankly don't: As I have expressed perhaps too brutally, it doesn't inspire my emotions or make me wish to propagate that religion: or impel me to self-sacrifice--or give me joy *at all.*

This without doubt has had its chance with me: to be taken in a system is to be impregnated with it. This surely again demands further study: from *two* points of view. If I can be shown that, on the whole, my intellectual conception of the appeal of moderate Anglicanism is wrong, and that all that I've said of the intellectual side is a false conception of the standpoint of the whole matter, then it is another question, but if words mean anything, the defenders of Anglicanism have always gone on the line of an appeal to Scripture interpreted by the Primitive Church &c. And it is that, as a whole, that I cannot believe.

As regards the Catholic party in the church of England, the reason I find it difficult, is that it is rejected universally, by Bishops, most of the clergy and very nearly all the laity. For a while I thought that this was one of the "Marks of the Lord Jesus": that the party was "despised and rejected of men," and I still believe that, *subjectively,* this is so. I still believe that the majority of the persons who compose that party are far closer to our Lord than, on the whole, any other party: and that their principles of supernatural religion are persecuted for the same reasons that our Lord was crucified. But I now take the rejection by bishops and people *as evidence* only of the *true position of the church of England,* that she, as a whole, doesn't own the "Catholic" souls as her own. And therefore the same result will follow in her case as in Jerusalem's. "Behold your house is left unto me desolate." Ultimately the rejected priests and people "shake off the dust of their feet" and "go to the Gentiles." (I hope this is not rhetorical. I don't mean it to be anything more than literal).

Things are moving on with me, fast, you see. I find it more and more inconceivable every day that I should minister again *publicly* in the church of England. Of course I may be quite wrong in this: and this may be the result of not doing it. But I must say that I am conscious that my soul has moved quickly since Easter--and that I'm appreciably further on than when we were together. And things seem dropping behind me. My ties with people seem loosening all round. (This may be pure fancy of course: but I can't help thinking that God is making it easier by this).

I am still *deliberately* waiting: not trying to push forward or back at all; but when I feel myself pushed I yield, and when the pressure stops I stop. (It's annoying how conscious one's soul can be of God and His guidance at times!) But I mustn't go on all day about myself. What I should ultimately do, and I feel I must, could be to go to a monastery for a week's Retreat, possibly in Gloucestershire to a Dominican House, because I'm greatly drawn to them. And even then I would not allow myself to go, decided: but deliberately went again for full and final confession. However, one knows nothing. I can't tell you how grateful I am for your letter. To have that sort of atmosphere around me, makes it possible to decide without cowardice or pain or rashness. If there were controversy or bitterness near one, it would mean acting impulsively one way or the other, just to dissipate the atmosphere. I am *so* grateful. . . . P.P.S. I haven't touched on what is really *the* controversial point at all: the Pope and his position in the scheme of Salvation. (After all, that is *the* thing).

3

Impressions of America 1912

[*This article written for the* New World, *the newspaper of the Chicago Archdiocese, emphasizes the openness and generosity of Americans. At the same time cultural differences between English and Americans are squarely noted. In an article written for a Liverpool newspaper* The Freeman's Journal, *Benson repeated his praise of Americans to an English audience.*]

Scarcely anything can be imagined more difficult than for an inhabitant of the Old World to assess his impressions of the New. When an American visits England he has a thousand aids and guides; the history of his own family it may be, or at any rate of his race, the story of civilisation and religion, the tale of the "old unhappy things" the reproductions, or specimens, of art that he has seen--all these matters direct him at least how and where to look for what he must ask and what expect. He may know little or nothing of the last five hundred years of European history, as the Englishman may know little or nothing of modern America, but both American and Englishman alike share in the heritage of the first fifteen hundred years after Christ: Rome belongs to them alike, both Imperial and Catholic; the saints and the kinds and the poets of Christian Europe have had as much to do with Chicago as with modern London or Paris. But the Englishman has no such advantages in America. To him, soaked as he is in unbroken tradition, the most venerable building in New York is of yesterday, and the Civil War is an unintelligible quarrel of the day before. He must begin all over again; there is no rhythm, to him, in American history, no gradual transformation from heptarchies to unity, from feudalism to constitutional sovereignty and from sovereignty to democracy. He is under extraordinary disadvantages--under the disadvantages that rest on a conservative son of an old house who meets for the first time his adventurous cousin returned from abroad.

As the American in Europe, therefore, is apt to pick out for notice first those things that are of the past, so the Englishman in America, believes first that those things are most characteristic of modern America are the rush and clatter of machinery, he is awed by the size of skyscrapers, by the distances over which he travels and the speed with which he goes, by the bulk of fortunes that are made and by the absence of what he knows as conservatism. This last point, in particular, strikes him: he notices how little, on the whole, family tradition counts, how a son will sell his father's house and set up elsewhere for himself without a qualm, how the gardens have no walls around them--a very significant symbol indeed--how men shake hands with their photographers, and have their boots blacked in public places--how, in a word, all that instinct which rises from a feudal past and which is in the very air he had hitherto breathed, has given place in America to a spirit, public and democratic in a sense of which he has never dreamed.

At first he is a little shocked and chilled. It seems to him as if there were no such thing as privacy or individualism anywhere--as if he had awakened in the morning, so to speak, and found his bedroom walls to be of glass. This is further driven home to him by the character of American journalism; he finds that he is not supposed even to resent having his personal habits described in headlines. The number of cigarettes he smokes in the day, the manner in which he turns his headphones as he speaks, his raids on grapefruit--all these things are proclaimed before him when he opens his morning paper.

Then, little by little, if he is not completely a fool, he begins to understand that it is not that there is no individualism, but that it is of a different kind; not that there is no home life in America, but that America itself is home life; not that the American house is not his castle, but that his country is. He begins to see that the children in the street look happier and the few beggars more self-respecting than in his own Whitechapel slums; that the national flag is not, like his own, brought out only on days of expansive festivity, but that it flies all the time; that travellers do not bribe the conductor to lock the door of their compartment, but, instead hang genially onto a swinging strap; in short, that individualistic life in America does not shut itself up within locks and bars, but had burst them and gone out into the street. He understands, in a word, that in spite of the palaces on Broadway, America is democratic; and that in spite of Mr. Lloyd George, and MM. Combes and Jaures, Europe is feudal.

After having done those things--after having ridden on an engine from New York to Albany, having sat in the electric chair, having been interviewed by brisk and charming journalists, having had a beefsteak supper in a chequered apron and walked up Fifth Avenue with a millionaire and a tailor's assistant--having understood something of that joyous, boisterous public spirit that lies at the root both of the virtues and the vices of America--so utterly alien from the melancholy happiness and the luxurious sorrows of Europe--he will, if he is a wise man, begin to enquire as to America's religion; for the religion of a country is its sole certain interpretation.

He will find first an immense activity; and that the same vital and unbounded rush that creates huge winking faces of electric light in New York by night, builds churches two or three stories high, creates orphanages that occupy five acres of ground, drives cinematograph lanterns in crypts, and creates Men and Religious movements in a thousand towns simultaneously.

At first, in spite of the lessons he has previously learned, he will be both bewildered and dismayed. It will appear to him that religion, as he knows it, with its silence, its dim-lit interiors, its haunted corners and its reveries, has no space to live in. He will ask, bitterly, why they do not have phonographs instead of pulpits, and steam-organs instead of orchestras: they would be entirely unwearying and quite as effective for this kind of thing. And then, little by little, he will begin to distinguish. He will see, first, that there is indeed in American towns a vast deal of religion that is scarcely at all religious. It is excellent in all other ways: it is a great social asset; it is sometimes quite artistic; it is unboundedly philanthropic and sincere and generous; it is even imitative--as in the Protestant Episcopal Cathedral of New York--of real cathedral life in England. Its ministers are active and zealous; the choirs sing beautifully in four parts; its dogmas have blossomed themselves away into the most exquisite sentiments; there is an abundance of good feeling and fellowship; its adherents are sincerely anxious to uplift the poor. But it is not religious; unless religion is but another name for philanthropy. He will see in this department of American religion, exactly that chasm into which so many streams of similar religious activity in his own country are tending--and that this end has been reached more swiftly in America exactly for the same reasons as those for which America was the first to simplify, by a process of amplification, certain kinds of machinery, and produces cold chisels more cheaply and better made than in England.

If he is a Protestant, therefore, he will leave America either confounded or delighted; for he will see his own timid principles worked out in their logical end. If he has given a red lamp to his church at home because it looks so nice from the road after sunset, he will be charmed, if he is logical, by the cinematograph as a principal instrument of worship; if he has endeavoured to cling to the belief that the love of God is more vital and fundamental than the giving of free breakfasts to poor children, he will be appalled by the absence of dogmas from American faith.

But if he is a Catholic he will carry away a very different impression. For he will find, in New York, for instance, that the same thoroughness and business-like activity that had driven Protestantism on to creedless sands, has embanked and cemented and scoured from weed the Rock on which the Church is built.

First, he will be amazed by the numbers of Catholics. "Who are all those men?" he asked one day, as an apparently endless stream marched by him eight abreast. "Those are the Holy Name Society," said his American friend, "Catholics, you know. "Catholics! I didn't know there were so many Catholics in the whole of America." "Why, but those are only the ones that don't curse," said the American. "You should see the others." He will find, then, that in this smallest parish in New York several thousand persons hear Mass every Sunday, and he will, amazed, compare with that the fact that in his own archdiocese in London scarcely a greater remember to make their Sunday duties.

He will see, from his window, the street thronged three times each Sunday morning; he will see that in church after church it is the same: he will learn that the Knights of Columbus could wield, if they chose, as great a social force in favour of Catholicism as Freemasonry can wield against it in France. He will hear from priests that lack of money need never be a real obstacle in any necessary work; he will find, in short, that there is one Church, at any rate, in America that is perfectly confident, that alone does not ask itself why its members do not attend public worship, that is an example of generosity to the whole world; and that this Church alone among all denominations still retains the Two Great Commandments of the Law in their divine sequence. And when he has learned this he will know more about America and her future than even Mr. Bryce himself, his own ambassador.

On the civil side he will have found, as has been said, a very vital public spirit, completely unlike that attitude which passes under the same name at home. At home in England we talk of the necessity of uplifting the masses; in America a millionaire's sister (let us say), takes a box for factory girls at the opera. In England we solemnly open Toynbee Hall in Whitechapel, and dressed in orange-coloured ties, administer artistic conversation to any tame costermongers we can allure within; in America a steel merchant and his clerk go honestly and together in the broad light of day to see Mr. Morgan's pictures. In England we live our real life in our houses surrounded by walled gardens and go out into the world to pretend; in America they live their real lives in the streets and squares and do their pretending at home. Public buildings, therefore, in America are magnificent, and private houses largely built of wood. Our private houses in England are beautiful and artistic, and our public buildings are deplorable and mean.

On the religious side, our Englishman will have found the same kind of laxishness and logic. Protestantism will be absolutely all that a human system of faith can ever hope to be. It will be splendid and glittering and artistic (within very clear limits), and unboundedly optimistic and philanthropic. But it will be devoid of dogma, since dogma is the one Divine thing we have left. And Catholicism will be fully as philanthropic, and as glittering, and as optimistic; it will lack, certainly, that intimacy and that remoteness and that contemplative attitude that are suggested (let us say) by the side chapels of Chartres Cathedral; but those things are not vital, however sweet and lovely they may be--not vital, that is, to the Church itself, however necessary to some churchmen.   For all that she asks is that the Rock may remain untouched, and God will take care of the building: that authority may remain unquestioned.   After that, God in her, will do the rest, will "bring the glory and honour of the nations into her," will work up into her fabric the joyousness and the generosity and the childlikeness of the American, as well as the patience and the silence and the feudalism of the European. And, it may be, one day He will shift the brunt of the battle from this side of the Atlantic to the other; from Europe who has played with the faith and already half forfeited it, to America, who has worked for it so nobly.

4

[In 1914 Hugh sat down to write a chronicle of his residence from the time he came to live at Hare Street in 1908, recording improvements made to the house and gardens, and naming the guests who came to visit, carefully handwriting this cover page--]

A
CHRONICLE
OF
HARE STREET HOUSE
NEAR
BUNTINGFORD

Written by ROBERT HUGH BENSON
(who bought it in 1907; and began this Chronicle in 1914)
AND CONTAINING

AN EXACT ACCOUNT
(so far as may be)
of the

CONDITION OF THE HOUSE
when he bought it
of the
THINGS HE DID IN IT
for its improvement
AND THE
MANNER OF THEIR DOING
AND THE
PERSONS
who executed the same
TOGETHER WITH

AN ABUNDANCE OF INFORMATION
AS TO THE

GUESTS
WHO CAME TO IT, AND AS TO

NUMEROUS OTHER DETAILS
BOTH INSTRUCTING AND DIVERTING

A Chronicle of
HARE STREET HOUSE

HERE BEGINS the Chronicle: June 1914

I bought <u>Hare Street House</u> from Miss Patten of Hertford in 1907; and put into it John Harris and his wife, who gave me much trouble in the following year when I came, having run up accounts against my name, without authority.   However, he repented and made sufficient restitution. <u>*IN 1908*</u>   At the end of August, I came to live in the house, having as my servants Joseph Reeman and his wife, and Reginald Port, a boy, who later went into the navy and was one of the sailors on the <u>King's</u> yacht when he went to <u>India</u> and <u>Medina</u>; also Mary Reeman.   The house was very bare and desolate. I had paid £800 for it; and it required another £200 before it was habitable.   I had the roofs repaired and many things put in order.   At this time I also bought <u>Hare Street Cottage</u>, for Miss Lyall's tenancy; her father Sir Alfred Lyall, also paying for its renovation with me. I paid, I think, £3000. She came there this year. I bought this year my horse Peter, who served me well, for £30.   Reeman, soon after our arrival, built the little cloister that unites the house and chapel. Before there had been an old bake-house, which I caused to be pulled down, and the sacristy to be built out of it. I had the whole of the cloister-floor paved with cobbles.   This year my dog <u>Kim</u> came to me from <u>Mr. Yarker</u> of <u>Cambridge</u>.   I had very little furniture when I came. I slept for a few days in the room now called the "tapestry-room" or the "middle-room"; or the "haunted room"--the first at the head of the stairs. The only trouble I had here is a dream, with an old man's groan in it. <u>Reggie</u> and I polished all the floors.   Among my guests this year were Mgr. John Vaughan now the auxiliary bishop of <u>Salford</u>, who said mass in the chapel, that had then nothing but an altar--(the Jacobean chest that still serves for an altar)--and a few chairs. He thought at this time of living with me; Mr de Havilland, a clergyman whom I reconciled to the Church; Torben De Bille, the son of the Danish minister to England, whom I also had reconciled; and Father Sebastian Ritchie of the <u>Birmingham Oratory</u>, then a layman and a convert. My brother Arthur gave me this year the Tuscan Madonna, in terra-cotta relief, which he bought for £20 in <u>Florence</u>; and we fixed it to the wall of the library. <u>*IN 1909*</u> I went to preach the Lent in <u>Rome</u>. When I returned, <u>Mrs Reeman</u> died immediately, while I was still in <u>London</u>: she died in the room over the kitchen, called "the doctor's room."   In May, <u>Kenneth Lindsay</u>, then my ward, came to live with me. He had for his room the large room, now called "The Nursery".   At this time I began to put in the hot-water system of warming. The house before had been bitter cold in winter. I also began to build "The Close", now occupied by Miss Lyall, having bought the land in this summer from Miss Patten of Hertford. The small tank for the house-water was put in. In the autumn Dr. Leonard Sessions came to live with me as my secretary; and occupied the "doctor's room" called after him. I pulled down at this time the old Nonconformist chapel on the cottage-ground; and turned the pulpit into a confessional. It now serves for the front of the organ-loft in my chapel.   Margaret Talbot, now my housekeeper came to me this autumn, as maid to Ken, and housemaid.   Fanny Reeman, who had come to me as housekeeper when Mrs Reeman died, left this winter.   Among my guests this year were Viscount Castlerosse; Bernard Merefield, the actor; Mgr Lindsay, Ken's cousin; the Princess Eleanore Salm-Salm; my brother Fred; and Mr Bowles, from Philadelphia.   This year Reeman re-polished all the floors. This year we made the mound in the orchard, of rubbish and earth, and erected the Cross on it. *IN 1910* Ken left me in January. I went to Boston USA for Easter.   Dr Sessions and I, in January, carved the figure of Xt crucified that is now on the Rood in the chapel.   Gabriel Pippet came to me this summer; and occupied the large attic that is approached through the tank-room. Captain Anderson came later this year; and occupied the "Captain's room", called after him. We began to clean the original panelling, to bring out the Georgian panelling now over the fireplace and opposite--all in my present room; and to add new panelling there, to finish it. I also turned the powder-closet opening out, into my dressing room: and when all was done, I occupied it. We found also, behind the cheap fireplace, a Gothic arch of plaster, which we restored. Shortly before I had stripped the fireplaces in the library and dining-room, and caused them to be built with bricks. Later I restored the old fireplace in the "parlour."   G. Pippet also began this year to carve the statue of B.V.M. that is now in the chapel. The jewels have been added to it gradually. Three of them were given me by my brother Fred. Reggie left me this year, in the spring; and entered the navy. Reeman, who married again at Easter, became my man-servant; and Alfred Turner, now sacristan at St Peter's Edinburgh became gardener.   The Close was finished. Miss Lyall went to live in it; and Mrs Hogge became my tenant at the Cottage. When the well was dug at the close, we presently closed the old well in my court, and connected my house with the new well.   This year we began the "Grail tapestry" that hangs in the parlour. Pippet designed it: Dr. Sessions and I executed it. We began and finished the chapel stalls and the screen and the organ loft. Pippet, who had made and given to me the little panel of glass B.V.M. gave me the old stall ends that enclose my stall--the decanal--

and we carved those on the other side, and painted in my own arms, the doctor's and Pippet's. The doctor had the stall corresponding to mine, and Pippet that next to him, beneath the windows. Captain Anderson had that next to him. We also made the confessional; and Pippet drew the large crucifix inside. He also painted and gave me the large Rosa Mystica panel in the chancel; and designed the St Matthew medallion in the large glass. The two panels of mixed glass in the chapel--from Canterbury, were given me by Miss Lyall. At this time we said Prime and Compline publicly. This year my dog Kim disappeared. I suppose she was shot. This year we made the pantry under the stairs: it had, before I came, been a lumber-room. In this year Reeman pollared the limes before the house. This year we made a door in the stable, to lead into the garden. This year Miss Lyall bought from Mrs. Lindsay the pony Paul, on which Ken had ridden. This year, when the statue of our Lady was erected, I caused the iron half circle with prickets for candles to be put up. This year we reorganised the kitchen back premises: dividing a largish room into Larder and lumber room. Reeman did the work. Reeman, after his marriage, went to live in the village at Moorfield House. Among my guests this year were Dick Howden, Chris Crofts my cousin; Austin Spare the artist (whom the ghost came to twice); Cyril Bickersteth, of Mirfield; Mr. Raupert the ex-Spiritist; Hector Tyler; Dr Herbert Vaughan; H. Shindler the artist. This year, I think, Miss Bull (now Mrs. Laurence) of Cambridge; made and gave me my cope-hood of the Rosary on the rose. *IN 1911* I went to Rome to preach the Lent; and was made Private Chamberlain to the Pope in May. I received the news the day after Beth died at Tremans, Horstead Keynes. At Easter Captain Anderson left. In this year I bought the two pieces of land of which I have the deeds-- one on the road to Barksway about 150 yards from my house, containing a gravel-pit from which ever since I have drawn gravel for my paths; the other on the road to Buntingford, containing many trees, about 200 yards up the lane from Hare Street. In the summer we painted and re-glazed the greenhouse throughout, by our own labour; and refitted the warming apparatus of it. This year Reeman gave me my dog Jack. This year we re-arranged the stable-yard first dividing it into a forecourt and a kitchen-court, and moving back the wooden doors, which before had given on the road to the new wall; and then preparing and planting by our own labour the bed in the centre of the fore-court, and the beds round about. We were forced to cut low many of the laurels we planted there, that they might take root. In this year Reeman made the great long oaken table now in the parlour, fitting an oaken top of old wood on to the old legs; and making a new kitchen table with the old top. This year came my new iron gates, with Heart of <u>Jesus</u> and <u>Mary</u> and the Priest's Hat wrought in the iron-work, to take the place of the old stableyard gates.   They were made in Campden, Glos. by my own designs, drawn out by Pippet.   This year in September I put in electric light, building the shed at the foot of the cottage garden, and connecting the water-supply from the new well in the <u>Close</u> garden, both for the House and the Close.   Miss Lyall would not have electric light for the Close, which I think a mistake.   In this year there fell down in a storm the northern end of the east-wall of the stable; which I rebuilt.   Its fall crushed some of the new yew-trees I had recently planted in this garden--for a hedge: and I planted more.   In this year I also made a new lawn in that part of the garden; but early in the year; and also planted the chapel-court with grass, and had a flagged path mad across it, and put flags for cobbles.   In this year I caused the parlour-window to be rebuilt, doing away with the French window that had been there; and inserting coats and emblems in the glass, designed by G. Pippet, and executed by his brother: viz. a swan for St Hugh: my crest, a bear: and a Priest's Hat; Our Lord in a chalice, and the Westminster coat.   In this year G. Pippet entered the Carthusian house at Parkminster, but came out again in a week.   This year Miss Lyall painted the portrait of me in my chamberlain's purple, now hanging in the dining-room.   This year <u>G. Pippet</u> carved, and I erected, the statue of St Michael in the chapel.   This year Miss Englefield at Rome gave me my curious waxen! crucifix, whose body opens, showing the entrails.   It hangs above the alterino of the Passion.   A nail fell on it from above and shattered its left hand.   Among my guests this year were Fr Maturin, Dr. Sarolea, the editor of "Everyman"; Lord Alfred Douglas; Dr. Jorgensen, the writer on Franciscan subjects, Rev. Dr. McMahon of New York, my mother and my aunt Nora Sidgwick, and my brother Arthur.   <u>*IN 1912*</u> I went to New York to preach Lent. While I was there <u>Reeman</u> made the oaken chimney-breast of the dining room; the small central face came from the Town-house, I am informed, of the Duke of Northumberland.   The two small faces above are ancient. Most of the mouldings are old; and came from a cow-house: probably originally from Hare Street House.   Also this year Reeman fitted into oaken mouldings the tapestries of emblems of B.V.M., designed by <u>Pippet</u> and executed by me, in the inner hall.   Also I made the tapestry of <u>Jeanne d'Arc</u> that hangs in the back-hall.   In the summer Dr. <u>Sessions</u> entered Parkminster as a Carthusian lay-brother.   This year I finished the "Dance of Death" tapestries, and hung them in the "tap-room" so called.   This year, in September, came <u>Fr. Watt</u> to be in charge of the district at Buntingford; and I put my chapel at the disposal of the <u>Cardinal Archbishop</u>, till Lady Gifford of the Glebe House <u>Hormead</u>, has built her chapel. Fr Watt is her chaplain and will be paid

by her. Fr Watt occupied the nursery in Hare Street House. Here he
presently heard the Ghost. I had heard vague stories of the Ghost
before. Sometime previously, I think in 1911, Reeman sitting on the
stairs while we were at dinner, heard the door of "the Captain's or the
"haunted" room open; the steps come out, and return. Also Austin
Spare the artist (once a prize-fighter) had, on two nights out of 3, while
sleeping in that room, heard steps come upstairs; the handle turn; the
steps enter: and a voice, as of a "tall old man: say either "is that you" or
"are you there." He felt no fear; but only an inability to move or to
speak, and a tingling in every limb, as of electricity. Father Watt to
whom I related this, told me that he, in the nursery next door, had heard
the steps, as if on plain boards, come up one night, enter the haunted
room: and go out and downstairs again. This year I caused a path
round two sides of the house and down to the old front iron gate to be
paved with flags. These flags came from the House of Commons.
George Thorogood did the work. This year Reeman began the
panelling of the staircase. I carved the emblems--those on the left (first
floor) are personal and historical. Reeman's own monogram is one of
these. The emblems on the second floor are of the Passion. In the
angle of one of the steps is "P.D" carved by a boy called Philip
Derriman, (while he stayed with me) a boy of the Westminster
Cathedral Choir (this boy played Our Lady one year at Westminster, in
my Nativity Play, I think in 1911). This work was not, I think,
finished till the year after. We also opened out the old hiding-place (as I
think it) over the door from the centre hall to the back hall: and fitted it
with a hinged door. It was, before, all plastered over. We found and
restored the steps on the second flight and landing and put in the first
flight steps of old oak. This year we built the little side chapel for
the relics and for the Crib of Jesus. The relic-chest had been made
previously by Reeman and me out of old carved wood found at
Tremans. We also fitted up the two altarini in the chancel; of St Hugh
and the Passion. Miss Lyall gave me this year; and I erected, the
statues of St Roch; St Gabriel (carved by Gabriel Pippet), St Sebastian,
St Barbara, St Thomas (to whom with B.V.M. the chapel is dedicated)
and St Anne. This year I caused to be half-cobbled the kitchen court.
In this year Gabriel Pippet [in 1913 he married a Frenchwoman], under
Miss Florence Leicester's orders, made, and erected, the statue of St
John. This year we finished the book shelves in the library. This
year I caused the inner walk of the cloister to be flagged. This year
Sir Charles Paston-Cooper gave me a great number of jewels for my
Madonna. This year Mrs Lawrence of Cambridge made for me a
tabernacle door of beaten silver, representing the Five Wounds with
carbuncles for the wounds: and I set it up. This year I brought from

New York my best set of red vestments, given by the ladies of the Church of Our Lady of Lourdes, and my silver and crystal cruets, with a silver lavabo basin.   This year I gave my first children's Xmas party. This year Fr John Gray of Edinburgh gave me my black little statue of B.V.M. behind the great one. I think it of the 14th century.   Among my guests this year were the Dow. Lady Gifford; Mr. W. Legge, Fr Vassall-Phillips, CSSR; Antoine de Geofroy; Lady Hadfield; and Rev. Dr. Havard.   This year Katie Hampsen was my housemaid. *IN 1913* I went to preach the Lent in Rome. This year I had to have Jack poisoned; and, later, Peter shot, and I had my operation. This year we erected the hen-house in the north-east corner of the garden; and planted laurels all along the eastern side of the garden. This year we pulled down the old sheds in the Cottage lands. This year my brother Arthur gave me a quantity of furniture from his house Hinton Hall in the Isle of Ely.   Including 2 brass candelabra, fixable to the wall; an oakbench; two coffin-stools; two brass candlelamps, rich silk curtains; carpets; a leather chair; a square bookcase of oak, and more besides.   This year we made the carpenter's shop at the head of the kitchen-stairs, into a Servant's parlour. This year G. Pippet designed and his brother made, the 7 armorial coats in glass, erected in the diningroom, front-hall and library.   This year we made the mahogany 4 post bedstead in the tapestry room, from old pillars and wood: and hung the curtains on it, which my brother gave me.   This year Turner left my service for the place of Sacristan (which I got for him) in St Peter's, Edinburgh. And Joe Reeman, my man's son, succeeded him.   Late in this year Dr Sessions came out again from Parkminster, and went as a ship's doctor to the Mediterranean.   This year we planted many fruit trees in the orchard and along the western and northern walls in the garden. This year Fr Watt again heard the ghost, in daylight. He went out of his room: and the steps came up to him: then the handle of the haunted room moved.   This year I painted 3 pictures, now hanging in the hall. My brother Arthur gave me this year the heads of game that are hung in the back-hall. A few came from Addington Park. This year Mrs Irwin gave me my tall silver flower vases for the high altar. She had before given me small ones: and a plaster statue of B.V.M. This year Miss Lyall gave me 4 oak reliefs of the Evangelists that are fixed to the east wall of the chapel: and the portrait of Sir Walter Raleigh in the old gilt frame. Among my guests this year were Fr Sheridan of New York; Cardinal Bourne; Mr and Mrs Bellamy Storer with the Marquis and Marquise de Chambrun; E. W. Hornung and his son Oscar; Dr. Langford James; Père Guillermin, S.J. and my sister for Xmas day. Mr. Dennys came to me as my secretary for a month, but went back to the stage again, which is a better place for him.   This year Miss Lyall gave me my gilt Agnus Dei and The <u>Pelican</u> in his <u>Piety</u>; both in my chapel. <u>*IN 1914*</u> I went to preach Lent in <u>New York</u>. While I was away Reeman finished the panelling on the first floor, so far as the tapestry-room; and put in 2 oak doors into the haunted room and the nursery. Also the library was painted white.   In June the brick-walls, round the paved walks, were built, and capped with stone. Also in this year the stone steps were put in, leading down to the orchard, and the ground levelled up. Also the concrete posts and wires were put in round both sides of the orchard, and roses planted there as well as in the kitchen garden for espaliers, and the archway there.   In this year I painted and erected the stature of St Anthony in the chapel, given me by Miss Lyall. This year Miss Lyall put the stone steps in the garden walk of the Close.   This year I bought my grand-piano, by Bechstein. This year Lady Kenmare gave me two flower vases for my chapel, of beaten silver. They were saved from the Chapel of Killarney House burned down last year (I was the last priest to say mass in it).   This year, in New York, I was given my best set of green vestments, of thin silk.   (This year on Aug 5. England declared war against Germany.)

5

Some Representative Novels

By What Authority?   Historical romance, set in England in the late 1500's during the reign of Elizabeth I. Two families, the Maxwells, Catholic, and the Norrises, Protestant, are neighbors. Young Isabel Norris and Hubert Maxwell fall in love, but religious differences create difficulties. In spite of a strict Puritan upbringing, Isabel's brother Anthony is drawn to the Catholic Church, as is Isabel, but by a different route. Both become Roman Catholics and witness religious persecution, first through the suffering of Hubert's brother James, who has returned to England a priest, and then personally in the imprisonment and torture of Anthony when he rejects the Queen's demand that he publicly renounce his vows. Amidst explanations of doctrinal positions of both religions there is keen analysis of character and motive, many suspenseful events, and breathless pursuits through secret meeting places and on country roads, as well as moments of tremendous pathos. Jesuit Edmund Campion's trial is powerfully dramatized from actual records. (1904).

The King's Achievement   Historical romance set in the 1530's during King Henry VIII's time.   Not only Henry, but Thomas More and to a lesser extent Bishop John Fisher and the Carthusian martyrs have a role, but the main characters are the Torrendon brothers and the main event the suppression of monasteries engineered by Thomas Cromwell. Christopher and Ralph Torrendon are set on separate paths, Christopher to become a monk and Ralph to enter service as Thomas Cromwell's secretary.   Both brothers are devoted to their calling, but is there any question which is the better? Against the blatant tyranny of the king are contrasted the martyrdom of Carthusians, the inquisition of monks, the sacking and destruction of monasteries.   Chris is turned out of Lewes but seeks to save his brother.   By that time, Cromwell, out of favor because of the Anne of Cleves fiasco, has been condemned; while Ralph imprisoned in the tower contracts a fever and dies, having first probably against his will received the Last Rites from his brother. (1905)

The Queen's Tragedy   Historical romance set in Queen Mary Tudor's times in the 1550's. This is Mary Tudor's life seen through the eyes of young Guy Manton who comes to court to serve her after she has married the errant Philip of Spain. He witnesses the brilliant pageantry of court, including the wedding at Winchester and the restoring of the Catholic faith in England. But Mary does not understand the will of the people, who though happy to be Catholic again, resent the Spanish marriage and the harsh methods Mary uses to stamp out sedition and heresy. Mary's personality is unforgettable--a woman of ardent nature brooding over her unhappy childhood, longing to bear a child who will truly unite both countries and reign in a Catholic England, and growing more and more bitter and repressive with every disappointment, not the least of them in her faithless husband. Her death in 1558 is poignantly described with haunting images drawn from inside her mind. (1906)

Richard Raynall, Solitary   A book purporting to be a translation of the life of Richard Raynall, a 15th century hermit. Richard is happiest in the midst of nature where he lives in the spirit of St. Francis of Assisi, dwells in a cottage in the forest, happy and blissful in the praise of God, and innocent. His is a perfect life of contemplation and prayer amidst the works of God's hands. Responding to God's call, he goes to visit Henry VI at Westminster Abbey to inform him of his imminent passion. Upon hearing the prediction, the king falls into an epileptic seizure with the result that Richard is taken for a lunatic and scourged. Finally, the king comes to understand and embrace Richard's message; and the hermit, his sanctity acknowledged, is laid in the king's own bed to die. (1906)

Lord of the World   A modern novel of the Antichrist. It is about the year 2000 and Julian Felsenburgh, freemason and socialist, virtually rules the Western world if not in name than by the force of personality. Percy Franklin is one of the last of the priests to remain faithful to Rome, most others having defected to the new world religion of humanism. Only Rome and Ireland remain wholly Catholic. Felsenburgh is hailed by all as Universal Peacemaker and hopes to convince Rome of the virtues of Humanity worship under the god and goddess of the generative power. Meanwhile, resistance to the new worship is suppressed. Mabel and Oliver Brand are faithful adherents until Mabel, disillusioned and depressed at the futility and purposelessness of life, has herself euthanized by special machine, a common practice. Felsenburgh is proclaimed President of Europe as the Pope announces the approach of the end of the World. Percy, now Cardinal attempts to stop a plot to blow up Westminster Abbey where the Feast of Maternity is to be celebrated. When the plot is discovered, Rome is destroyed by Felsenburgh's air fleet in retaliation, and the persecution of Catholics is put into full force with many martyrdoms. Percy, now Pope, is betrayed and killed as ominous clouds form signalling the triumph of Antichrist and the coming of the end. (1907)

The Mirror of Shalott   The set of short stories is framed by an afternoon symposium of priests of various nationalities discussing supernatural or preternatural events in the Canadian college of San Filippo (really San Silvestro, Rome). Each is called upon to tell a tale from his experience: two are accounts of diabolical possession, one of recall to life, and others are ghost stories. Among them are Mr. Perceval's Tale is about an iron mine in Wales where the ghosts of lost miners dwell, and Father Girdlestone's tale about a demonic force imposing itself subtly into a priest's will to kill his faith. (1907)

The Necromancers   A young man Laurie Baxter cannot get over the death of his love Amy, the grocer's daughter. Following a conversation with a friend Mrs Stapleton, who had journeyed to "the other side," Laurie tries to make contact with Amy's spirit through a medium, Mr. Vincent. He is discovered to be exceptionally sensitive, falls into a trance at once, and spends an hour with the spirit of Amy. Despite warnings, Laurie insists on continuing these contacts at the cost of eroding his Catholicism and the gradual separating of his soul from body to the point that a "presence," the Devil himself, threatens to enter his body. Only with the help of an ex-spiritualist, does he free himself from the demon leading him to disaster. It is expelled after a terrifying confrontation with the powers of Good. (1909)

None Other Gods   A modern novel. Cambridge student Frank Guisely has shocked everybody first by becoming a Roman Catholic and then by leaving Cambridge to take to the life of the road as a tramp. What his purpose is no one knows, not even Frank. After knocking about, he meets the Major, another vagrant with a shady past who is traveling with Gertie. Frank proves a good friend when he goes to prison for a crime committed by the Major, but on his release they all go off together as before. Frank's motive now is to wrest Gertie away from the Major and send her back to her family. Meanwhile his fiancée Jennie had married Frank's father Lord Talgarth, but at the old man's death Frank inherits the estate. It makes no difference, for his interest remains the welfare of Gertie. He manages to free her from the Major and send her home but at the cost of his life. (1910)

The Dawn of All   A futuristic novel full of spectacle and polemics written as an antidote of the depressing *Lord of the World*. The events are the opposite of those in the earlier novel, and Rome has become the triumphant power. Father John Masterman awakens from a deep sleep to find himself in the future in a Catholic England. Socialism has been tried and has failed. Getting adjusted to the change, while observing first hand life in Rome including a trial and execution for heresy of a gentle monk, Masterman is overwhelmed to the point that his faith is undermined. Not everyone in the world is quiescent, however. Socialist opposition rises in Boston, and the Freemasons threaten to overturn the Christian emperor, but are put down under threat of aerial bombardment by volors (aircraft introduced in *Lord of the World*). Eventually Father Masterman is made Cardinal Archbishop of England and with the king at his side goes into the skies on an aerial barge to welcome an airship carrying the Pope and world leaders making a world tour. (1911)

Come Rack! Come Rope!   Historical romance of the 1580's during the reign of Elizabeth and time of the English martyrs. Robin Audrey and Marjorie Manners are in love, but human happiness will be denied them in exchange for happiness achieved through suffering and death. When Robin's father yields to demands by the State to take Communion in a Protestant service, he and Robin argue and Robin leaves home. At Marjorie's urging, he decides to become a priest, leaves England for the Continent and returns a Jesuit, knowing that if caught he will be killed. Meetings with Father Campion and with Queen Mary Stuart are memorable. The persecution of Catholics guiltless of treasonable intent is carried through in the capture and ordeal of Robin. He is sentenced to death by his own father and dies after being tortured in the usual horrific manner of the day. (1912)

The Coward   A modern "psychological" study. Valentine Medd, the delightful second son of an old English family, cannot live up to the family code of honor in which cowardice is *the* unpardonable sin. Cursed with a vivid imagination that magnifies danger, Val is put to the test twice--first in an Alpine descent, and after that by an incensed Italian he has accidentally insulted. Both times he fails and is disgraced in the eyes of others and in his own eyes. He grows to hate himself. The family, his fiancée, and his inherited religion have no comfort to give him; the only relief from despair comes from the sympathetic Catholic priest who understands the problem, and advises him to "starve the imagination and feed the will." At the end Val is caught in a fire and killed trying to escape. To all but the stony Medds who, in their pride, blame him for cowardice, he has redeemed himself. (1912)

An Average Man   A modern novel, demonstrating Benson's technique of creating effective propaganda by showing the effects of faith or backsliding on character. After hearing a lecture by a Carthusian monk, Percy Smith is on the verge of converting, when he suddenly and inherits a lot of money. He gives up the girl he has fallen in love with to marry the daughter of a Protestant peer, and his religious intentions turn to ashes as well. In his new circle of wealth and position, Catholicism is the wrong religion. Here as elsewhere the secondary characters have their own tale to tell, which throws new light on the decision of the hero. In deciding Catholicism will handicap his career, Percy is proved right, for his opposite Mr. Main, an Anglican curate married to a shrew, loses all prospects of employment (even as a grocery vendor) in order to become a Catholic. (1913)

Initiation   A modern novel, very strong, with a clear theme: pain and suffering are proving grounds of character. Sir Nevill Fanning, a nominal, pagazised Catholic, has been doomed to suffer for the sins of his father. In Rome he meets Enid, an irritating and selfish egoist, who as a Protestant shares his views of sensible religion. They plan to marry. When his severe headaches (described in extraordinarily lifelike imagery) lead to blindness, surgery provides a temporary cure. By this time Nevill and Enid have parted, and Nevill now blinded by the tumor and knowing he is to die soon seeks comfort first in Nature, which fails him, and then in the suffering Christ. Nevill's devoted Aunt Anna (an unforgettable character) wants to care for him, but he will not let her. How Anna overcomes her jealousy, first of Enid, then of God to whom Nevill turns in his last months of life; and how Nevill meets his death (minutely detailed) are extremely moving. (1913)

Oddsfish! Historical romance, set in England in late 1600's during the reign of King Charles II (the word "Oddsfish!"--"By God's Flesh"-- was Charles II's favorite expletive). Roger Mallock, an ex-Benedictine novice returns to England sent at his own request by Pope Innocent XI to rouse the Catholic tendencies of the notorious but likeable king and curb the zeal of James, his brother. He becomes involved in the infamous Titus Oates plot, witnessing the king's promise and subsequent failure to intervene to stop the execution of Jesuits and other Catholics on trumped-up charges of conspiracy to commit treason. All the plots and counter-plots of a dark and sensual age in which the Church appears to be gasping her last breath inject a good measure of excitement into the narrative. In the midst of it the woman Roger has fallen in love with is killed in a treacherous attack. In spite of Charles' moral weaknesses, sensuality and backsliding, Roger remains loyal to him and reconciles him to the Church on his death-bed. (Early in the novel Benson describes the interior of Hare Street House. He had done the same for Tremans in *By What Authority?*) (1914)

Loneliness? A modern psychological novel (Benson's last) touching upon Church law governing marriage, and containing as an incidental event a detailed description of a performance of Tannhaüser. Marion Tenderton has returned from voice training in Germany to take an engagement in London. She is a Catholic, and the protégée of an older woman, a strict Catholic who is like a mother to her. When Marion and Max fall in love, his family begin to worry about getting a Catholic daughter-in-law, a situation made worse by her stage career, even though it is the operatic stage. Marion learns from her priest that she and Max must marry in the Catholic rite and her fiancé must promise to raise the children as Catholics. Fearing his reaction, she begins to waver in her resolve to remain a Catholic. When she sings Wagner despite warnings from her doctor, her voice is permanently damaged. She decides to defy the Church and marry in a Protestant ceremony. When her dear friend is killed, Marion realizes she is about to make a mistake and releases her fiancé from his promise, turning at last to her Church and her Lord. The yoke of Catholics is sometimes difficult, but when understood proves well worth the trial. (1915)

A Chronology of
Robert Hugh Benson's Published Works

1899 *Archbishop Edward White Benson's Prayers Public and*
Private.

1903 *The Light Invisible*; Preface, *Bands of Love.*

1904 *The Book of the Love of Jesus; By What Authority?*

1905 *An Alphabet of Saints; The King's Achievement; Papers of a*
Pariah (first serialized in *The Month*).

1906 *History of Richard Raynal, Solitary; The Queen's Tragedy; The*
Religion of the Plain Man; The Sentimentalists; "The Sanctity of
the Church"; "The Death-Beds of 'Bloody Mary' and 'Good Queen
Bess'"; "Christian Science"; "The Hermit and the King"; "The
Catholic Point f View"; "The Conversion of England."

1907 *Lord of the World, A Mirror of Shalott, Papers of a Pariah*,
"Infallibility and Tradition, "Mysticism"; "A Modern Theory of
Human Personality."

1908 *The Conventionalists, The Holy Blisful Martyr St. Thomas of*
Canterbury; A Mystery Play in Honour of the Nativity of Our Lord;
Preface, *Jeanne d'Arc, Maid of France;* Preface, *A Torn Scrap-Book.*

1909 *The Necromancers*, "Dissolution of the Religious Houses" for
The Cambridge History of English Literature; "Spiritualism";
Preface, *The Angelical Cardinal: Reginald Pole.*

1910 *The Cost of a Crown; Non-Catholic Denominations; None Other*
Gods; A Winnowing; Life of Archbishop Beckett; Preface, *Back to*
Holy Church; "The History of Religions"; "The Life of Jesus Christ
in His Mystical Body"; "Catholicism and the Future."

1911 *Christ in the Church; The Dawn of All; The Maid of Orleans*;
Preface, *St. Pius V of the Holy Rosary;* Preface, *The Life of St.*
Teresa; Preface, *Roman Catholicism.*

1912 *A Child's Rule of Life; Come Rack! Come Rope!; The Coward;*
The Friendship of Christ; Preface, *The Mustard Tree*; Preface,
Roman Catholicism; Preface, *A Modern Pilgrim's Progress*; "Eton."

1913 *An Average Man; Confessions of a Convert; Old Testament*
Rhymes; Paradoxes of Catholicism; A City Set on a Hill;
"Optimism"; "The Beatitudes"; Preface, *Imitation of Christ;* "Eton"
(2).

1914 *Initiation; Lourdes; Oddsfish!; Poems; The Upper Room; Vexilla*
Regis; "Spiritualism"; Preface, *Thesaurus Fidelium*; Preface, *War*;
Preface, *A Modern Pilgrim's Progress*; "Pius X"; "Some Reflections
on the War."

1915 *Loneliness?; Spiritual Letters*; "Catholicism."

Bibliography

Asquith, Betty. *Two Victorian Families.* London: Chatto & Windus, 1971.

Benkovitz, Miriam. *Ronald Firbank.* New York: Alfred Knopf, 1969.

Benson, Arthur Christopher. *Life and Letters of Maggie Benson.* London: John Murray, 1917.

--- *Hugh: Memoir of a Brother.* London: Smith, Elder, 1915.

--- *Life of Edward White Benson.* 2 vols. London: Macmillan, 1899.

Benson, Edward Frederick. *Our Family Affairs,* 1867-1896. London: Cassel, 1920.

--- *Mother.* London: Hodder & Stoughton, 1925.

--- *Final Edition.* New York: George Doran, 1940.

Fontmell, E[ustace] V[irgo]. *Life at a Venture.* London: Eric Partridge, 1930.

Gorce, Agnès. *Robert Hugh Benson, prêtre et romancier.* Paris: Plon, 1928.

Le Bour'his, Jean Morris. *Robert Hugh Benson, Homme de Foi et Artiste.* Lille: Université de Lille, 1980.

Leslie, Shane. *The End of a Chapter.* London: Constable, 1916.

--- *The Cantab.* London: Chatto & Windus, 1926.

--- *The Film of Memory.* London: M. Joseph, 1938.

Marshall, Archibald. "Robert Hugh Benson. Some Early Memories." *Cornhill Magazine,* 38 (1915): 161-71.

Martindale, C. C. *Life of Monsignor Robert Hugh Benson.* 2 vols. London: Longmans, 1916.

Newsome, David. *Godliness and Good Learning.* London: John Murray, 1961

--- *On the Edge of Paradise.* Chicago: The University Press, 1980.

Parr, Olive K. *Robert Hugh Benson, An Appreciation.* London: Hutchinson, 1915.

Spiritual Letters to One of His Converts. London: Longmans, 1915.

Warre-Cornish, Blanch. *Memorials of Robert Hugh Benson.* London: Burns & Oates, 1915.

--- "The Death of Mgr. Benson." *Dublin Review* 156 (1915): 122-134.

Watt, Reginald J. J. *Robert Hugh Benson, Captain in God's Army.* London: Burns & Oates, 1918.

Weeks, Donald, ed. *Robert Hugh Benson and Frederick Rolfe's St. Thomas.* Edinburgh: Tregarra Press, 1977.

Index

Reeman J. 98, 175, 191,
213, 216
Respighi, Cardinal 69, 74
Roddy (pet dog) 113, 121
Rolfe, Frederick 80, 81-83,
84, 89, 92n5, 94n13&14,
97, 117, 126,150, 176n5,
182, 192
Rome ix, 27, 33, 43, 46,
47, 48, 50, 51, 55ff, 76,
96, 118, 121, 127, 145,
157, 160, 161, 163, 167,
187, 192, 212, 214, 216

St. John Lateran 60, 61, 69,
70
St. Lydwine of Schiedam 127,
149, 150
St. Peter's (Rome) 57, 61
St. Thomas Becket 25n7
94n14
Salford Cathedral viii, 169,
173, 179, 190, 194n4, 212
San Silvestro 55, 58, 62,
134, 140n10
Scripture x, xiv, 1, 52n2,
33-36, 41, 63
Sessions, Dr. Leonard 116,
117, 155, 176n6, 213,
214, 216
Sharrock, Canon 170, 172-
74
Shaw, G.B. ix, 149
Sidgwick, Henry 4, 99, 190
Silverstone, Miriam 118, 120,
124-26, 135
Skarratt, rector of Kemsing 31,
33
Spare, Austin 148, 214, 216
Spiritualism viii, 136-38
Storer, Bellamy and Maria
151n1, 153, 157, 217

Sulpician Order 59n10, 55
Swedenborgism 16

Tait, Lucy 27, 30, 36, 51, 97
Temple, Archbishop 33, 34
Theology 16, 24, 56, 59, 63
65, 69, 77, 78, 159
Theosophy 88, 136-37
Titanic 156, 157-58
Tremans 35, 44-46, 48, 50
51, 56, 72n6, 97, 98, 99,
100-102, 104, 118, 113n2,
131
Trinity College 13, 14, 15,
16, 19, 31, 117
Tyrrell, Fr. George 43-44, 51,
51, 52n4, 62-63, 72n2, 77-
78

Vaughan, Fr. Bernard 58, 131
Virgo, Eustace (Fontmell) 80-
81, 91n4
Von Hügel, Friedrich 77-78

Watt, Fr. Reginald 118, 155-
56, 164n6, 166, 175, 215,
216
Waugh, Evelyn 9n4, 52n3,
81
Wells, H.G. xi, 149, 183
Westminster Abbey, 34, 42
Westminster (Archdiocese)
69, 72n3, 74, 172, 177,
185-86, 191
Westminster Cathedral viii,
216
Wilde, Oscar 36, 25n5, 117
Woodchester 49, 56, 68, 96,
159
World War I viii, 1, 61, 127,
136, 144, 157, 168-69,
183, 189, 218